The Making of
Swallows and Amazons (1974)

The Making of
Swallows and Amazons
(1974)

For Fima
Swallows & Amazons
Forever!

Sophie Neville

with love

from
Titty,

Sophie Neville

Ⓛ
The Lutterworth Press

Sophie has reminded me of one of the happiest times I ever spent on a film. The fun that was had, the friendships forged, the challenges overcome, are all delightfully recalled with a freshness and sense of adventure that has made me smile all over again.

Virginia McKenna OBE,
'Mrs Walker' in *Swallows & Amazons*

Amazing. It brought so much that I had forgotten flooding back. Thank you! My father will love it, too.

Simon West,
'Captain John' in *Swallows & Amazons*

Looking at your pictures, I relive all the thrills, wearing the costumes, the people and the lovely carefree, but caring, atmosphere. Extraordinary, extraordinary how it all comes back.

Suzanna Hamilton,
'Mate Susan' in *Swallows & Amazons*

A smashing book about childhood adventure. . . . It is a truly touching read and I'm sure fun for the newcomer as well as those who lived through it. LOVED it.

Richard Pilbrow,
Producer of *Swallows & Amazons*

Sophie brings to life all the many memorable characters who worked on the film and in particular the other children, the Director Claude Whatham who developed a great relationship with his young cast and the stars Virginia McKenna and Ronald Fraser. . . . The result is compulsive reading as she recalls that cold wet summer, while the camera crew wrapped up warm and she shivered in her skimpy dress as Able Seaman Titty Walker.

Roger Wardale,
biographer of Arthur Ransome

A fascinating insight into filming on location in the Lake District.

Classic Boat

Sophie's magical *Swallows* tales . . . a heart-warming account of making the movie.

Daily Mail

Sophie Neville, who played Titty in the film based on the classic Arthur Ransome books, has revealed the behind-the-scenes secrets in her new book, released to coincide with the anniversary of filming.

The Telegraph

. . . My ultimate adventure dream, as that of a whole generation, was one of playing Titty in a film!! So your account is recounting that dream for all of us.

Jill Goulder,
The Arthur Ransome Society

You don't need to be a *Swallows & Amazons* fan to enjoy this book – it's universal!

Winifred Wilson,
Editor of *Signals*

A fascinating insight into behind the scenes of the film world. Sophie cleverly intersperses entries from the diary she wrote at the time into her amusingly written memoir of playing Titty. Lots of photos throughout the book bring the scenes to life – a delightful read.

Celia Lewis,
author of *An Illustrated Country Year*

Your reminiscences are a treasure-trove.

The Arthur Ransome Trust

Gorgeous.
Yours magazine

A delightful book.
The Lady

The Lutterworth Press
P.O. Box 60
Cambridge
CB1 2NT
United Kingdom

www.lutterworth.com
publishing@lutterworth.com

ISBN: 978 0 7188 9496 2

British Library Cataloguing in Publication Data
A record is available from the British Library

First published by Classic TV Press, 2014

Reprinted in a new edition by The Lutterworth Press, 2017

Copyright © Sophie Neville, 2014

Original illustrations © Sophie Neville, 2014

Front cover photograph © STUDIOCANAL Films Limited

Quotes from Arthur Ransome © The Arthur Ransome Literary Estate
Use of Arthur Ransome's crossed flags motif by kind permission
of The Arthur Ransome Literary Estate

Swallows & Amazons (U) 1974 – a Theatre Projects Films Ltd
production. All rights now held by STUDIOCANAL Films Limited

For my ever patient husband Sim
'He's winged his arrows with the parrot's feathers'

Claude Whatham with the Swallows.

Note to the reader:

Sophie's childhood diary entries are presented
in a sans serif typeface.

Contents

Director Claude Whatham showing Simon West and me
how to use the 16mm camera.

Opposite: returning to *Swallow* with our purchases from Rio.

The Cast and Crew
of *Swallows & Amazons*

The Cast

Mrs Walker   VIRGINIA MCKENNA

Uncle Jim   RONALD FRASER

John Walker,   SIMON WEST
Captain of the *Swallow*

Susan Walker,   SUZANNA HAMILTON
Mate of the *Swallow*

Titty Walker,   SOPHIE NEVILLE
Able-seaman of the *Swallow*

Roger Walker,   STEPHEN GRENDON
Ship's Boy of the *Swallow*

Nancy Blackett,   KIT SEYMOUR
Captain of the *Amazon*

Peggy Blackett,   LESLEY BENNETT
Mate of the *Amazon*

Mrs Dixon	BRENDA BRUCE
Mr Dixon	MIKE PRATT
Young Billy	JOHN FRANKLYN-ROBBINS
Old Billy	JACK WOOLGAR
Sammy the Policeman	DAVID BLAGDEN
Nurse	KERRY DARBISHIRE
Baby Vicky	TIFFANY SMITH
Mrs Jackson	MOIRA LATE
Mr Jackson	BRIAN ROBEY JONES
Native on the Rio Jetty	MR PRICE
Shopkeeper	MR TURNER
Polly, the green parrot	BEAUTY PROCTOR

Supporting Artists

Visitor at Railway Station	MRS PRICE
Native on the steamer	MARTIN NEVILLE
Steamboat owner	GEORGE PATTINSON
Motorboat mechanic	STANLEY WRIGHT
Boat mechanic	JAMES STELFOX
Casual holiday-maker	HERBERT BARTON
Man just returned from abroad	L. LUCAS DEWS
Cyclist at Rio	SARAH BOOM
Motorcyclist	JACK HADWIN

Rio Visitors

JANE GRENDON	JANE PRICE	SIMON PRICE
TAMZIN NEVILLE	PERRY NEVILLE	PANDORA DOYLE
ALAN SMITH	JANET HADWIN	PEGGY DRAKE
WILLIAM DRAKE	JILL JACKSON	LINDSAY JACKSON
NICOLA JACKSON	FIONA JACKSON	SHANE JACKSON
MAGDA KHAN	LORNA KHAN	ZENA KHAN

and the
KENDAL BOROUGH BAND

The Crew

Director	CLAUDE WHATHAM
Producer	RICHARD PILBROW
Screenplay	DAVID WOOD
Associate Producer	NEVILLE C. THOMPSON
Original Music	WILFRED JOSEPHS
Conductor	MARCUS DODS
Art Director	SIMON HOLLAND
Costume Designer	EMMA PORTEOUS
Set Dresser	IAN WHITTAKER
Sailing Director	DAVID BLAGDEN
Director of Photography	DENIS LEWISTON
Production Consultant	HARRY BENN
Production Manager	GRAHAM FORD
Film Editor	MICHAEL BRADSELL
First Assistant Director	DAVID BRACKNELL
Second Assistant Director	TERRY NEEDHAM
Third Assistant Director	GARETH TANDY
Continuity	SUE MERRY
Camera Operator	EDDIE COLLINS
Focus Puller	BOBBY STILWELL
First Assistant Cameraman	DAVID WYNN-JONES
Assistant Cameraman	CEDRIC JAMES
Sound Recordist	ROBIN GREGORY
Boom Operator	JOHN SALTER
Camera Boat Advisor	MIKE TURK
Sound Editor	IAN FULLER
Dubbing Mixer	BILL ROWE
Wardrobe Master	TERRY SMITH
Make-up	PETER ROBB-KING
Hairdresser	RONNIE COGAN
Chief Electrician	MARTIN EVANS
Grip	DAVID CADWALLADER
Electrician	PETER BLOOR
Best Boy	DENIS CARRIGAN
Property Master	JOHN LEUENBERGER
Action Props	BOB HEDGES
Stand-by Props	TERRY WELLS
Carpenter	BILL HEARN
Scenic Painter	MICK GUYETT

Stills Photography	ALBERT CLARKE
Publicist	BRIAN DOYLE
Production Associate	RICHARD DU VIVIER
Production Accountant	BOB BLUES
Production Secretary	SALLY SHEWRING
Producer's Assistant	MOLLY FRIEDEL
Chaperones	DAPHNE NEVILLE
	JANE GRENDON
Unit Nurse and Driver	JEAN MCGILL
Tutor	MARGARET CAUSEY

Other crew members

Lee Apsey	Richard Daniel	Craig Hillier
Ron Baker	John Pullen	Harry Heeks
Graham Orange	Mike Henley	Joe Ballerino
Ted Elliot	Eddie Cook	John Engelman
John Mills	Ernie Russell	Toni Turner
Phyllis B	Nick Newby	Les Philips
Gay Lawley-Wakelin		

Clive Stuart of the Keswick Launch Company
John and Margaret of Pinewood Caterers
Robert Wakelin, David Stott and other drivers
from Browns of Ambleside
Mrs Dora Capstick, who gave Ronald Fraser accordion lessons
John Foster, snake handler

Lighting Equipment by Lee Electric (Lighting) Limited
Sound Equipment by Delta Sound Services
Construction by F.T.V. Scenery Limited
Film Processing by Technicolor
Filmed in Eastmancolor

Made on location in The Lake District National Park, England
by Theatre Projects Film Productions Ltd.
10 Long Acre, London WC2, England

With grateful thanks to The National Trust, The Lakeside and
Haverthwaite Railway, and the folk of the Lake District

Originally distributed by ANGLO EMI Film Distributors Ltd.
Currently distributed by StudioCanal Films Ltd.

ELTERWATER

NATIVE SETTLEMENT of
Ambleside

Skelwith Fold

N

W   E

S

Steamboat
Museum

RIO
Bowness

MAP
OF
WINDERMERE

M.V. TERN

Low
Ludderburn

Silver Holme

Blake Holme

Lakeside +
Haverthwaite
Railway

River Leven

0   1
ONE NATIVE MILE.
CHART DRAWN BY SOPHIE NEVILLE.

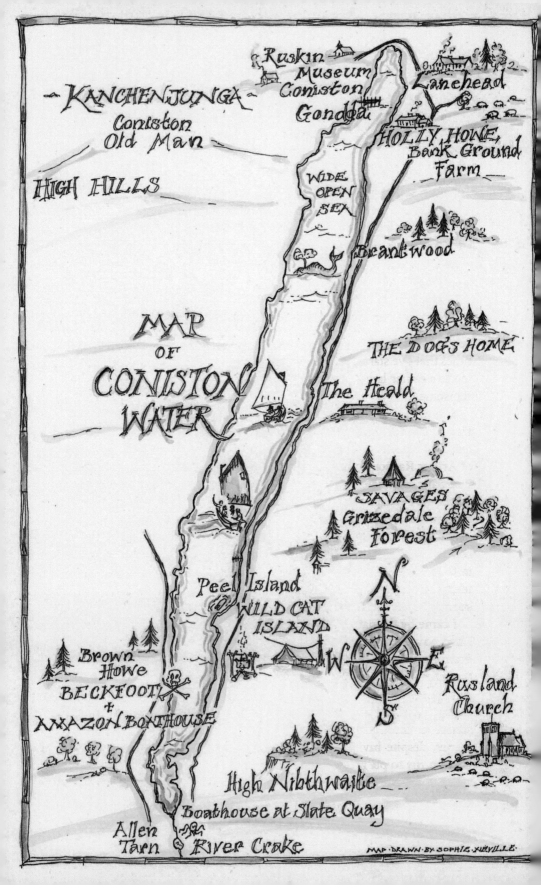

Introduction
Serendipity

serendipity /ser-uhn-dip-i-tee/ *n.* an aptitude or faculty for making desirable discoveries by accident.

Serendipity, indeed. The word has been brought to my attention so many times that I've started to take note. The serendipity in question connects me to a rather large, bald man with a massive moustache called Arthur Ransome.

Sometimes extraordinary things do happen to ordinary people. Little girls can find themselves becoming film stars. Long ago, and quite unexpectedly, I found myself appearing in the EMI feature film of Arthur Ransome's book *Swallows and Amazons*, made for a universal international audience. I played Able-seaman Titty, one of the four Swallows. Perhaps it would be more accurate to say that I became Titty for a while, wearing thin cotton dresses and elasticated navy-blue gym knickers, which the camera crew soon referred to as 'passion killers'. The book was written in 1929 and although the film adaptation was made in the early 1970s it has an ageless quality and has been repeated on television year after year, typically on a Bank Holiday between movies starring either Rock Hudson or Doris Day, sometimes both.

I came by the part of Titty because I could play the piano. Although I had no ambition to be an actress, at the age of ten I was cast in a BBC dramatisation of Laurie Lee's *Cider with Rosie*. I played a little girl from the valley of Slad called Eileen Brown. Laurie Lee told us she was the first person he'd ever fallen in love with. He knew my parents and was around during the filming since he had a cottage nearby. I'd been to a village school in the Cotswolds myself and enjoyed being in the classroom scenes, despite having to wear a drab and rather itchy green dress. I was too shy to put myself forward when the director, Claude Whatham, asked if anyone knew the chants to playground skipping games, but I

1

Me as Eileen Brown with
Claude Whatham in 1971.

coped with having to fall in love. It only involved smiling broadly. The difficult bit was that I had to accompany the eleven-year-old Laurie Lee on the piano while he played a violin in the village concert. I plodded through *Oh, Danny Boy* at an agonising pace.

'Do you think you could play a little faster?' the director asked.

'No,' I said, flatly. 'These are crotchets, they don't go any faster.'

Claude Whatham must have remembered my crotchets, for two years later, in March 1973, a letter appeared, addressed to my father. It arrived completely out of the blue, from a company called Theatre Projects:

Dear Mr. Neville,

Claude Whatham has asked me to write to you concerning
Sophie.

We are at present casting for a film version of SWALLOWS
AND AMAZONS which Mr. Whatham is going to direct.   We
were wondering if you would be interested in your daughter
being considered for one of the parts in this film.

If you would like to telephone me at the above number,
I would be delighted to give you all the information about
it.   I look forward to hearing from you.

Yours sincerely,

NEVILLE C. THOMPSON.

Amazing!

To gain a part I had to be able to swim. I think this was to do with ensuring I would not drown. As it happened I could row, sail and swim quite well. My parents had taught me. I can't remember Claude asking me about this when he interviewed me. He only wanted to know what my favourite television programme was.

'*Blue Peter!*'

'Why?'

'Because they show you how to do things.'

It was exactly what Mr Whatham wanted to hear. Why? Because that is how Arthur Ransome wrote his books. He doesn't tell. He *shows* his readers how to sail, how to camp, and how to fish. I had already read most of the twelve books in the series and loved the stories. What I didn't know then was the effect they would have on the rest of my life.

I couldn't envisage myself as Titty at all. The illustrations show her with dark hair, cut in a bob. Arthur Ransome had described her as 'a little eager imaginative child of about nine'. I was now aged twelve, and thought myself far more like the practical Susan, Titty's elder sister. However, I was soon persuaded that I could climb into the character and *play* the part of Titty. I took this assurance on board and did my best to behave like a nine-year-old with a vivid imagination. Thankfully they cut my straggly blonde hair, and I soon started singing out the dialogue that I already knew off by heart from reading the book: 'I expect someone hid on the island hundreds and hundreds of years ago.'

While Arthur Ransome was obviously impervious to the cold, I was not. I shivered terribly in the sleeveless cotton dress I was given to wear as we sailed off to Wild Cat Island, but otherwise I enjoyed playing Titty and soon became her in every way. She was a child who took to telling stories and drawing maps, her mind entering that of an imperialist explorer of the early twentieth century.

'Here we are, intrepid explorers, making the first ever way into uncharted waters. What mysteries will they hold for us? What dark secrets shall be revealed?' Titty wondered, transforming the English Lake District into an exotic land inhabited by natives and savages, some of whom used bows and arrows, while on a houseboat in a desolate bay lived Captain Flint with his green parrot. A parrot that she wanted very much indeed.

The letter from Theatre Projects came while my father was away on business in South Africa. Mum never, ever opened his mail, but made an exception this time. Had she not done so, I would have missed the opportunity to be considered for the part. She replied on his behalf, and Dad took us all into London the morning he stepped off the plane.

Chapter One
Preparations for Filming

By May 1973 I was on my way up to the North West of England to take a leading part in the feature film of *Swallows and Amazons* that the producer, Richard Pilbrow of Theatre Projects, had somehow persuaded Nat Cohen of EMI to finance. I had no idea of the responsibility being laid on my shoulders, or of the huge sums of money involved. I was just doing it for fun.

My lack of concern emanates from the pages of the diary that I kept. I have three volumes, in readable italic hand-writing, detailing what we did, and indeed what we said, on every single day. The wording is childlike but, as a little bit of film history, the diary provides the facts from an interesting angle. My mother was pleased when I started to type them up forty years later. She'd been nagging me for years.

On the inside cover of the first volume, I wrote:

> I had been very lucky to be picked out of all those hundreds of children for one of the six who were cast. I had been in a film with Claude, the director, before but only for three days. He short-listed me for the part of Titty. I was then chosen with 22 others for a sailing holiday [a cold weekend in March at Burnham-on-Crouch] to see how we reacted and sailed.

This weekend had proved something of an endurance test. It was miles from where we lived. The weather was awful, with driving rain falling on rough seas. The only warm piece of clothing I took was a knitted hat. We slept in cabins aboard a permanently moored Scout boat with flowery orange curtains. There were no parents around to boost our morale, the sailing was challenging, and I felt bitterly cold the entire time.

Richard Pilbrow brought his two children, Abigail and Fred. With him was Claude Whatham, Neville Thompson (the associate producer), and

The final audition at Burnham-on-Crouch in March 1973.

David Blagden who, as Claude was no sailor, was to be the film's sailing director. He told us that he had read *Swallows and Amazons* forty-two times, which sounded daunting.

Out of an initial 1,800 who applied, twenty-two children had been short-listed and were effectively auditioning for the six parts. I still meet people who went up for them. We didn't read from a script, we weren't asked to improvise or act out a scene and there was no film test, but 8mm movie footage was taken. I wonder if it still exists.

While there were only two or three boys up for the role of Roger, there were five girls auditioning to play Titty. At one stage Claude had a chat with the five of us in our cabin, all the Tittys. The others were so sweet that I didn't think I stood a chance. I was undeniably gangly and felt that I kept saying the wrong thing. One of the other girls looked incredibly together. She had pretty, fashionable clothes and would make a point of brushing her hair and wearing jewellery, just as Mummy would have liked me to have done. While I was used to boats my sailing wasn't up to much. I was completely in awe of the seamanship of Kit Seymour (who would land the part of Nancy) and how fast she got the dinghies to whizz through the driving rain.

We were all lucky to be the right age at the right time. I was perhaps the most fortunate because at twelve-and-a-half I was really too tall for the part of Titty. I was a year older and a good two inches taller than Simon West, who played Titty's older brother, John, but Claude must have known that he could cheat this on-screen. I wrote: 'In about a week's time they rang up to say I had got the part and Mummy a chaperone.'

One of Arthur Ransome's most famous quotes is: 'Grab a chance and you won't be sorry for a might-have-been.' The chance was grabbed.

The Lake District gets very busy in July and August, so busy that the production team were advised to film during the summer term. This was a bit of an issue as I was at boarding school, a conventional Anglican convent. By law, before I could work as an actress, my parents needed formal written permission from Sister Ann-Julian, my headmistress. This seemed unlikely. She wrote back, saying that she had prayed about it with my housemistress Sister Allyne. They gave us the go-ahead.

The filming was to start on Monday 14th May 1973. We were told there would be forty-six days on location with a full crew for a ninety-minute movie.

Friday 11th May – First day in the Lake District

On that Friday, Mum saw my father off to work, dropped my two little sisters at their village school and took me for a medical to satisfy our local County Council. What they would have done if I had been deemed unfit I do not know, but I had already passed stringent medical tests for the company insuring the film, who'd sent me to the grandest doctor in Harley Street. My mother then bought me a stash of hay-fever pills before driving from Stroud in the Cotswolds to Ambleside – a journey of about two hundred miles. Her small, rattling, red Renault Four hatchback was packed to the gills. My diary entry, spelling mistakes and all, reads as follows:

> We got to the motor-way and travelled up to Westmorland and the Laks. Half-way we stopped at a motor-way service station and filled up with petrol. We had lunch. I had steak followed by a nickerbockerglory. We went of again. We turned off and wound our way through the county until we found the guest-house.
>
> Mummy and I unpacked. When we had finished all the others came. They unpacked and we watched television until a minnibus took us to the hotel to see Claude. When we went in before us lay a magnificent tea. We ate a fair amount and then Claude came and talked to us about the

> film and told us we would not have a script. We watched
> color television there and went back. We had super I went
> to bed and Suzanna came later and went to bed too. (She
> slept with me poor soul!). We rote our dairys and slept a
> well-earned sleep.

The film company took over the rather grand hotel on the lakeside. They booked us children into Oaklands, a solid stone Edwardian guest house above the little town of Ambleside. 'To separate you from the hurly-burly of the crew', was how my mother saw it. The others had all travelled up by train, via a last minute costume fitting at Morris Angel and Son Ltd, Theatrical Costumiers, Shaftesbury Avenue in London. The Evening Standard took a shot of them on the station platform.

Kit Seymour, who came from Middlesex, was playing Nancy Blackett, 'Captain of the Amazon and terror of the seas.' Her sister, Peggy Blackett, was played by Lesley Bennett, who was often described as being talkative and bubbly.

Simon West, who was cast as my brother John Walker, Master of the *Swallow*, was from Abingdon in Oxfordshire. His father worked at the nuclear research station nearby. He had only auditioned because his sister had been keen to be considered for a part herself. Claude said that Simon was everybody's idea of the perfect son. 'He has only to be told anything once.' He was both bright and practical, exactly like the character he played. I never had a brother in real life so it was quite interesting to gain a ready-made one.

Suzanna Hamilton took the role of my sister Susan. She went to the Anna Scher after-school theatre club in Islington and was the only one of us who had a pronounced ambition to act. She explained that she would have to be credited as Zanna Hamilton as there was already a Susannah Hamilton registered with Equity. Suzanna would have preferred to use her full name but was glad she had been christened Suzanna with a z. Most people called her Zanna anyway. I grew aware that we were having to make decisions that would affect our future.

The part of my younger brother Roger had been given to Stephen Grendon (always known as 'Sten'), with whom I'd appeared in *Cider with Rosie* when he played young Laurie Lee. Sten, who was now aged eight, couldn't swim well, but Claude adored him and was determined he should take on the role. He had travelled up from Gloucestershire via the costume fitting in London, with his mother Jane, who was to act as an official chaperone along with my mother. I wasn't quite so sure about having a little brother. He seemed very energetic.

And me? What did people think of me? Documents from the producer's office described me as 'a skinny, wide-eyed, little girl who loved to have a sketch pad near at hand'. They were right. While Mummy had been buying antihistamines at the chemist, I was choosing a paintbox and brush.

As my diary relates, we were taken for tea at the Kirkstone Foot Hotel to meet Claude. He was a small man, habitually clad in jeans, with a denim jacket. He seemed young and trendy for an adult. We had all got to know him a little during the weekend sailing in Essex, which had served as our final audition, but he was more respected and revered now, surrounded by assistants of different kinds, all anxious to please.

I can only think that we were thrilled to hear that we would not be learning lines, never realising it was Claude's key to getting natural performances out of us. I knew from my parents that Claude had decided not to cast children from stage schools who were trained to deliver dialogue in a theatrical manner. We, who were full of high spirits, were encouraged to start adopting our character names, which was something we enjoyed. Claude's other secret was that he never allowed us to see the 'rushes' – recently recorded film, newly returned from the developers – as he thought it might make us self-conscious. I learned later in life that he was quite right. It's dreadful seeing photographs of yourself, let alone un-edited film clips.

Claude Whatham, Sten Grendon, Simon West, myself
and Suzanna Hamilton at Derwentwater.

From the moment Richard Pilbrow gained the film rights from Mrs Ransome, he had been keen to cast children who were all confident in boats. I don't think Claude fully appreciated how deeply he would value the experience that both Kit and Simon had with sailing dinghies until we were out on the lakes in gusty weather. They were so good he later admitted there were times when they advised him what to do, which both stunned and amused him.

The thing that fascinated us above all else was watching the large colour television in the plush hotel lounge. I'm not sure if I had seen one before. They were hugely expensive in 1973 and considered a great luxury. The set, which had a wooden veneer, stood on legs and showed all three channels – BBC1, BBC2, and ITV, a channel we could not receive at home. We all thought it was phenomenal, including Claude.

Saturday 12th May – Second day

I woke up at about 6.00. Suzanna was already awake. We lay in bed for a part of time. Kit and Lesley came in fully dressed. They had been woken up by the clock in the hall at 4.00. They played Suzanna's ukelele until Mummy came in and told us to try to go to sleep, as we had a tiring day ahead of us. Then we had breakfast with the rest. We collected sailing gear of our own and set off to the hotel. We played in the garden until we were called to have our hair cut.

In the early 1970s most people had long hair. Ours had to be cut and bobbed to match the 1929 hairstyles in Arthur Ransome's well-known illustrations. Mum said that Sten really did have long, flowing hair, which looked extraordinary on an eight-year-old boy. He wrote in his scrapbook, 'When the hairdresser had got halfway through my hair he said let's wash it now. So he washed it with nice smelly shampoo.'

Sten went first and came out looking much older with all his locks cut off! Simon was next. He looked much the same, except with his ears showing.

We thought he looked so much better with a short back and sides, but such haircuts were a big issue. My mother had huge reservations about my hair being chopped off and said she nearly refused to let them. I am very glad she didn't. It was wonderful having it short. My hairstyle proved such a great success that I believe it may have set a fashion for having a graduated bob or 'Titty Haircut'. I noted, 'We all looked much different except Kit.' Suzanna thought, 'We all looked very funny!'

After that we hopped in the mini-bus and went to the dentist
to have our teeth polished. I was first, the others went later. It
did not take long. We went back to the hotel and had lunch with
Claude, David, Neville and Richard. After that we went sailing.

We had met our sailing director, David Blagden, at the audition weekend
in Burnham-on-Crouch. He was a tall, dark, good-looking actor who
had been in the film *Kidnapped* and was to play the part of Sammy the
Policeman. David was well known for having sailed across the Atlantic in
the 1972 Observer Single-handed Race. He made the crossing in *Willing
Griffin*, a Hunter 19, the smallest yacht ever to officially participate, and
came in tenth out of fifty-nine competitors.

David took us out on Windermere in *Swallow* that day, as we obviously
needed to get used to handling a clinker-built dinghy. It was thrilling to
be out on the water.

David was with the Captains and mates first, so Mummy,
Richard, Sten and I went for a ride in a motor-boat. I steered
and Richard took the controls. Then all the Swallows were
taken out in '*Swallow*'. Then the Amazons went out in '*Swallow*',
with David like us.

Richard Pilbrow's motor boat was a hired Capri, one of those hideous
orange and white fibreglass ones with a small cabin that were thought so
snazzy, but at least we could take shelter from the elements.

I faithfully recorded how we spent the rest of the day:

We went to the hotel and then to the Church Hall to have
gum-shoes fitted. We came back and I wrote my diary as
Mummy and Suzanna went to the book shop.

Next we had supper. Straight after I went up-stairs with
Mummy. We washed my hair and went down-stairs to dry my
hair under a funny hair dryer. I went up and this time slept
with Mummy to get more sleep. I wrote up the rest of my
diary while Mummy talked to Jane. I settled down and went
to sleep looking on the next day.

Sunday 13th May – Third day

A wet day on Windermere.

We went straight to the Lake. We got in the motor-launch
and went to *Swallow's* and *Amazon's* moorings. We hoisted sail
and went for a long run, where I got very cold.

Back then I only had a terrible blue nylon anorak that provided so little insulation I was unable to enjoy the sailing. It hadn't occurred to us to pack winter clothing or thick woolly sweaters. Richard Pilbrow realised he had also been over-optimistic about the leaf cover in the Lake District, where even the vegetation was still visibly underdressed.

> We went back and had soup. We went out again and practiced coming into the jetty and going out. We did this three times and then had a race. The Amazons won.

Although they were old boats, the lugsail dinghies could go at quite a lick. The *Amazon* had a centreboard and was proving much faster than *Swallow*, whose long keel made her roomy and stable but held her back when we were running with the wind. Both were difficult to turn unless you had a bit of speed up. We were used to modern rudders that dropped down into the water, whereas *Swallow* and *Amazon* had shallow ones shaped like the letter 'b'. They had no added buoyancy, but had pig iron ballast under the floorboards.

> Then we had lunch with Virginia, Claude, Richard and David. We collected stores and sailed off down the Lake. David was with the Amazons, Virginia was with us and Mummy and Jane in the chaperone boat. We went a long way down the Lake. We landed on the stoney shore and found a lovely little headland and ate our tea. We went back as before except with Virginia with the Amazons. We sang sea shantys. Half way back the motor-boat gave us a tow. We took down the sail and went straight to the waiting mini-bus.

Virginia McKenna

Virginia McKenna was to play our Mother, 'the best of all natives', Mary Walker. I did not know it, but another reason we had to start filming on 14th May was to fit in with her availability. She must have been very busy but was completely focused on us, sweet and enthusiastic about what we were doing. I remember her instigating games of Consequences. We all roared with laughter, startling other hotel guests, as she unfolded the strips of paper and read out the results.

'Virginia McKenna was completely right to play the part of a Naval Commander's wife,' said my father.

'In just a week's stay she managed to win everybody with her kindness, concern, and the ease with which she works so hard,' wrote Molly Friedel, Richard's girlfriend.

A darling of the British public, Virginia was the star whose name was intended to carry the film. We knew her from having loved the animal movies she'd been in – *Ring of Bright Water*, *An Elephant Called Slowly*, *Born Free* and the WWII classic *A Town Like Alice*, for which she won the BAFTA Award for Best Actress. Married to Bill Travers, she had four children of her own when she made *Swallows & Amazons*. I don't know how she managed to do so much.

Neville Thompson was also with us that first weekend. He was a director of Theatre Projects and experienced in making movies. He'd been the production manager on a number of Ken Russell's films including *The Devils* (1971) starring Vanessa Redgrave and Oliver Reed, *The Boyfriend* (1971) which featured Twiggy, and the biographical movie *Savage Messiah* (1972) with Dorothy Tutin and Helen Mirren. Here, he was responsible for most of the preparations before we arrived in Ambleside. As the associate producer, he was in charge of the budget, schedule and practical aspects of production, a good man to have on board. I always remember him wearing a sunshiny yellow shirt.

That day, signs reading 'T.P. LOC' – the secret code for 'Theatre Projects Location' – were being driven into the verges of the road leading to the south of Windermere with large black arrows pointing the way to the first location. The cameras were ready to roll.

Chapter Two
First Days on Film

Arthur Ransome's book was adapted for the big screen by David Wood. David had appeared opposite Malcolm McDowell in the somewhat shocking feature film called '*If. . . .*' about a boys' public school. Neville Thompson had also worked on this movie and, knowing that David had written several plays for children, invited him to dramatise *Swallows and Amazons*. It was his first screenplay. 'I was twenty-nine years old,' he told us later.

The first time I saw the script, with its dark orange cover, was early in 2011 when my mother pulled it from the back of a wardrobe. I had literally not been allowed to set eyes on it as a child. It is only now that I fully appreciate how beautifully it was crafted.

The film opens with a shot of a steam train passing through North Lancashire. This does not feature in the book but was a powerful image and a good way of introducing the Walker family, setting the period and the very Englishness of travelling up to the Lake District for the summer holidays. It was a wonder that this was possible: the Lakeside and Haverthwaite Railway, with its restored steam train, had only been open and running for two weeks – since 2nd May 1973, to be precise. It was a private concern run by a bunch of enthusiasts on the old Furness Railway branch line. The engine was an eighty-four-ton Fairburn 2-6-4 tank locomotive, of approximately 1930s vintage, standard gauge and coloured blackberry black.

As the producer, Richard Pilbrow was given the honour of calling the first take. He'd never made a film before and was lying in some tall weeds trying to keep out of the way as the camera focused on a wavering dandelion. He recalls:

> Denis Lewiston and the camera crew were in a pit to the side
> of the railway tracks; the train puffed away around the corner.

Neville said quietly to me, 'Richard, we're ready.' I declared, 'Turnover!' The camera turned. 'Action.' The train whistle pierced the morning sky, the huge locomotive lurched into sight around the bend and thundered towards us.

Being inside the railway carriage was equally exciting. What I never knew until I read the third scene recently, was that we added quite a bit of dialogue. I don't know if it was improvised or given to me by Claude but I said more than was scripted. I recorded the details in my diary.

Monday 14th May – First day of filming – the train journey

I woke up and dressed quickly because we had slept late. We went down to breakfast. We got into the mini-bus with our school books. This time we were joined by Mrs Price and her three children, who were to be Extras, and the school teacher, Margaret.

We arrived at our location which was an old railway line. The Extras were there changing and the crew were getting ready. We had our own bus for resting and doing our school work. It was a converted double-decker. We put our books down-stairs and changed into our costume up-stairs.

From 9.00–10.00 we had lessons. Then we had a rehearsal in the steam train for the day's filming. After that we had another hour of lessons. Then we had our lunch which we ate in our bus. We had a short rest and afterwards we did art. I drew an old car which we later drove in. After that we rested. Later Susan, Mother and I were filmed in the train compartment. This went on for some time. These were my lines:

> *Titty:* The endless treck through the Sahara desert. See the
>   camels bravely plod through the sand.
> *Susan:* Titty!
> (Mother, John, Roger speak)
> *Titty:* Do they have sheep in China?
> *Susan:* Of course.
> *Titty:* Well even if Daddy misses this holiday, he'll see
>   Chinese sheep when he gets to Hong Kong.

Claude's original intention was to shoot the film in 'story-order' as much as possible, as he thought this would be easiest for us to comprehend. Scene 3: INT. RAILWAY CARRIAGE DAY was, however, difficult to execute and proved a challenging first scene for us children. Once the railway carriage contained movie lights, the director, a huge 35mm Panavision camera, the cameraman, focus puller and assistant, with microphones and an assistant sound recordist, there wasn't any room for me. It also became extremely hot. When it was time to take shots of Titty, I had to give my lines to imaginary family members. They were no longer there – the camera had taken their place.

When I look back on these scenes , I feel our opening performances were rather wooden. Fortunately this didn't matter too much, as we were meant to be bored children on a long train journey. It was natural for Virginia to carry the scene. But what with Mother's magazine, our picnic and Susan's tapestry, the matter of continuity in the railway compartment was important. We greatly enjoyed learning about this technicality, which was vital if the shots that made up the scene were to cut together smoothly. Numerous Polaroid photographs were involved, which we found deeply interesting. These cameras had not been around for long, and we enjoyed watching the pictures develop.

We did our best to be helpful and keep an eye on the picnic, but somehow we got muddled and the continuity in this opening scene is out. This was probably because the continuity girl could not get in – into the railway carriage, that is. There was simply no room for her.

Simon, Virginia, Suzanna, Lesley, Kit and me outside the carriages.

On that first day of filming, a huge effort was made to 'dress' Haverthwaite Railway Station, at the southern end of Windermere, to bring across the feel of a bustling 1929 holiday destination. Local people, including our Oaklands landlady Mrs Price and her children, had been fitted with costumes in the Ambleside Church Hall. There were old bikes, a horse and cart, two period vehicles, and a porter's trolley laden with trunks. What I didn't know was that this was the documented intent of the producer:

> The setting of the book in its original period is important to heighten the sense of adventure. The imaginative use of period clothes, props, sailing boats and action vehicles (i.e. cars, bicycles etc) will also add another interest in the subject.

Having stepped down from the steam locomotive, we were piled into an open-topped motor for publicity photographs. I liked being in the car but thought the photograph was silly, especially since the Amazons were in their ordinary clothes. Surely they could have changed? Lesley had a red smock top with long flared sleeves, and Kit wore a ribbed polo-neck sweater. The result was later published in *The Guardian*, *Homes & Gardens* and *Woman's Realm*. Virginia McKenna was interviewed by a journalist from *The Times*, while we were hurried away to get on with our lessons. Our tutor just let us draw. I painted a picture of the train.

The yellow motor used in the film for our taxi was superb. It was far grander than a real Lakeland taxi would have been. Sten hung out of the window as Claude 'filmed us driving out of the station, along the platform at top speed'. This sounds bizarre. It wasn't until I returned to the station recently that I could see that he used the platform for this shot, instead of the less interesting forecourt on the other side of the building.

By this stage, other members of the crew had set up the camera in the corridor of the train and lit the compartment, so that we could be seen as a family while moving along.

Sten, Simon, Suzanna, Kit, Lesley and me.

> Next we filmed a scene in the train, in which Mother, who was
> talking about father says 'He'd say, just look at that scenery,'
> and at that moment we went in to a tunnel, and all started
> laughing.

Kerry Darbishire, the shy girl in a brown dress who played Vicky's Nurse, told me that she was very impressed that we were all able to burst into spontaneous laughter. She'd found it impossible.

> After that we went back and took home a few Extras (support-
> ing artists who appeared at the station). After supper Mummy
> and I washed our hair. After writing my diary I went to sleep.

Although Titty was the one who always kept the ship's log in Arthur Ransome's stories, we girls all kept journals during the filming as part of our schoolwork. It was quite a task.

Suzanna's diary gives the story of making the film from the perspective of an actress, recording each day from a different angle. Her God-given sense of humour fills the pages. When she lent it to me, along with a bundle of photographs, I immediately recognised the blue-bound book bought with my mother in Ambleside.

Tuesday 15th May – Second day of filming

If you ever go to Bank Ground Farm above Coniston Water – the inspiration for Ransome's Holly Howe – you must run down the field to the lake as we did. As soon as you arrive. And at top speed. As your lungs take in the mountain air, you will be filled by the same feeling of elation that we experienced playing the Walker children. The slope, formed by glacial scouring and subsequent deposits long ago, is steeper than you'd think. You soon learn the art of galumphing. As the ground levels out you reach the stone boatsheds, where you might even find a little ship called *Swallow*.

Most Arthur Ransome devotees will know of the Peak at Darien, where once stood stout Cortez. It is familiar to readers, since it appears in two of the illustrations in the book, but it cannot be found below the farmhouse. Mrs Ransome told our Producer Richard Pilbrow that he would come across the rocky peninsula at Waterhead on Windermere. However, he chose Friar's Crag on Derwentwater for the location. I didn't know it, but Christina Hardyment writes in her book *Arthur Ransome and Captain Flint's Trunk*, that the production team had found the very place Ransome had in mind, 'without the slightest idea that they were quite right to be doing so'. She discovered a postcard of Friar's Crag that he had marked up for Clifford Webb, the 1930s illustrator. It feels completely right when you are there, with the iconic view of an island under towering peaks. It was over this view that Claude would add the opening titles.

When he'd been making preparations for the film, associate producer Neville Thompson managed to take Mrs Ransome up to the Lake District to help him and Richard find the locations. Evgenia Ransome was Russian and reputedly six foot three, although in photos she looks about the same height as Arthur who was just under six foot. She had been Leon Trotsky's private secretary. Described as a 'tall jolly girl', she'd captured the heart of the pipe-smoking English journalist covering the events taking place in Petrograd in 1917. Arthur Ransome ended up accompanying her to the Baltic, fleeing the revolution. Some say she left with Bolshevik diamonds sewn into her knickers, but no one can deny the romance of their great escape, which eventually brought the couple to the Lake District.

'She was a pretty tough old lady, but with limited mobility,' Richard told me. 'It was quite a palaver talking her on the trip, but we did it. Where we stayed and how long we were there escapes me. Molly reminds me that she also came up during the filming. This made us very nervous because she'd taken such a violent dislike to Roger's photograph. She didn't like his dark hair. I was afraid she might cause a scene in front of you kids. However, her visit passed off without incident.'

Looking at a letter sent to a solicitor that Richard kept for posterity, I can see that 'the casting requirements of every character and their clothes and hair styles' had been discussed with her 'at length'. She had several meetings with David Wood, the writer, as the story had to be condensed. She was 'an enormous influence on the shaping of the script, a substantial portion of which is now directly based upon her suggestions . . . she immediately agreed to certain alterations that we proposed and gave us, on our meeting of 3rd April, a great number of detailed and useful comments, a very large proportion of which we incorporated in the second draft of the screenplay. Some points of mild disagreement Mrs Ransome accepted, but the vast majority of points that she raised we were very happy to go along with.'

David Wood remembers:

> After I had written the screenplay, she was given time to read it before joining Richard, Neville and I in the Lake District to discuss it. She even came in a boat to Peel Island and excitedly

showed us the original places in the book! Then she and I
spoke in a room at the hotel. She didn't have many comments
to make, I'm glad to say! But she did question one particular
line – a line I had given to Susan. She said that Susan would
never have said that. Luckily I was able to find the line in her
husband's book – spoken by Susan! Mrs Ransome smiled and
said, 'I think it will be alright!' From then on, I liked to think
she trusted me . . .'

Returning to the Lakes must have been evocative for Evgenia. It was the
last time she went. Neville returned her to the nursing home, Aynhoe
Park near Banbury in Oxfordshire, where she quietly spent her last,
lonely days.

If you take the East of Lake Road along Coniston Water, you will
soon find Bank Ground. In 1973 it was leased by the redoubtable Lucy
Batty, who was bringing up seven children. The farm lies between
John Ruskin's former home, Brantwood, and Lanehead where Arthur
Ransome's friends the Collingwoods lived. Ransome was a particularly
good friend of Dora Collingwood, to whom he casually proposed
in his youth. She ended up marrying a good friend of her brother's,
an Irish-Armenian doctor keen on sailing, called Ernest Altounyan.
They went to live at his family home in Syria but every five years or
so they would bring their five children to visit their grandparents for
the holidays, often staying at Bank Ground Farm next door. In 1928,
Arthur Ransome helped Ernest to buy two fourteen-foot dinghies
called *Swallow* and *Mavis*. They were probably kept in the low stone
boathouses on Coniston Water.

It was for the Altounyan children, four girls and a boy – Taqui, Susie,
Titty, Roger and Brigit, the ship's baby, that Arthur Ransome wrote
Swallows and Amazons, after they had given him a pair of bright scarlet
Turkish slippers as a present for his forty-fifth birthday in January 1929.
I hadn't known that Titty was a real person when I played her in the
film. I only knew her character from the books. I've been told they were
very similar. Titty Altounyan was looking after her family and painting
seriously in 1973, but had distanced herself from the character she
inspired and I never met her.

The story is firmly set in August, an idyllic childhood summer when
the water was warm enough to swim daily and the only disappointment
was a total lack of wind. On 15th May 1973 it was grey and raining.
Instead of filming the sequence when Roger runs up the field, Denis
Lewiston, the director of photography, lit Mrs Batty's living room for

an evening scene. Simon Holland, the art director, dressed the low-ceilinged room in the style of a Westmorland farmhouse of the 1920s, with oil lamps and sombre furniture. Bob Hedges and his prop men brought in the camping gear we were supposed to be packing, while Virginia McKenna was having her hair done. Meanwhile, we were given lessons in the red double-decker bus, described by Geoffrey Mather in the *Daily Express* as being 'surely the most remarkable classroom ever'.

Then we filmed a short scene, which I recorded in my diary:

> I was making a flag. I said –
>
> *Titty:* We need a dictionary.
> *John:* Why?
> *Titty:* For talking to the natives of course.
> *Susan:* Should I pack bandages and medicines and things?
> *Titty:* Oh no! On desert islands they cure everything with herbs. We'll have lots of plagues, fevers, illness and diseases and cure them with herbs that the natives give us.
> *Mother:* No medicines or herbs. Anyone who wants doctoring is invalided home.
> *Titty:* Oh of course, if it's really serious but we can have one or two plagues by our-selves.

If you do not immediately recognise the dialogue, it is because it was never used in the finished film. You do see Susan packing bars of soap. There is also a shot of me making heavy weather of sewing our flag, my hair pinned back rather aggressively. A modern reel of white cotton is lying on the desk. John stowed the telescope in a biscuit tin, which to me now seems a mistake as we used it on the voyage, very much not in a tin, but then one always re-packs many times before an important trip.

After lunch, we shot the scene when Mother is teaching us how to erect a tent on rocky ground, saying, 'Father and I often slept in one when we were young.' Titty asks if she is really old. 'Not really. But I was younger then,' Mother replies, looking dubious.

The weather must have cleared up a bit by teatime as we recorded the scenes in the boathouse when John discovers *Swallow*, brings her out to the stone jetty and steps the mast. I'm pretty sure that the sunlight comes from an arc-lamp. They must have driven the generator down to the lakeside. Suzanna got her shorts wet as she pushed out the old clinker-built dinghy, but we loved being by the water.

Wednesday 16th May – Third day of filming

The Amazons' time had come. In the script, the short scene where Nancy and Peggy careen their dinghy is set in the *Amazon* boathouse, but Claude shot them scrubbing the underside of their dinghy on the lakeside, with Beckfoot, the house where the Blacketts lived, standing behind. Kit threw a bucket of water over him for his pains. It was a complete accident. She actually chucked the water onto the bottom of the boat, but it splashed back. Claude was squatting below the camera and got well and truly soaked by what must have been very cold lake water. Kit flung back her head and roared with laughter. He took it in good spirits but only up to a point. I don't think he had anything else to wear.

A later article in *The Times* included an extract from Kit Seymour's diary:

> This is the day I had been waiting for. The Amazons had at last begun filming. We got changed and had to be made up sunburnt. We then rehearsed what to do. We did the second scene. I quite accidentally threw a bucket of water at Claude. After lunch we had to film the interior of the boathouse. Peggy had to say: 'Not a breath of wind.' This was quite funny because our hair was flying about everywhere. They had to film this scene quite a lot of times.

I was a conscientious child and keen not to fall behind with my schoolwork. Children under the age of sixteen have to be issued with a licence by their local education authority before they can act professionally in the United Kingdom. This comes with strict regulations. My mother interpreted these her own way, deciding it would be quite fine if we did fifteen hours of school work a week rather than a minimum of three hours a day, as the rule book stipulated. I spent my time catching up in our bus, recording that 'We went home at about half past four and I was very pleased because I had done seven hours proper schooling.' I sound like a terrible goody-goody. Kit relished the prospect of only having to do three hours of lessons, although she often did much more.

Mum was equally fluid about the time we spent on set – or, indeed, on location. Sten was aged eight. I now know he was meant to go home promptly at 4.30pm, but we all returned together whenever it was deemed practical. However, his mother was with him and if ever there was a child who needed to let off steam it was Sten. Sending him back to the Oaklands guest house early could have endangered

David Blagden with my mother at Brown Howe.

the people of Ambleside. It did us a lot of good to work hard, and cope with real, if channelled, responsibility. We were all bursting with energy, so much so that I grazed my leg badly when climbing a tree at lunchtime that day. Claude put a stop to that as a result. He couldn't risk any of us getting injured. My sister Tamzin broke her ankle when she was in the middle of filming once. It could have been a disaster, but luckily the drama was set in 1904, and her long Edwardian petticoats covered the splint. My legs were on full display. If I hadn't been wearing dungarees when I climbed that tree, the whole world would have seen my scratches.

I was intrigued by the large house featured as Beckfoot and enjoyed wandering past the towering rhododendrons in the garden. We used Brown Howe on the west side of Coniston, south of Peel Island, as our location. The Edwardian boathouse is also there on the edge of the lake. Christina Hardyment felt that Arthur Ransome must have modelled Beckfoot on the Collingwoods' house Lanehead, but the film required a big house with lawns going down to the water. Brown Howe and its gothic boathouse somehow felt right.

That same day, my mother wrote to my father at home in Gloucestershire:

Oaklands,
Millans Park,
Ambleside

May 16th 1973

My darling,

Here we all are eating Kendal Mint cake – sitting on the lawn facing a beautiful lake – in the blazing sunshine. . .

I have to keep a log book of each half an hour of work and lessons. The one teacher is just like Muriel with bright red hair and loads of eye shadow and quite good except she can't do modern Maths.

All the kids are being very good. S. got very tired yesterday with lots of lines and four hours of work, so I had to 'cook the books'. I have her in my room as the three other girls are a bit wild and much more robust. Tomorrow they do the island scene.

We go very early to bed. No hi-jinks. Up at 6.30 for 7am breakfast. At eight the mini-bus collects us. Jane Grendon is really a very nice person and we get on well, but she does get easily agitated and gets very nervous, so she's had today off and it's much calmer without her.

The script is super. Very cleverly constructed and very exciting at the end. I don't know how they'll do the pearl diving scenes in this icy water. Claude got a bucketful on his head from Nancy today. Our Sten is causing a little hoo hah. I find him a very interesting child. I've ordered fresh fruit for them all as we get a lot of packet soups and tinned food from Mrs P. who gets a bit fraught.

The phone number of the dinghy hire place is Windermere 2121 (Windermere Aquatic). I cannot phone as I am not here in the evening. I will have rung by the time you get this but you could phone them to check. I have sent off two films but I expect they will be awful. Don't forget the projector. Virginia McKenna is here for one week and will miss seeing you so you'll have to leave the projector here so she can see the audition. She comes back again on June 16th. She is super. It's a pity you'll miss her.

All love, Daphne xxxx

Ha! Mum was finding how biddable and compliant I was in comparison with other girls of my age.

The food at the guest house was taking its toll. It was not a good idea to feed children on packet soups and baked beans in the days when 35mm film stock was so extremely expensive. No one realised why, but the chemical additives and preservatives made Sten hyperactive. A visiting journalist wrote: 'By the end of the day Roger, aged seven, had mown down the entire film crew using a hammer as a mock machine gun. He had fallen down several times and emerged with grazed knees all splattered with mud.'

Suzanna simply refused to eat processed food. 'I couldn't get her to eat anything,' Mum told me. Location catering is excellent now – exquisite – but back in the early 1970s it could be pretty basic canteen food produced from the back of a grey 'chuck wagon'. We'd queue up in the rain for a tray of meat and two veg, which was usually consumed in our school bus. The crew very kindly let us eat first, pushing us to the front of the queue, which was a huge relief if it was chilly. They used a second red double-decker that had been converted into a dining bus with the same scratchy old seats either side of small tables. You could help yourself to knives and forks, tomato ketchup and little paper napkins on the way in. The call sheet always specified: 'LUNCH for approx 70 persons', so the budget must have been considerable but there was no salad table, just a working man's meal with coffee in plastic cups and paste sandwiches provided later with tea. The tea itself was good.

Mum started to order fruit for us and we relished it. It was a huge treat back then to have bananas or melon, oranges and grapes. Most families only had a fruit bowl at Christmas. Ours seemed to refill as if by magic while we grazed on the contents. As soon as we had eaten, Mum tried to make us rest in the fitted bunk beds at the top of our bus. I don't think she could pin down the Amazons easily but she made me get between the sheets with a hot waterbottle. I know I objected at first but I must have needed to lie down properly, especially when it was cold.

Apart from Sue Merry, the 'Continuity Girl', the film crew consisted entirely of men, forty-five of them. This included the hair and make-up designers, the wardrobe master, the art director, set dresser, prop men, a carpenter and a scenic painter, the sound recordist and boom operator, the director of photography, camera operator, focus puller and grip in charge of the camera-mounts with the electricians from Lee Electric, who looked after the lights and generators. The director, with three assistant directors as well as the sailing director, production associate and producer, had the job of organising all the others, along with a number of lorry and bus drivers. I didn't know it at the time, but there was a film accountant and location manager and, being a feature film, we also had a permanent stills photographer and a publicity manager. And this was a *small* crew. Terry Smith, the wardrobe master, seemed to cope without assistants or dressers by roping in Mum to help now and again. Everyone knew each other pretty well from having worked together on previous movies. Whenever we needed boats, up to six local boatmen would also join the queue for the chuck wagon – and the mobile loos. Mum wouldn't let me use these lavatories. She had reservations about the ratty-looking chap who serviced them.

Neville Thompson had a production secretary called Sally Shewring, but she must have been stuck in the production office back at the unit hotel as we never saw her. Molly Friedel, Richard's girlfriend and assistant, was often on location. She was American, tall with long brown hair and always had time for us. Molly was one of the few female lighting designers in theatre. While we milled about, playing on the rocks by the shore of Coniston Water, she was working on the lighting plot for the next Rolling Stones concert.

We were also looked after by our tutor, Mrs Causey, and a wonderful minibus driver called Jean McGill. She had been a top BOAC flight attendant but had returned to Westmorland to care for her ailing mother. She took the job of driving us around the area to keep busy. As soon as Mum found out that she was also a qualified nursing sister, she made

Molly Friedel with Richard Pilbrow and his dog.
Our double-decker buses can be seen in the background.

sure that Jean was taken on as the official unit nurse. This was a great improvement as it meant she could be around the whole time and we never had to wait for the bus. We soon found that we needed a nurse, too. People were always hurting themselves.

So all in all, with our chaperones there were usually about six women around as well as journalists, friends and relatives who came to watch. It was a huge circus with sixty to eighty people milling about, with more joining us when we had crowd scenes, such as the day we explored Rio, but that comes later.

Thursday 17ᵗʰ May – Fourth day of filming

It looks as if Mum had had a word with someone about the food. I noted that we had turkey for lunch on location that day, which was almost unheard of back then, but the improvements came too late for Mate Susan.

> I woke, dressed, went down to breakfast, and with the others, into the minibus. We drove off to Coniston. Suzanna started off feeling ill. When we got there we started to change into our costumes as the first scene we did was sailing to the island. I was awfully cold but survived. The second shot was landing and the third exploring. We had turkey for lunch. After lunch Nancy (Kit) broke a swing. I finished my fifteen hours of school work and so did most of the others. I missed tea. Suzanna felt even worse. We were taken home. Mummy put her straight to bed with hot soup. We had a super salad supper made by Mr Price. Suzanna was taken to the doctor. Simon and I felt ill too.

My mother wrote to Dad in a much lighter mood:

My darlings,

On the shore of lake Coniston today. Very windy but sunny. . . . The Swallows are sailing to their island. Poor Titty in a thin cotton dress, navy blue knickers and nothing else! We are longing for you to come up. I had dinner last night, great treat, with Brian Doyle, the publicity man. He says you <u>must</u> bring your 16mm Bolex camera and take a film. He would know how to sell it for you. They offered the taking of the film-making to *Blue Peter*, giving John Noakes a part, but they turned it down. You could probably do everything you'd need in the 2 weeks. My one (8mm ciné camera) wouldn't be good enough.

Susan is not very well, which is causing a bit of worry. I have to continually cook the books with work time, but they really are having the time of their lives, and Sophie is surviving best of the lot so far.

All love to all – Ruth and Gertie and co, and dear Lupy,

Daffy xx

I did not know until I read Mum's letter that *Blue Peter* had been given a chance to document the making of the film. I wonder if John Noakes, the presenter, even knew that he'd been offered a part. Biddy Baxter, then editor of the programme, was keen on 'behind-the-scenes' items. Lesley Judd had made one earlier about *Dad's Army*, the wartime sitcom starring Arthur Lowe and John le Mesurier, who happened to be a vague cousin of Dad's. My father accepted Brian's advice, bought 16mm stock for a borrowed Bolex movie camera, and took on the task himself.

As to the navy-blue knickers that Mum refers to, the crew took great delight in the sight of my passion killers. Claude had me tuck my dress up into them. Apparently the Altounyan girls had done this, since they usually wore dresses in the 1930s rather than shorts. I was never allowed to untuck mine between takes for fear of spoiling continuity. It made me feel that I was wearing much less and haunts me still. A photograph of us sitting around the campfire, featuring my long white legs, was recently published in *The Daily Telegraph*.

I first met Emma Porteous, our costume designer, at a fitting in Shaftesbury Avenue , when I tried on the ivory-coloured silk dress and buttoned shoes which I wore in the train. She then had my cotton frocks made up, apparently without a thought to the Westmorland climate. The fact that they were rather short was in keeping with 1970s fashion, rather than that of 1929. Emma confided in Mum that they would cheat on the length a bit. Arthur Ransome would have turned in his grave. Luckily Titty's dresses just look a little outgrown. It was Claude who insisted that we all – boys and girls – wore original 1929 knickers. Mum approved of the gym knickers, having made me wear them to school from the age of seven to eleven despite knowing how I withered with embarrassment when they were scrutinised by other girls every time I changed for Games. She also found us woollen vests to wear once everyone realised how cold it was out on the water. I had to beg Terry to let me wear a grey cardigan in subsequent sailing scenes.

Emma Porteous must have been too expensive and too busy to be with us the whole time. She'd been making *The Lovers!* written by Jack Rosenthal and starring Richard Beckinsale, and *Dr Jekyll and Mr Hyde* with Kirk Douglas, Susan George and Stanley Holloway.

Mum with me and Simon in our tracksuits and BOAC buoyancy aids.

The terrible royal-blue or scarlet nylon tracksuits with 'go-faster' stripes down the arms that we wore on location were bought to keep us warm during rehearsals. Rather than Wardrobe, the assistant directors Terry Needham and Gareth Tandy were sent to buy them for us in Ambleside, probably by my mother. This was a huge mistake, firstly because they were ineffective waterproofs, and secondly because they found their way into the publicity shots. They even made their way onto the cover of the VHS tape of the movie released in 1999. I thought at the time that they were a misguided purchase (and please note that I was twelve) but we were so grateful for the meagre covering that we willingly climbed into them. Everyone on the crew was wrapped up warm and well equipped with wet weather gear. They needed to be. There was so much hanging around.

While it took time to line up a dinghy for a shot, Denis Lewiston was very strict about waiting for clouds to pass so that it looked sunshiny on screen, even if it wasn't that sunny in reality. This could take ages and 'takes' were often snatched between scudding clouds. When it was sunny we'd have to wait around while a vapour trail from an aircraft faded. I have a vision of Denis in a navy-blue raincoat peering at the sky with a shaded eyeglass that he wore on a long cord around his neck, while we shivered and shook beside him.

Denis Lewiston with the Panavision 35mm camera.

I now gather that there was both a Production Office and Accounts Office at the Kirkstone Foot where Richard Pilbrow retreated at the end of the day. He found an old *Theatre Projects Newsletter*, which described the scene:

> In the front sitting room of the hotel now sits a 35mm projector and screen for the evening ritual of watching rushes. In the yard is a 35-foot radio antenna for communication with the locations . . . the production office is a hectic place, where two phones constantly ring, a shortwave radio receiver crackles, and a copying machine endlessly runs off call-sheets, movement orders, script revisions, numerous "very important" charts, reports, and lists. Sally Shewring is the ever-cool production secretary who seems to know where everything and everybody is at a given time. Production Manager, Graham Ford, and Associate Producer Neville C. ('You can't have it, it costs too much') Thompson also occupy the office and are administrative masters of the monster.

'Making a film,' he wrote later in his autobiography, 'is really quite like fighting a war – it requires strategic planning. Every night we watched the rushes and planned options for the morrow. Every morning before dawn, Neville and I reviewed the weather and decided what we were to shoot and where. Before seven, convoys of vehicles left the Kirkstone Foot Hotel, where we all stayed, and rolled towards the chosen location.'

And yet, even with this carefully considered planning, things could go awry. . . .

Friday 18ᵗʰ May – Fifth day of filming

Jane woke us up at quarter past seven. Suzanna was in bed ill. We went down to our late breakfast. Everybody else was halfway through. The location had been changed many times because of weather, and poor Suzanna, but it ended up at Holly Howe.

We arrived there before the buses and saw them coming down the hill. We finished off our fifteen hours' school work and did some more as well. Before lunch I changed into a nightie, and we did the bed scene where I was reading *Robinson Crusoe*.

After lunch (which I didn't want to eat) the Amazons went sailing, John acted, and Sten and I did art. I drew some horrible leaves and some lovely hens, except that they kept moving.

If you ever go to Bank Ground you must stand outside and imagine the sight of two red London Route Master buses making their way down the drive. They swayed from side to side. We thought it comic. No one could work out how the drivers managed to avoid bringing down the dry stone walls. While sheep grazed around us outside in the rain, we made ourselves comfortable at the Formica tables in our school bus and settled down to our lessons. I am sure it was good for us to be kept busy.

Meanwhile Simon Holland, the art director, and Ian Whittaker, the set dresser, transformed two of Mrs Batty's upstairs rooms into the bedrooms used by the Walker children in 1929, one for girls, one for boys. I changed in the cold and was rushed through the rain with a coat over my high-collared flannel nightie to the magical atmosphere of the set, warmed by the lights, with everyone's focus on what was just in front of the camera: me reading a beautiful hardback edition of Daniel Defoe's classic. Claude needed to establish that *Robinson Crusoe* was Titty's hero and that she was a voracious reader. I had to hold the book in a special way so that the cover could be seen clearly. It is interesting that I described this as a 'bed scene', something which might amuse some actors, especially those who are not at all keen on undressing for the camera (every actress I know).

'Each day the goal is to put between 2 and 4 minutes "in the can". That is to say, 2 to 4 minutes of useable film footage,' Molly explained in her letter to Theatre Projects' London office. Even with all the difficulties and delays, we probably achieved more than four minutes that day. They had already taken the shot where John was learning Morse code before lights out.

While the camera crew were in my bedroom, Simon was being made brown, very brown indeed, for the uneasy sequence, much later in the story, when John comes to explain himself to his mother and apologise for sailing at night. This was shot with Virginia sitting at a writing desk in the square bay window, with the view of Coniston Water beyond. I'd sat at the same desk while I was making *Swallow*'s flag.

The Amazons went sailing while all this was going on.

> Some people of the Press came and took a photo of Roger, Nancy, Peggy and me as the Amazons arrived back. They went off again. After seeing some sweet ten day old calves and mucking around, Sten, Simon, Mummy and I went home in the minibus. When we got back we found that Claude was just going from seeing Suzanna. I went in to see her too. She was looking very ill.

Saturday 19th May – The First Weekend

Suzanna was still ill.

'I told Claude that it was because she wouldn't eat anything,' my mother said. 'Ooh, she was difficult.'

But it can't have just been that. The handwriting in her diary looks very shaky: 'When I got back there was a doctor there, waiting, he was horrid and creepy and said there was nothing wrong with me,' she wrote. 'I went to another doctor who said I had septic spots on my tonsils so I immediately went back to bed.' Graham Ford, our production manager, called a unit day off. This decision probably cost thousands.

'The sun shone through the thick curtains as I woke up,' I wrote in my diary. That Saturday was a glorious day, one of the few we had in May. It rained on the Sunday, when the crew were originally scheduled to take their day of rest. I had no interest in resting at all, and made the most of our free time in the sunshine. 'After breakfast, we decided to go into the town.' And what fun that was. 'We looked around Ambleside, into craft shops and the newsagent to buy some copies of the *Daily Mirror*, which we were in.'

I wrote that 'Garth' brought Suzanna a pocket chess set. I'm afraid I couldn't spell properly. This was meant to read Gareth. I have known two Gareths in my life, a Gloucester Old Spot pig, living in North Wales, and Gareth Tandy, our third assistant director. His aunt Jessica Tandy was the famous Hollywood actress who had appeared in Alfred Hitchcock dramas such as *The Birds* and is now best known for her Oscar-winning role in *Driving Miss Daisy*. Gareth had acted in all sorts of things as a boy from *Oliver Twist* to *Dr. Finlay's Casebook*, but in 1973 he donned a blue cagoule to look after us. He acted as unit runner with a walkie-talkie strung around his neck, stopping unwanted traffic, cueing various boats and lugging tea urns about. It was also his job to get us through costume and make-up, and onto the set at the right time. He fielded stress with good grace and we all loved him. And no wonder, seeing as he'd given us a chess set just because Suzanna was stuck in bed.

> We came back and the doctor said it would be all right to visit Suzanna. Just as we were sitting down to lunch a lovely pink and blue bouquet came for Suzanna from her father. After that, Jane, Sten and I walked up the Fells.

I had been brought up in quite an isolated valley deep in the countryside, much like the Blacketts. Mum hardly ever took me and my sisters shopping when we were children, but Jane Grendon was quite happy to take us around Ambleside and up into the fells. I am sure it was just what we needed while Mum stayed with Suzanna, and I expect had a snooze herself. Mum was the better chaperone on location, where she felt happy and relaxed; Jane enjoyed other activities. She had bags of energy and would encourage us to sing during the seemingly endless minibus journeys. *Blue Lake and Rocky Shore, I will return once more.* . . . When Simon and Kit went sailing, Jane would go with them. My mother doesn't like getting cold feet.

Me and Jane Grendon.

When the sun came out that Saturday, Richard and Molly took Virginia up into the mountains for a picnic. It must have been a relief to get high into the hills. I am sure they could have spent all

Molly Friedel and Virginia McKenna on a picnic.

day relaxing with the newspapers but instead Virginia came to Oaklands, bringing Suzanna strawberries and a large book of animal stories. She even took us out to the cinema. This was a huge excitement for me. I had only been a few times before. *Ring of Bright Water*, *Swiss Family Robinson* and *The Sound of Music* were the main filmic influences on my life to date. 'It was a sweet little place and very few people there,' I wrote. 'We saw *The Cowboys*, a film about a man taking out some small boys.' After what had been a very full day, I recorded in my diary that 'We had milk and biscuits. Mummy and I rang up daddy, and went to bed.'

Meanwhile, out on the lake, Wild Cat Island was waiting for us.

Chapter Three
On Wild Cat Island

Sunday 20th May – Sixth day of filming

I woke up and ran down to breakfast. We went off in the minibus to Holly Howe. It was a rainy day and first they filmed all they could of the interior rooms. I stayed inside while some of the others filmed and some went for a walk in the rain with Jane. I wrote a copy of my diary and read my book. The others came back and we played Consequences. I was set to draw three maps of Wild Cat Island. Lunch came. I had spaghetti. After lunch I played Consequences with Virginia, Emma, Peter, Ronnie, Lesley, Kit, Mummy, Suzanna, and Simon. I then read more of my book. After that I was called to do some filming. We did a short scene with a tatty flag. In the middle of the rehearsal some sheep came into the boathouse and I (who was the only one who noticed) burst out laughing. We went home in a fully laden van.

It was quite amusing when Mrs Batty's sheep walked into *Swallow*'s boatshed, lifting our spirits on that rather gloomy day on Coniston, but I have no idea if it was caught on film. I don't suppose our out-takes were ever kept.

This time, we roped Hair and Make-up into playing Consequences. It seems Emma Porteous, the costume designer, was on set with us that wet day in May. We never saw her again; presumably she was on to her next job. Claude was busy filming scenes in the kitchen with Suzanna, Sten and the wonderful lady who played Mrs Jackson. Someone asked why Susan never thanked her for lending her the frying pan, as it seemed out of character. I expect it was because Suzanna still wasn't feeling that well.

Ronnie Cogan just about to trim
Sten's hair.

Ronnie Cogan was the quiet, gentle man, usually clad in a grey tweed jacket, responsible for our hair. Foregoing the use of wigs, so very much in use on earlier costume dramas, he simply did up Virginia's lovely thick hair, and cut ours, giving the whole film a classic feel. He was a true movie hairstylist of the old school. In the early 1970s Ronnie worked on *Follow Me!* with Mia Farrow, Michael Jayston, Annette Crosbie and the Israeli actor Chaim Topol, whom Richard knew well from producing *Fiddler on the Roof* in the West End. Topol had unexpectedly taken a week out to go to war. He literally flew to Israel to play his part in the Six-Day War and returned an international hero.

We were not so thick-skinned. After that sunny Saturday in Ambleside it was clear that sunscreen was extremely important to our work. Mum slathered it on, much to Kit's disgust. If even a tiny bit of us had turned red or peeled, the film would have been put in jeopardy. Predicting that we would turn vaguely brown once we started filming out on the water, Peter Robb-King, our make-up artist, decided to give us a bit of a tan when scenes were shot out of sequence.

Peter, Ronnie and Terry the wardrobe master were also responsible for the continuity of how we looked so that the shots would cut together. My fly-away hair was well-monitored. Mum had to wash it every other day, which was a chore. Sten seemed to be forever having his hair trimmed. There are quite a few photographs of this particular activity in progress.

While the sunscreen was ever in her handbag, my mother was on a mission to build up Suzanna's health. When she asked her to name her favourite food, the emphatic answer was 'Steak!' Mum booked a restaurant.

'When we got back I went out for a lovely dinner with Jane and Brian,' Suzanna wrote later. 'I had prawn cocktail first and steak and chips afterwards. The restaurant was lovely it was painted white with red curtains and it had lots of Caesar's heads round it.' She must have felt better straight away, since her ending comment was: 'When I got back I had a lark around with Kit and Peggy.'

Arthur Ransome's description of Wild Cat Island is based on two real islands. The landing place and open grassy campsite illustrated in the books can be found at Blake Holme Island on Windermere, but when Richard Pilbrow went there in 1972 he was so disappointed by the sight of caravans, and the fact that it was so near the shore, that he decided to make the film almost entirely on Peel Island, where you find Ransome's Secret Harbour. We never went to Blake Holme.

Arthur Ransome and the Collingwoods camped with tents on Peel Island, once known as Montague Island or the Gridiron. The Altounyans occasionally spent the night there beneath *Mavis*'s sail slung from a tree. The girls complained that they'd wake up to find slugs in their hair. In 1932 the 7th Duke of Buccleuch gifted the island and land nearby to the National Trust who prohibited camping. Roger Altounyan told my friend, Bill Frankland, that he secretly spent the first few nights of his honeymoon there none-the-less. It must have been magical. Something about the steep sides makes it like a fortress, the ancient Viking settlement that Roger's grandfather, W.G. Collingwood, believed it to be.

Had I been producing *Swallows & Amazons*, I would have chosen Peel Island for Secret Harbour, but used High Peel Near for the landing place. There is a nice open beach there and we wouldn't have had to lug all the heavy paraphernalia of filming over the water. You can imagine the time and effort involved in hauling a 35mm Panavision camera across with its mountings and track.

We loved crossing over to the island, but getting us back for lessons and lunch wasn't easy. There was no loo. It could be chilly out there, but we were getting used to coping with our unusual way of life.

Monday 21st May – Seventh day of filming

The mini-bus took us off to the island. We changed into our costumes, piled on jumpers. So far the morning had been raining and wet. After half an hour of making my scrapbook and filling in my three hours' work I did the scene of exploring by myself. After lunch we did the scene where Roger discovers the camp and finds a fireplace there. Then I say: Natives.

After that we did close-ups of that scene.

The wonderful thing is that now when children reach Peel Island they can find most of the locations there, although the Landing Place has nearly washed away. One great secret is that it was created especially for the film. They must have dumped a huge amount of shingle to build up the beach. We never knew.

The other secret is that there weren't actually enough trees for the Swallows to erect the tents that their mother had made for them. Two had to be added by the construction team. Arthur Ransome's design of tent is not easy to put up. It is difficult for children to get the rope taut enough between the trees to take the weight of the canvas. You need to use wagon knots or twist it with a stick. If you tie the rope too high, the tents ruck up. The reality was that Suzanna had Bobby Props, Bob Hedges, to help her.

> The cameras were moved again and a shot was taken of Roger and I picking up sticks. Roger then had a scene and then they shot Susan and John pitching tents.

One thing that is not a secret, but which might take you unawares, is that there never seems to be any firewood on Wild Cat Island. It is the reason why the Swallows rowed to the mainland in the book. Roger really did struggle to find sticks to pick up. Mine were carefully set out for me to find by the art director. Poor Sten did fall over and he did get quite badly scratched by thorns. Claude gave him a bit of 'Danger Money' for being brave about it and not complaining.

> We came off the island and went home. We had supper. I had a bath. Then we went downstairs and watched *Cider with Rosie*, which Sten and I were in. I went straight to bed, so as not to be really yawning.

I don't know if Sten had ever received Danger Money when he played Laurie Lee two years before. It must have been shown quite late that evening as it had been labelled 'avant garde'. We were allowed to stay up, as of course television recording machines had not been heard of.

A number of actors who appeared with us in *Swallows & Amazons* had also been in *Cider*, as the director called the play. Mike Pratt, who played Mr Dixon the dairy farmer, was 'Uncle Ray', and John Franklyn-Robbins, who we were to know as 'Young Billy' the charcoal burner, had been the 'Stranger', a WWI deserter living in the woods, his face 'red and crinkled, brilliant like fungus'.

Tuesday 22ⁿᵈ May – Eighth day of filming

> I woke up feeling very tired after last night. We had breakfast and drove off through the mist to the island. We arrived at our bus, which stank of gas. It was aired out, but later in the day leaked up-stairs. We did two hours of lessons and went

Bringing *Swallow* into Secret Harbour.

over to the island and filmed a scene when we were all in
one tent with the camera at the back. We returned for lunch.
After resting, John and I went over to the island. The first
scene was looking for a harbour in which I said:
'We ought to have brought machetes like Red Indians use.'
The next scene was going into the harbour in *Swallow*. We
had to wait a long time for the sun to come out.

It seemed that we had another wet day, but what Claude did shoot was
excellent. It was the day John and I discovered the Secret Harbour and
took *Swallow* around from the rather exposed Landing Place. I looked
out for rocks, while John sculled with one oar astern, making careful
figures-of-eight in the water. Somehow, between scudding clouds, they
captured those limpid, watery scenes.

The Secret Harbour looks very different over the course of a year. It
is at its most dramatic when the water levels are low and more rocks are
exposed, but one thing is certain, it is always a safe haven for a dinghy. I
was sad that the sequence in the book where Titty watches a dipper from
her rock was never in the film, but then I have never seen a dipper there.
I rather think they prefer shallow, fast-flowing streams where caddis fly
larvae can be found, but I am sure that if Arthur Ransome wrote about a
dipper, he must have seen one there.

Terry Smith with Kit Seymour. Albert Clarke can just be seen
sitting behind them by Coniston Water.

The stills for the film were taken by Albert Clarke. This must have
been tricky as his large-format camera clicked loudly. He had to grab
shots while not intruding on the soundtrack, which was not possible if
Claude wanted to shoot the rehearsal. Reams of black-and-white contact
sheets were brought for our appraisal. Although many proved beautiful,
iconic images, the odd thing about the official photographs was that
we always looked incredibly serious in them, if not melancholic. The
newspapers battled to use them, often extracting my face from a shot
taken when we are reading the 'If not duffers' telegram, as it was the
only vaguely smiley one. It is difficult to capture laughter but somehow
my mother's Instamatic caught the joy, humour and closeness of our
relationships.

After filming the Secret Harbour scenes, I recorded in my diary that
'we went home in Terry Smith's Range Rover. I took the gears and he
went very fast.' I can't believe Terry let me travel in the front of his white
Range Rover, let alone change the gears. I can only think that Simon and
I were taken back after the other children had gone home, and can just
imagine us swinging around the lanes, between the high stone walls, on
that beautiful road back to Ambleside.

Terry must have had an annoying day, if gas had been leaking into his
bus. He never hung up our costumes even though we had hanging space

Perched on a Capri waiting to go out to Peel Island. A journalist is talking to us while Mum and Brian Doyle stand on the jetty.

next to our bunkbeds on the top deck. 'I don't want them to look ironed,' he explained, bustling John's clothes into a suitcase, which I suppose he took back to the hotel for laundering. I can only imagine that he dried our shoes out in front of the gas heaters. We were always getting wet feet.

Wednesday 23rd May – Ninth day of filming

Breakfast, and away to the island. On the way we bought some sweets and some fresh fruit to store in the bus. When we got there I did three hours' schooling.

In real life Peel Island is a long way down Coniston Water from Bank Ground Farm, but it is not that far from the shore. Richard had permission from the Lake District National Park for the crew to gain access and use the fields opposite the island as a base. One proviso was that our two red double-decker buses had to be swathed with army camouflage netting in an attempt to make them less conspicuous. As a result, they looked like huge monsters from *Doctor Who*. In addition to these we had a caravan for make-up and hair, the caterers' mobile kitchen or chuck wagon, and a black lorry full of lights, stands, cables and huge reflector boards belonging to Lee Electric and known as an Electric Truck. The grey Lee Electric generator and the very basic mobile loos were tucked in under the trees. I am not sure what kind of camera van David Cadwallader, the grip,

used, but I half-remember a Land Rover. Alongside these were parked
a carpenter's truck, three props lorries, our minibus, the unit minibus,
everyone's cars and various boat trailers with the occasional white Jaguar.
Mum thinks that Terry Smith's Range Rover could have been orange.

'He was a very orange man.'

'No, it wasn't, Mum. It was white.'

'After lunch we went to the island,' I wrote. 'The first shot was of John
and I taking *Swallow* out.'

It must have been a bit of an effort to avoid getting the whole entourage
in shot when John and I rowed around to the harbour. You can tell that
it was a greyer day than the one before.

You may wonder why we needed a carpenter. The crew always seemed
to be making jetties. There are many more on the lakes now but they
had to build a temporary one, made from scaffold and planks, so that we
could climb into boats going to the island without getting wet. It must
have been quite something lugging the camera to various woodland
locations. It travelled in a big black wooden box lined with foam rubber
that David Cadwallader had fitted with strong handles. The Panavision
was thus transported by two men like the Ark of the Covenant, holy
and revered. Once on the island it would be set on a complex mounting,
which enabled it to pan and tilt. This in turn usually sat on sections of
track so that moving shots could be achieved.

Sten eating in the camera box wearing David Cadwallader's cap.

Denis Lewiston had Eddie Collins as his camera operator but insisted on doing most of the camera work himself. If you watch the scenes of the Swallows making up camp you can see that he must have just followed what Susan and Roger were doing. It has a wonderful, busy, natural quality with the result that all one wants to do is to leave real life behind and go camping. I imagine that the scenes when the kettle is being filled were shot in the morning, while I was at my lessons, as I joined them after lunch.

> The second scene was in the camp. Susan was passing round the end of our supper. I was eating an apple. These were the lines I said:
>> *Titty:* And we'll invent our own names.
>> *Susan:* Mother says we have to eat plenty of greens or we'll get scurvy.
>> *Roger:* What's scurvy?
>> *Titty:* Sailors died from it like flies.

We loved shooting any scene at our camp on the island, especially when we were eating. Nothing else seemed to matter. When Suzanna swung her frying pan of buttered eggs she did burn Sten on the knee but he was very brave about it and hardly flinched. It was a heavy pan.

As anyone who has read Arthur Ransome's books will know, the Swallows were very organised when it came to provisions. Mate Susan's diktats must surely have been modelled on the ideas of Ransome's own efficient wife Evgenia. Milk from the farm, buttered eggs, seed cake, apples, molasses (toffees) and grog – I savoured it all. I wasn't too sure about fried perch or pemmican, but I relished the buns from Rio. We didn't have peas to shell on the film. Apples must have seemed a realistic alternative. Sten enjoyed them.

Suzanna would detail whatever she ate in her diary. 'For lunch I had plaice which wasn't very nice but better than nothing.' On another day, the location caterers treated us by cooking spaghetti. It was considered exotic dinner-party food back then, but there was still no salad, which irked her. Meals were hot, on time and hearty whatever the weather, but without optional alternatives. Suzanna couldn't bear the thought of mushy vegetables. But when they made salad, she declared herself to be full of breakfast. Time and time again, she'd write, 'For lunch I had two tomato sandwiches.' Once she wrote, 'For lunch I had Leasly's tomartos (from her salad) in a sandwich.' As a result she was often given steak for supper back at the Oaklands guest house, while the rest of us had whatever was on offer, which was a bit of a swizz. I have evidence:

'For dinner I had steak and chips,' Suzanna noted, 'while the others had cornish pasties and baked beans.'

She single-mindedly chivvied, encouraged and begged John and Margaret, the location caterers, and our landlady Mrs Price for more and more fresh raw food, particularly strawberries, which she loved with a passion. These would have been early English strawberries and a great treat in 1973. They managed to find enough for us all later in the summer, but they were presented in a manner that Mate Susan wasn't too happy about: 'We had strawberries and artificial cream. Kit has just told me it was condensed milk or evaporated milk. She wasn't sure which.'

Thursday 24ᵗʰ May – Tenth day of filming

The first scene of the day was the one when Titty emerged from her tent in her pyjamas, wiped the dew off the top of a large biscuit tin and started writing her diary. I now regret writing *Titania Walker* on the cover. Mum encouraged this because my contract for the film stated that I would be playing the part of TITANIA. Did Richard Pilbrow, who is quite theatrical, have Shakespeare's *A Midsummer Night's Dream* on his mind? Was it something Evgenia said? In the book *Discovering Swallows & Ransomes*, John Berry claims to be witness to the fact that Mrs Ransome thought the name Titty was 'ridiculous' and it was she who sold Richard the film rights.

Arthur Ransome never wanted his character's name changed. He was most upset when the BBC altered it to Kitty in 1962, when Susan George played the part. I've seen the series and it does feel wrong. People were concerned that I would be teased for being associated with a name like Titty, but I never was. It's a sweet name and somehow reinforces the innocence of the age. We thought that Titty Altounyan was called Titty as a shorter version of Beatrix Potter's character 'Mrs Tittlemouse', but in fact her name was actually adopted from a horrible story of mousey death entitled *Titty Mouse and Tatty Mouse* from *English Fairy Tales* by Joseph Jacobs. Her family called her Tittymouse, then Titty for short. Her Christian name was Mavis, but she loathed it. When *Swallows and Amazons* was adapted for the big screen in 2016 the character's name was changed to Tatty. The press had a field day, running the headline Tit for Tat.

Our knitted swimming costumes, with their little legs, were a novelty for us. I do wish mine hadn't been red. It was such a cold day I turned blue. The entire crew were clad in overcoats – even parkas with fur-lined hoods. Looking back, it was silly to have gone ahead with a swimming scene in May, but we survived.

Claude in waders, filming the swimming scene from
the Landing Place on Peel Island.

Claude shot the scene wearing waders and using two cameras, as the continuity would have been impossible otherwise. While Denis operated the Panavision that was planted on the beach, Eddie Collins had a 16mm camera in the water with us. He was being steadied by another chap in a full wetsuit. Fitted neoprene was quite an unusual sight then, when divers were known as frogmen. Suzanna was stoic, but it simply wasn't possible to pretend we were enjoying ourselves. My rictus smile was not convincing.

> I have never been so cold. It was not only that we had to look happy and enjoy it, we had to run in without hesitation and swim. That was all right, it was having to dive under and stick up my feet. After doing this again for the second time, over and over again in front of the camera I couldn't do anymore.

Later on in the summer, the Lake District became so hot that we begged to be taken swimming in rivers on our days off. I wish we had re-shot the scene in July with an underwater camera capturing my pearl-diving antics. I was a good swimmer. I still love snorkelling – but only in warm seas. As it was, I had to be extracted from Coniston Water by Eddie's frogman. I'd almost passed out. And did Terry Smith have a hot water bottle for me? No.

Filming from the Landing Place.

> They dragged me out of the lake. We were rolled up in towels
> then blankets. We were fed lunch we were so cold. I said 'it's
> cold' on tape and I meant it. Susan had to say 'but no it isn't
> it's loverly and warm'.

Suzanna wrote, 'It was terrible, but a lot of fuss was made of me after and
Claude gave me £1.00 every time I went in.'

Quite a few people almost learned how cold we had been for themselves
later that day. The boats used to ferry us back and forth to the island were
blue Dorys with outboard motors. You don't want too much weight in
the bows when you are travelling in one of those. Water can come in
very quickly.

> On the way back from the island, Mummy, Terry, Claude, Ernie
> the boatman, Suzanna and I were in the motor-boat. Suddenly
> we put on speed. Because there was too much weight in the
> front the water came in over the bows. We all climbed to
> the other end. The motor-boat was half full of water. Mummy
> had been giggling just before it came in. As she was sitting in
> the bows the water came in on top of her. Her face changed
> from pink to white so suddenly. We laughed all the way home
> (except for her).

Friday 25ᵗʰ May – Eleventh day of filming

Titty: It'll have to be Arctic for north and Antarctic for south.
Susan: What about the town there?
Titty: What about Rio?
Roger: Rio? Why Rio?
Titty: Because of the song, Away to Rio.
Roger: What about the bay where we fished?
John: Dixon's Bay. It's very near the farm.
Titty: No, Shark Bay – because of Roger's great fish.
Susan: What about where we saw the houseboat?
Titty: Houseboat Bay.

I loved drawing the map. I had prepared it earlier with Simon Holland and always regret pressing too hard with my pencil. If you look very carefully you can see that I had already written 'Rio' and rubbed it out, only to write Rio again when it came to the take. I also wish that I had been taught the song *Away to Rio* before this scene, as I would have delivered that line differently.

After close-ups on that scene we heard a big bang, which was the Amazons firing the firework. After that we did a little school work.

We were whisked off to the island and rehearsed a scene but could not film it because of the sun. Next we had lunch break and then did some art by the lake side. After that we went back to the island. We were jumping to the morning when I got up

Me strangling Terry Smith,
our wardrobe master.

early, and went to wake Roger to go off to find Captain Flint's treasure. Terry took Kit, Mummy and I back to Oaklands. After supper we watched television for a while. I changed for bed and moved all my things into the girls' room. Mummy packed her things as well. We had to move out of our rooms because they had been let out for Whitsun.

Saturday 26ᵗʰ May – Twelfth day of filming

I woke up, breakfast and away to the sweet shop. The mini-bus took us to the island. We changed into our costumes. Some other children came, we played with the swing. The first scene we did was when we saw the Amazons sailing around the island.

> *Titty:* If they're pirates, why does the pirate in the houseboat fire at them?

After that scene we did a scene in the camp, where I said,

> *Titty:* Perhaps this is his island.
> *Roger:* What was that?
> *John:* Nothing. Must have been a bird.
> *Susan:* If this is his island, why doesn't he live here?
> *Titty:* Much nicer for his parrot.
> *Titty:* Don't touch the point, it might be poisoned.
> *John:* Shhh!
> *Titty:* It's him again, he's winged his arrows with that poor parrot's feathers.
> *Susan:* Shut up, Titty.

Then we had lunch. I fell off the swing and hurt my leg. After this we did a scene down on the beach again when *Swallow* had gone and Roger found the Amazons' knife. These were my lines:

> *Titty:* Roger and I pulled her right up. She couldn't have drifted. She couldn't.

We rehearsed a scene in the camp, and because the sun was shining we went back to the harbour. My lines were:

> *Titty:* I expect someone hid on the island hundreds and hundreds of years ago.
> *Roger:* What did you put the cross on this tree-stump for?
> *Titty:* Natives again. Or cannibals. This marks the spot where they ate six missionaries.

'Natives again. Or cannibals. This marks the spot where they ate six missionaries' has to be the best line that *anyone* in the history of film-making has ever had to utter. It is not in the book. Titty, having digested huge helpings of Daniel Defoe, declares, 'they might have been killed and eaten by other natives,' revealing herself as the most ardent imperialist of all time. But she has such fun doing so. I have always liked the talk of 'the powerful native' (Mr Jackson the Lakeland farmer) and the savages living around Rio. I hope it has shocked lots of people.

A blurry memory of trying
to hoot like owls.

In many ways the Swallows were missionaries. The Amazons, Nancy and Peggy Blackett, although energetic tomboys, had lost their father. It goes unsaid in the movie, but Nancy very touchingly lets it out in *Swallowdale* when they find a hidden tin on the peak of Kanchenjunga. Their mother's brother, Jim Turner (Captain Flint), had taken them sailing and did things with them initially, but then decided to concentrate on writing his book. Nancy and Peggy feel so rejected that they light a firework on his cabin roof. The Swallows, who know what it is like to live without a father around as theirs is in the Navy, somehow manage to come alongside the Amazons. They give them a reason to keep going and live life to the full. Nancy and Peggy excel – they find life-long friends and blossom. The Swallows are challenged and have more fun than if they had travelled in a structured way, intent purely on their own enjoyment. They have great adventures and do more things than they ever imagined possible, fulfilling their potential and developing strength of character.

Arthur Ransome was only thirteen when his father died. Cyril Ransome, a Professor of History, incurred a fatal infection after injuring his leg in the Lake District. He was particularly disappointed with his son for doing badly in the entrance exam for Rugby School. I can now see that *Swallows and Amazons* was written as a subconscious outpouring of grief and loss, an insistence that a boy like John could be trusted without his parents around. Arthur's father was a great fisherman keen on catching pike and walking on the high fells. They were footsteps any son would long to fill. How much of the stories are a description of Ransome's own childhood when he, his brother and his two sisters, on holiday at Nibthwaite, met the two local Collingwood girls when they rowed down to Peel Island?

Cyril Ransome had also been an author, churning out history textbooks even when on holiday. Was he as crabby towards his children as Uncle Jim is towards the *Amazons*? If there was any guilt or regret it is fully embodied by a certain retired pirate and put to good use in the plot.

I, too, had been fatherless for a while, but as we left Peel Island that day, there was a surprise waiting for me.

> Simon saw Daddy, Perry and Tamzin. I got off the boat and said
> hello to them. We went home and helped Perry and Tamzin
> unpack. Mummy took Daddy out (or the other way round).

My father had left the dogs at home on 26th May so that he could drive my younger sisters up to join us for two weeks, and watch the filming. He found Peel Island on Coniston Water and was there to meet us when the boat came in at the end of the day. My sisters, Perry and Tamzin, stood smiling on the rocks, dressed for the weather in matching red jerseys, duffle coats and gumboots.

My father loves the Lakes. He has always grabbed any chance to visit Westmorland. As a young man he once took advantage of a military travel warrant to climb in the hills and later made it his job to visit the Colfast Button factory in Maryport, every month, when he worked in the plastics industry. He would stay at the Pheasant Inn at Bassenthwaite Lake, latching visits onto a weekend so he could explore or go sailing. This was in the late 1950s. When I came along he took us to stay at a place called Goosemead Farm. We climbed Castle Crag and you only have to glance at the photographs to see how happy I was to be there. Our sheepdog, called Lupy, came too. She was a great character and much loved. Found as a stray before I was born, she was still around when we left home to drive up to the Lake District.

Arthur Ransome had been Dad's favourite author as a boy. He said that he used to wait in anticipation for another book to be published in time for Christmas.. After his aunt bought him a clinker-built dinghy he began to live the life, albeit on the mudflats of the south coast where he lived from the age of eight to fifteen. He kept sailing and bought me the whole set in hardback, collecting them from various secondhand shops.

My parents had booked a bed and breakfast in Ambleside across the road from the Oaklands guest house. I immediately noticed a sign declaring that you had to pay 10p to have a bath.

'Ten pee!' I shrieked.

Mum glared at me, furious.

'Do be quiet, they'll hear you.'

I had moved into Suzanna's room, as Mrs Price had a long-standing booking for the quiet back room that Mum and I had been using. The guest house was full to bursting since she had students from the Charlotte Mason College of Education lodging with her as well as all of us and her own three children. The only problem was that we had nylon sheets and the bedding kept snagging on our toenails.

My sisters Perry and Tamzin waiting for us on the mainland.

My sisters, Tamzin and Perry, who must have been about eight and nine, struck up an instant rapport with Suzanna Hamilton when she asked them to babysit her pet slow-worms. These had come up from London with David Blagden in a small glass aquarium, which she carefully placed in the disused fireplace in our bedroom. I don't know what Mrs Price thought. I wasn't very keen on handling them and have no idea how they were fed, but Perry was intrigued.

Suzanna was meant to be practising her oboe but preferred the ukulele. She would sit on her bed playing *Ain't She Sweet, Sunny Side of the Street, When I'm Cleaning Windows* and other classic numbers, completely fluently and with great gusto. My sisters were entranced. They even shared the room with us and the slow-worms, although I don't think I slept terribly well as a result: 'My Slumberdown fell off twice in the night.'

My father, Martin Neville, with his dog Lupy in 1963.

Dad had already made plans for sailing that Bank Holiday, when Graham Ford had scheduled a two-day break in the filming.

Sunday 27ᵗʰ May – Unit day off

We got in the car and drove off to Keswick, and to Derwentwater where we hired a boat from Nick Newby. We took a picnic lunch and sailed off in our Turtle. We sailed on and landed on an island in the middle of the lake. We left Perry and Mummy there, and sailed off to the end of the lake and back. We had lunch and watched some hula-hula girls bathe (they infested our island).

I remember the hula-hula girls well. Although it was still only May, they suddenly appeared on what seemed to be a remote, inaccessible island, clad in garish, brightly-coloured bikinis – the kind that had little frilly skirts to them. We watched them splash about and swim in complete wonder as, although it was sunny, we knew how cold the water was.

We had seen something of the same kind of savage the day before. The dismay on the first assistant director's face when he realised it was a national holiday weekend epitomised our feelings. We'd had Peel Island all to ourselves, indeed it had become ours – our special place, our magical camp, our home. And suddenly it was being invaded by brash women from Manchester who certainly had no respect for anyone making a film. They seemed to arrive from nowhere when we were in the Secret Harbour, suddenly a secret no more. It was their holiday and there was no stopping them or their overweight and noisy children. They were quite terrifying.

Me in 1963, with Lupy the sheepdog just behind me.

The horrific Bank Holiday queues were also unexpected, but my father took us up into the mountains and out on the water. He had been trying to teach my mother to sail since they first met but she never even began to get the hang of it. She was in mourning that weekend as she had watched her favourite hat blow across the water and sink to the bottom of the lake. It was a bulbous pink and white flowery Donny Osmond cap that Claude had enjoyed wearing on set to amuse us. She was able to find a yellow and white one to replace it, but he never liked it as much. He said it didn't suit his colouring.

Chapter Four
The Amazons Attack

My father said that his first impression of the film crew was 'What an awful mess of trucks and weird people!'

He'd just come from his office in the electronics industry where everybody drove smart cars and wore suits with neat ties. Dad didn't even own a pair of denim jeans, let alone purple bell-bottoms. One of The Arthur Ransome Society members took one look at his home-movie footage of the making of *Swallows & Amazons* and said, 'It looks like Woodstock.'

Woodstock on wheels, except that unlike a music festival everyone had to keep quiet when filming was in progress, which was hard for my little sisters. As the notion of 'Free Love' was virtually typed on the call sheet, their eyes, ears and mouths had to be sealed. Goodness knows what the crew got up to in Ambleside. None of the men on the crew wore peace pendants, or behaved like Dylan the Rabbit from *The Magic Roundabout*, but they smoked cigarettes continuously.

We children were all staunchly anti-smoking, particularly Sten, whose father had a 'No Smoking' sign on the front door of their house in Whiteway – even though it happened to be called *Lucifer Lodge*. Kit showed us how to sabotage a cigarette. We would use the tweezers on her Swiss Army knife to remove a bit of tobacco from the end, and would insert an unlit match-head before stuffing the tobacco back inside. The cigarette would then be returned to the victim's packet. Soon after the cigarette was lit and a good smoke was being enjoyed, the match-head would suddenly ignite and flare up, terrifying everyone in the vicinity. 'We got Gareth Tandy good and proper,' was the cry.

Dad couldn't bear the notion of hanging around all day, so he brought some watercolours with him to do what he never normally had time for while he was looking after us. My mother had to leave that Tuesday to

Dad and me painting on the shore of Coniston Water.

spend four days at the Bath and West Show – a long-term commitment that could not be cancelled. By this time she had been working for Harlech Television (or HTV, as the station became known) for about four years. She started with the company as an 'In Vision Announcer', reading the News with Martyn Lewis from the studio in Cardiff, before moving on to present her own children's programme called *It's Time for Me*. By 1973 she was presenting a women's afternoon programme made in Bristol called *Women Only*, with Jan Leeming. They were obliged to host the HTV stand at regional agricultural shows. I'm not sure what the farmers thought. It was meant to be a celebrity highlight for rural communities.

I have a horrible feeling that in this Woodstock-like atmosphere, where my father was feeling out of place, I took on my mother's role and got a little bit too bossy in the school bus. Sten didn't respond to my command that we needed to get on with our lessons, so I took his books out of my desk, where they'd been kept for some reason. The result was a head-on attack from Sten, who must have been so offended that he not only fought me but would not let go. Perhaps this was a good sign, in that we had become like a real family. Perhaps it was because the balance had been tipped by our real families turning up. Sten's father had arrived with his little sister, Jo. My little sisters were playing outside too. Perhaps it had something to do with the red and yellow sweets we had started eating on the bus.

Dad said that Sten was always picking fights. He *was* an eight-year-old boy. 'Lessons went on till lunch,' I wrote. 'We were just settling down and Mrs Causey went upstairs to get Sten down for more lessons. A fight started again.' This time Sten attacked poor Mrs Causey but he calmed down a little in due course. 'More lessons came after that excitement.'

Luckily for Claude, we were filming the scenes on Wild Cat Island where the Amazons attack, 'when we fell flat on our faces and the Amazons' arrows flew over our heads'. Our aggression could be constructively utilised. We loved this scene, and it was good that Nancy and Peggy had at last arrived on the island. They were using the hazel bows made for them on site by Bob Hedges, which can't have been very flexible, but my parents both knew how to use the longbow. They had been taught how to shoot in about 1958 by their neighbour Tony Norris and his wife Cecily who encouraged them to practice every evening on their long and beautifully cut lawn in the village of Clent in Worcestershire. They joined the Worcestershire Archery Society where they gained further experience, while making life-long friends shooting with a certain Olympian archer on Sunday afternoons. I had no idea that archery would play a pivotal role in my life but years later I ended up meeting the grandson of this Olympic archer at a bow meeting held at Hagley Hall, only a few miles from where I was born. He had become the Chairman of the Worcestershire Archery Society and came over to

Mum teaching Lesley how to shoot.

ask me to make a speech. We were married four months later, walking through an arch of longbows as we came out of church.

Arthur Ransome enjoyed playing Red Indians as a boy. His great-aunt Susan was a great toxologist who wore lodden green to shoot on Belle Isle on Windermere. Mum had only given the Amazons basic archery lessons in the field outside the bus but they did well and were truly threatening. It looks pretty scary on the big screen when those arrows, fletched with green parrot feathers, zip over our heads. Much to Kit's disappointment, these were actually fired by Terry Wells and another prop man. They strung up fishing line in the direction and precise angle at which the arrows were to fly and pulled it taut. Next, they firmly attached loops of nylon to the arrows and literally shot them down the invisible line. This ensured that we would not actually get hit, but it was quite thrilling. The shot, in both meanings of the word, looked so dangerous that it was actually cut from the TV version of the movie.

After being on location for more than two weeks, this was only the second day that Kit and Lesley had appeared in front of the camera. The waiting around must have been pretty frustrating for them.

'David Wood came up today,' Suzanna noted in her diary. 'He was

On Peel Island with David Blagden, the sailing director.

the writer of the script. He knew Anna and Marilyn. Anna is my agent and drama teacher and Marilyn was the producer of the Treasure Seekers, a *Jackanory* I once did.' Mum was sorry to miss him. She was rather in awe of David Wood, since he had played Johnny in *Z Cars*. She hadn't actually seen *If. . .* but had watched him on *Jackanory*, the BBC children's programme, when Suzanna appeared in the photo captions illustrating the story. Suzanna had also taken part in an episode of the 1972 anthology series *The Edwardians* about the life of the author E. Nesbit, who happened to be a friend of Arthur Ransome. That episode and another, about 'Daisy', Countess of Warwick, played by Virginia McKenna, were directed by James Cellan Jones – another film-maker who was passionate about classic book adaptations.

Wednesday 30ᵗʰ May – Fourteenth day of filming

I woke up and dressed. After breakfast the mini-bus took us to our usual location. It was horribly wet. I did one and a half hour's lessons and was then taken to the island to clean fish. In this scene we could talk to each other about them.

Although we had a late start it was a good day, a day when Claude encouraged us to improvise. The dialogue about preparing perch, in the little scene set on the rocks at the northern end of Peel Island, is our own.

Suzanna was very good at gutting fish. She is not a remotely squeamish person; in fact she loves snakes and other reptiles. A stoic, *who would valiant be 'gainst all disaster*, she is probably the most gutsy film actress there is. No fuss or over-long scenes for her. I was more interested in examining the high dorsal fin of the perch and could have spent all morning standing on the rock. I knew Arthur Ransome used a line drawing of one of the perch he caught as a book illustration, a perfect one.

Claude did not go for many 'takes'. His aim was to get fresh performances. He wanted us to react rather than act. By this time, he had started to film the rehearsal, and then one 'take' as a back-up, to give his film editor an option. Then he would change the camera angle. It is probably a good policy when filming with children, as charm is difficult to replicate. Richard must have been pleased to hear that we gained a reputation as 'One Take Wonders' on *Swallows* because cans of 35mm film stock did not come cheap.

When it came to the scene in which we returned to the camp to find an abrupt note from Captain Flint, Claude took me to one side and suggested that I add a line of dialogue at the end without letting the others know. He told me to say – 'And he used my crayons, too.' I wish he hadn't. The secret made me self-conscious, and I did not deliver the line well.

We stayed on the island while they set up for the night scene when the Swallows are huddled together, under canvas, discussing by candlelight how they could win the war. Looking back on it, my line was straight out of a guidance manual on how to conduct naval warfare. 'If there was only something we could do that they could not. That would help.' That was the last scene of the day, and this speech was key.

I'm not sure why but I described it as being 'very strange in the tent'. Unlike real siblings, the four of us had never been together in such a confined space. It was a bonding experience.

Thursday 31ˢᵗ May – Fifteenth day of filming

After leaving Oaklands, we arrived at the location. We changed into our costume. After some lessons we did some filming but not much. We had lunch. After lunch we filmed on the pontoon. It was the dawn scene when the Amazons were calling us in.

With Suzanna Hamilton in our tent.

Me with our safety officer.

It was the first time we shot a sailing sequence using the camera pontoon. The film crew put on their life-jackets, trudged down the jetty with all their equipment and settled on board before we were brought along by my mother. She handed me over and, looking down at the crew, asked in her loud, clear voice, 'Have you all done wee-wee?' The crew looked at Suzanna and me, looked at each other and all got off again. Claude was not amused.

How do you film two girls sailing a thirteen-foot dinghy, talking to their brothers who are sailing along in another small dinghy, while calling out to two other girls in red bobble hats dancing about on a wooded island that both the small boats are approaching? The scene looks so simple on paper. It is the one when the Swallows sail back to Wild Cat Island with the captured *Amazon* to find Nancy in a fury and Peggy anxious to get home. A single page of script. I noted the event carefully in my diary:

> My lines were –
>> *Titty:* Nancy looks as if she's dancing with rage. What's that thing fluttering?
>> *Susan:* It's one of our blankets.
>> *Titty:* They're surrendering! They're surrendering! It's a white flag.

Claude soon discovered that he was shooting the most complicated of sailing scenes, on that cold grey day in the Lake District. It is extremely difficult to describe how he managed this, but I will attempt to do so. There was no room in the dinghies to film us sailing, unless a cameraman was sitting in the bows. For this scene and others, a decent 'two-shot' featuring the characters sailing one dinghy calling to another beyond them needed to be captured from a third vessel, preferably one lashed alongside.

Swallow lashed to the camera pontoon on Coniston.

The production had a pontoon especially built for this purpose, skippered by Ernie Russell who was in charge of the support boats. It was basically a twenty-foot raft, equipped with outboard engines and surfaced with a number of standard flat camera boards. It was rectangular but with added arms on either side. The idea of this cross-shaped platform was to enable Claude to film us either side-on, from astern, or across the bows of the dinghy, which was wired by its keel to the pontoon. The camera was normally on a tripod but could be mounted on a short section of track.

Electric lighting was not something that could be used on the water, but two large reflector boards were always deployed to ensure our faces were not hidden in shadow. The sound recordist and 'boom swinger' needed to be aboard this pontoon as well as the director and camera crew, Sue the continuity girl, a stills photographer taking shots for the cover of a book, obviously the two boatmen who drove it, and David Blagden, the sailing director. He had to work with Claude, the wind and the boatmen, so that we were sailing while the pontoon travelled with us. This was tricky enough on open water. If we were near the shore it could become more difficult.

As you can imagine the dinghy could easily start to sail away from the clumsy pontoon – or worse. Our mast socket broke that first day. They should have had my father advising them. He was an expert at handling lug-sail dinghies with years of experience racing on the Solent, but all he could do was sit there, quizzically watching from the shore.

Although we had all read the book *Swallows and Amazons*, and were devoted to adhering to every detail, no one remembered that John and Titty sailed the captured *Amazon* back to Wild Cat Island. She had a centreboard which was a new thing for the Walkers, so in the book Mate Susan opted to helm *Swallow*, their familiar boat. Arthur Ransome wanted to establish Titty as the heroine. It was no wonder that this scene was chosen by Puffin to be on the cover of their next edition of the book.

I wish this had been detailed in the script. In the film, John was with Roger in *Swallow* while Susan and I were in the *Amazon*. Claude endorsed this because he was trying to achieve a very difficult 'three-shot' featuring Susan in one dinghy, the boys in another and the Amazons on Wild Cat Island. He was relying on Simon, who was eleven, to keep sailing *Swallow* in exactly the right position while a stiff wind was blowing up Coniston Water. This wasn't as easy as it looks. *Swallow* kept racing ahead of the pontoon. It can be gusty around Peel Island and the rocks can be lethal. Donald Campbell had lost his life nearby only six years previously when he tried to set the world water speed record in 1967. Sten was on lookout, but he also had to deliver his lines. Simon had wind and was on a broad reach. Suzanna did her best. We were suddenly whizzing along and she had no previous experience of sailing the *Amazon*. No one had remembered this sequence when we practised before filming began. David Blagden had not analysed or 'broken-down' the script as he should have done.

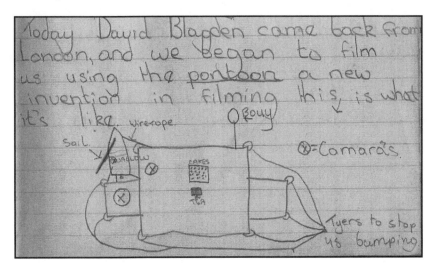

Suzanna's sketch of the pontoon in her diary, 1973.

The camera pontoon on a sunnier day.

Meanwhile, Gareth Tandy, the third assistant director, was standing-by on Peel Island with Kit and Lesley. His job was to hide in the bushes for ages, and cue them at just the right time. The girls had to deliver their lines while jumping from rock to slippery rock to keep up with *Swallow*, the camera and the story. Claude somehow achieved the sequence.

In the photograph above, you can see the pontoon with its outboards and odd cross panels, while Susan climbs onto the *Amazon*. Here there are at least twelve crew on board. Costume, Make-up and our chaperone would have been in a separate safety boat, which would mill about with the life-jackets, sunhats and warm clothes that we wore between set-ups. The crew soon discarded their life-jackets. We had been issued with old BOAC inflatable vests with so many flappy straps that you were at risk of being trapped underwater. Dad thought they were dangerous things.

Claude also had the inevitable problem of modern boats coming along. To avoid this we had one or two men in zoomy motorboats that could zip across the open water to ask vessels to move clear of the shot. Even with this control you can imagine what happened. We would rehearse, line up ready to go for a take, with everyone in position – and a fibreglass motorboat would roar across the lake, leaving us all rocking in its wake. Then it rained.

Friday 1ˢᵗ June – Sixteenth day of filming

We woke up very late but I did remember to say 'rabbits'. We arrived and changed into our costume. The first scene we did was day-night filming in the harbour. We had the 'leading lights'. After lunch we filmed with the Amazons, when we gave them back their boat. Day-night filming was done again. I did my big scene when I captured the *Amazon*.

The Secret Harbour looks south over Coniston Water to the hills of North Lancashire. It has to be one of my favourite places on Earth. Bringing a small dinghy in there gives you a special feeling either of exploration or of coming home. You need to go there when no one else is about.

Our secret of Secret Harbour was that although many of the scenes are set at night we only ever filmed them during the day. This was achieved by using the technique called 'Day-for-Night' filming. Filters were put over the camera lens so that it looked as if we were in the dark even though the scene was shot in broad daylight. This had some obvious advantages.

Filming at night is exciting, but very tiring. It demands considerable lighting set-ups, which would have been impossible on Peel Island as

Wearing our life jackets in the safety boat.

they could not get a generator out there. In mid-summer, it doesn't begin to get dark until very late in Cumberland. Children are only permitted to work certain hours, and need to be given several rest days after any night-filming, by law. And yet much of *Swallows and Amazons*, including the most dramatic scenes, takes place at night.

I remember Claude and Denis Lewiston being intensely absorbed in perfecting our Day-for-Night sequences, which were particularly tricky as many of them were set out on the water. Denis started the day with a scene that was on the island, yet demanded that the camera looked out across the lake. He explained that ideally he needed constant, bright sunlight, which would look like moonlight reflected on the ripples of the water. What he didn't like were cloud banks. For this we would wait, and wait and wait. And waiting, while out on the water or in a confined space, can be hard for children. In the scene where the Swallows set up the leading lights, Denis had to accept the clouds. It looks fine, as the sequence is set as it is getting dark rather than at the dead of night. However, the fluffy white clouds in the scene where the Amazons arrive do look a bit odd.

Even at the camp site, the Day-for-Night shots would take some time to line up. The candle lanterns had to be boosted with battery-operated light bulbs. If you look at the lantern in Susan's tent you can see a black electric wire coming off it, and even spot a small light-bulb if you are watching on the Big Screen. You don't notice this because your attention is on the dialogue but it can easily be spotted. You might think it would be a distraction for us children but we were all quite down-to-earth and the technical detail kept our minds on our work.

It was the Amazons' big day, with Kit emanating leadership as she portrayed Nancy Blackett, with all the confidence, grace and rugged beauty Arthur Ransome must have either known or envisaged. She displayed both authority and kindness with a bit of audacity thrown in for good measure: 'By thunder, Able-seaman – I wish you were on my crew.'

There was quite a bit of dialogue for Lesley who played Peggy. She did well, but acting opposite Suzanna Hamilton is always easy. It's like rowing in a crew led by an excellent stroke or having a good man at the helm. The part of the practical Susan was not a charismatic one, but Suzanna anchored us all. Her own performance was absolutely faultless.

I had much to react to but not much to say. I did manage to handle the *Amazon* by myself and the long shot when I captured her was achieved in one take. A triumph at the end of an exhausting day.

Saturday 2nd June – Seventeenth day of filming

After waking, dressing and eating we went off in the mini-
bus. Sten was sick on the way. We changed into our costume.
It was a horrible day. We put on oilies and went sailing. We
rehearsed the scene when the Swallows set off to capture
Amazon. After lunch we filmed that scene. As I was pushing
them off I slipped on a stone and fell in the water up to my
waist. Everybody laughed but I went on waving them goodbye.

If it is tricky navigating in and out of the Secret Harbour, leaving from
the Landing Place under sail can prove even more hazardous. You need a
decent shove to get going so you can catch the wind, escape from snaring
tree branches and avoid the danger of flat rocks lurking just under the
surface. This was my job on a rainy, grey day with a telescope in one hand.

In the finished film you don't see the shot when I slipped in the water
up to my waist, and kept on shoving. The 'Don't forget about the lights'
scene had to be re-shot on a sunnier day.

What you see is a long-shot, with Titty waving furiously from the
shore as *Swallow* flies away from Wild Cat Island. You cannot see that my
dress is soaking wet, but the trees on the island indicate just how windy it
is. While Susan is waving back, Roger is looking out for rocks for all he is
worth. John is sailing hard, running with the wind, with the boom right
out and white water on his bow. He hung on, as he had to, until *Swallow*
passed the big rock, before coping with a massive, dramatic jibe. You
see him rise to handle this, while Susan ducks. She needed to. It was so
violent the mast nearly broke, but John 'scandalised' and, spilling excess
wind, sailed on. The film cuts to two closer shots of the jibe taken on
the sunny day, then cuts back to the long-shot when Susan bobs up and
Swallow sails at speed, north up Coniston towards dark clouds and rain
over Langdale. It's very exciting.

My father watched all this from the shore, knowing the risks, knowing
Sten wasn't a strong swimmer. I'm afraid that he thought that Claude
overestimated David Blagden's abilities. Dad was of the opinion that
crossing the ocean was not quite the experience needed for sailing
dinghies, which could jibe viciously without warning when wind
blustered down from the fells. He was concerned about our safety. But
Simon was proving himself yet again as a very good sailor. He was totally
confident. You can tell – even from a distance – how calm he was, how
instinctively he read the wind. He knew it would hit him with force as he
left the lee of the island.

These wet windy days were a worry to the producer and a challenge for the crew. They had already lost quite a bit to the rain. Claude was always trying to find a way of making the best use of his time, while David Bracknell, his first assistant director, had to make things happen. The practicalities of each day rested on his shoulders. Co-ordinating our transport out to the pontoon so that while the camera crew were never waiting for us, we were not missing time at our lessons, would have been difficult. Even getting the tea urns out to the island twice a day must have been a struggle. I'm not sure what we did about anyone wanting the loo while we were out on the lake. Working in mauve trousers, with a Motorola on his hip, David maintained safety and kept things going, whatever the weather.

'Quiet. Quiet, please!' he would call before each take, then 'Camera? Sound?'

'Running,' the sound recordist would confirm.

'Mark it!'

The clapperboard would be named.

'Scene one hundred and twenty-one, take one!'

It was snapped shut before Claude whispered, called, or at times shouted, 'Action!'

Then off we'd go, in this case simply to fulfil the stage direction '*Swallow* speeds towards Rio'. The rule was to keep going – whatever happened – come the hell of slippery rocks or high water.

Claude finally barked, 'Cut!'

David would then take over command and set up either for a re-take or a subsequent shot. Once a scene was completed he'd move the crew on for a new sequence.

David Bracknell was very experienced. He'd worked on a number of hugely popular *Carry On* movies, which were made at a terrific rate. Prior to *Swallows & Amazons* his credits included *Carry On Abroad, Carry On At Your Convenience* (I'd seen this at school; it's all about lavatories), *Carry On Henry* and *Carry On Loving*, with Kenneth Williams, Sid James and Charles Hawtrey. He'd worked on *Far from the Madding Crowd* with Julie Christie, Alan Bates and Terence Stamp, *A Day in the Death of Joe Egg* with Janet Suzman and Peter Bowles, and *Battle of Britain*, which starred Michael Caine, Susannah York and Laurence Olivier. We were in capable hands. My father recognised this, watching patiently from the base camp with my younger sisters. I fear it must have been cold and boring for them, but we were all together and did have a chance to explore Westmorland at the weekend.

Sunday 3ʳᵈ June – A day spent exploring with my family

It was Sunday and a much-needed, formal unit day off. It was also a day of rest for the 'artistes', as Claude called us. The crew called us 'saucepans': saucepan lids, Kids. There was a lot of Cockney rhyming slang about in Ambleside that year.

When I wandered across the road I found my parents still in bed, exhausted. To keep me busy, Mum had me writing letters to my Headmistress, Sister Ann-Julian, and to my Housemistress, Sister Allyne. Amazingly, I did.

Hardknott Fort, which Titty Altounyan's grandfather
W.G. Collingwood helped to excavate.

My father's idea of a day out in the Lake District was to drive over the hills and up the Hard Knott Pass, taking car rugs, a picnic and his volcano. This is a brilliant item of equipment with which you can boil enough water to make a cup of tea using an old newspaper. I am sure I've read somewhere that Arthur Ransome had one. My mother just pulled on her Charlotte Mason College of Education sweatshirt and came too.

The highlight of the day was a trip on the Ravenglass and Eskdale Railway, through the National Park to the sea and back. The historic line was opened in 1875 to ferry iron ore from the mine near a place called Boot to the coast by steam locomotive. My father has always loved steam. He was also thrilled about the self-timing gadget on his new camera.

We went the rest of the way back. Again we travelled through the pass. On the way back we made some tea. We went back and met a sheep on the way and fed him. We went to the hotel and Mummy got her camera back. We went home to supper and went to bed.

I seem to have done a lot of went-ing in my diary. I was reading Charlotte Brontë, and you can find 'again we travelled' strains of English nineteenth-century writing reflected in my literary output at the time.

With my mother on the Ravenglass and Eskdale Railway.

Chapter Five
Away to Rio

Monday 4ᵗʰ June – Eighteenth day of filming

Richard said that the most fantastic thing about filming *Swallows &
Amazons* was that breakfast was served on location every morning,
without fail, sending 'a wonderful aroma across the set'. Huge English
breakfasts were dished up by John and Margaret, the couple running
the location catering company from Pinewood, who greeted the film
crew every morning with bacon and eggs, mushrooms, sausages and
tomatoes, and fried bread that was well fried. It didn't really matter if we
missed breakfast at Oaklands, because a bacon butty would be placed
into my hand as soon as we reached the base camp. I only wish our guest
house had been nearer Peel Island, where we spent so much of our time
filming, or that we could have stayed at Bank Ground Farm.

You can see in the movie how much we were enjoying the iced buns
before the Amazons attacked. 'The film scenes we did meant eating 4
buns and 3 bottles of grog and I felt very ill afterwards . . .' wrote Suzanna
in her diary. 'For lunch I tried to have a salad but there wasn't room for it
as we had had all the buns and ginger beer.'

I recounted the detail of the Parley scene in my diary:

> All morning we filmed the Parley. My lines were –
> *Peggy:* How long have you been here?
> *Titty:* Days and days.
> *Nancy:* This is Wild Cat Island. It's been our island for years
> and years.
> (Others speak)
> *Titty:* Is he your uncle? I thought he was a retired pirate.
> *Nancy:* That's quite a good thing for him to be. He can be
> Captain Flint.
> *Titty:* But you're pirates too.

The Parley scene had been of particular concern to Mrs Ransome. She did not want there to be any sexual frisson between John and Nancy, and quite right, too.

By now other members of the crew had been joined by their own children. Our friends the Selbys, with whom I had learned to sail, also joined us on the shore of Coniston Water with their little dog Minnie. They brought a memorable picnic lunch. They always do.

My parents were very keen on picnics. It was how families ate out in those days. It was always carried in a wicker basket and set on a car rug with cold squash in a thermos flask. No cool bags or bottles of wine. We'd have triangles of processed cheese and honey sandwiches which tended to get rather sandy. You couldn't buy ready-made sandwiches from petrol stations or supermarkets then but if you went to a bakery they would make you a filled bap while you waited. My favourite was egg and cress. We liked crusty baps when we were little but I soon preferred the soft ones.

That evening Mum went to help Terry Smith, the wardrobe master, sort out costumes to fit the supporting artists. Perry and Tamzin went with her, unaware that they were about to earn their own breakfasts. They were soon to become film extras.

Tuesday 5th June – Nineteenth day of filming

> We got up very late. As soon as we arrived after make up and costume I did a tiny day-night scene in the harbour. I went back and did more school work. Next we went on to the landing stage and filmed pushing *Swallow* off. I said,
>> *Titty:* Aye aye Sir. Oh, oughtn't I have the telescope for keeping watch?
>
> We went back for lunch. I did a lot of school work. We were called back for close-ups for the Parley again. I changed in the middle of the set, got into *Amazon* with Claude and Denis. We filmed me rowing *Amazon* away from the island.

When David Wood constructed the screenplay he introduced dual action soon after the Swallows arrived at the island. By this I mean that he split us up a bit – John went to fetch the milk from Dixon's Farm while Susan and Titty were teaching Roger to swim. This isn't quite as Arthur Ransome wrote, but it added vitality to the script, moving it along. I reckon Claude needed to avoid a gang scenario of Enid Blyton's Famous Five at all costs. He needed to make the most of any action or jeopardy

Ransome could offer to appeal to an audience more sophisticated than children of the 1930s. It also enabled us to get on with our school work since no one actor was in every scene.

I was in all the scenes shot on this day, but went back to my lessons for a short time. Claude was out on the pontoon filming John and Susan jibing *Swallow* – a pick-up sequence to intercut with Titty waving them goodbye from Wild Cat Island, which was recorded on 2nd June.

At this stage in the story Arthur Ransome actually did divide the action into three. John, Susan and Roger sail off to find the Amazon River, Titty is left alone on the island with her telescope, while the Amazons are busy plotting and planning at Beckfoot.

Up until the early 1970s, most films followed linear stories – this happened, then that happened – a bit like my diary. *A Town Like Alice* is an example of this. It's a road movie. Lovely – but slow. I need to watch it while doing my tapestry. I am sure this was because most movies were adapted from theatre plays, which are usually linear because it is difficult to bounce from one location to another on stage, let alone cope with different time zones. There is nothing wrong with this. *The King's Speech* was originally written for the theatre and so is structured in such a way. As it happened, the method of running three storylines at once became popular in television dramas of the 1980s and 90s, so when *Swallows & Amazons* was first broadcast on television it felt fresh, even though it had been made six or seven years previously.

The playwright John Mortimer said that when he first started writing three strands of action for *Rumpole of the Bailey* it terrified him. Would the audience be able to follow what was going on? Nowadays every detective story breaks into three as soon as possible, while soap operas keep a number of storylines boiling furiously. Arthur Ransome, who had studied storytelling in depth and loved detective novels, must have recognised that the technique helps to pace the action, create suspense and keep readers guessing. In film, it gives the director much more flexibility in the cutting room.

Meanwhile two or three things were also happening behind the scenes. Terry Needham, the second assistant director, found that most of the men who had come forward to be supporting artists for the scene soon to be shot at Bowness were refusing to have their hair cut. My mother was astonished. They couldn't portray the Lake District unpopulated by men. Only a few very elderly gentlemen, who didn't have much hair anyway, agreed to a short back and sides. My father was more than happy to receive a free haircut without having to go to the barber's. Ronnie

Cogan brought out his scissors and snipped away there and then on the shore of Coniston Water. After that, 'Perry, Tamzin and Daddy went off for a costume fitting.'

As a result, Dad missed seeing me capture the *Amazon*. Although it seems I was all alone in the storyline, this was not the reality. I rowed away from Peel Island with Denis, his 16mm camera and a reflector board held by Claude who was also tucked into *Amazon*'s stern. No wonder I was tired by the end of the day. I certainly had to be carried ashore that evening.

'Today was a failure,' Suzanna wrote. 'We had to do parts of the Parley again. The mast floorboards broke when the Amazons were filming and so poor old Claude was in a bad mood all day.'

Although we had achieved quite a bit, we were way behind schedule, and Claude must have been feeling the pressure.

Wednesday 6ᵗʰ June – Twentieth day of filming

A hot sunny day in the Lake District, at last. Mum had a blue sunhat firmly wedged onto my head. I suppose this was so that I wouldn't go pink. It was lovely to be able to eat lunch outside under the rhododendrons with my sisters but I started to roast in my stripey acrylic polo-neck jersey and begged to be able to wear something cooler. Terry Smith was not pleased when he found me wearing a white blouse that happened to be one of Suzanna's costumes, especially since I was eating a choc-ice.

Mrs Causey, our long-suffering tutor, was helping me to swot for the summer exams that we knew were being sent north from my school. These were taken very seriously. My father was still paying my fees, which amounted to as much as I was earning for appearing in the film. I don't think my little sisters had any formal education at all that week. I can only suppose that they learned a little more about being in films.

This is my diary entry for the day in full:

I woke up dressed and ate. We played a trick on Jane and Kit, driving off without them. We arrived at Beckfoot. I was the only one not filming that day. I did school work all morning. Sometimes I was alone and sometimes with the others. We all had lunch outside. In the afternoon we worked outside. I did an awful lot of school work, like the last time at Beckfoot.

Mrs Causey left and the Amazons and I went on to the lawn in front of the house and enjoyed the sun. I ate an ice cream and had some Coca-Cola the boys gave us. When the rest of the Swallows ended filming we went home. We had supper and went to bed.

The boys mentioned were rather too old to be called boys. Why did we call them prop boys? Is it something left over from the theatre?

I know Bobby Props – Bob Hedges – must have been well over forty. He was regarded as the father figure of the unit. Bobby worked out of

Bob 'Bobby Props' Hedges.

a lorry with a transparent sun-roof together with John Leuenberger, Terry Wells and Bill Hearn the carpenter. Dad caught them on film when they were having lunch on the tailgate of their truck. They later drove to Bowness to help set up for our big scene the next day and kindly returned with ice creams and fizzy drinks, which were a great treat. They were generous to a fault.

The prop men on *Swallows & Amazons* all had movie credits to their names that would delight any actor. They never seemed to stop working. Claude may well have asked for them to join us, as they'd all been on the crew of his first feature film.

If you look at our call sheet for the day (opposite) you can see how important the property master's job was. *Swallows & Amazons* was an unusual film in that the dinghies were technically action props. *Swallow* had to be kitted out with exactly the same rigging, plus the same 'continuity props' (the torch, compass, whistle, charts, blankets and provisions originally listed by Arthur Ransome) that were in the little ship when she left Wild Cat Island, in the scene when John gave me the telescope. The safekeeping of these items was paramount. In Scene 135, the envelope containing the Amazons' message is key to the action, thus an 'action prop'. If we'd seen it before it would have been known as a 'continuity action prop'. You can see it pinned to the post in the film. Simon Holland, our set designer, under whom the prop men were working, had a number of identical envelopes made. Lesley wrote

the message in her clear italic writing, making enough duplicates for any number of re-takes after John scrunched up the first one and flung it in the water. There were times when a continuity action prop such as our telescope, which was irreplaceable, would become very precious indeed. Had it been forgotten or lost it would have caused major disruption to the filming.

There was very little 'set dressing' for many of our scenes but you can understand that it was crucial that the carpenter mounted Captain Nancy's skull-and-crossbones on the *Amazon* boathouse. He would have taken this off at the end of the day and stored it in case retakes were needed, which is why the

Kit and Lesley at the Amazon boathouse.

```
                              T.P. FILMS LIMITED
CALL SHEET no. 20

PRODUCTION: SWALLOWS AND AMAZONS          DATE: WEDNESDAY JUNE 6th 1973

LOCATION:   BROWN HOWE                    UNIT CALL:
            WEST SIDE, CONISTON
                                          07.30 leave Car Park, Compston Road
                                          07.15 ferry from Kirkstone Foot Hotel
SETS:                     SC.NOS.
1.  EXT. AMAZON RIVER     135,136pt. EVENING
2.  EXT. LAKE             149,151 NIGHT
3.  EXT.LANDING PLACE     157,159,161 NIGHT

DIRECTOR: CLAUDE WHATHAM
```

ARTISTE	CHARACTER	LEAVE HOTEL	ON SET
SET 1. EXT. AMAZON RIVER SC.NO. 135, 136pt. EVENING			
SIMON WEST	JOHN	08.00	09.00
SUZANNA HAMILTON	SUSAN	"	"
STEPHEN GRENDON	ROGER	"	"
KIT SEYMOUR	NANCY	"	"
LESLEY BENNETT	PEGGY	"	"

```
ACTION BOAT   SWALLOW

WORK BOAT     2 DORYS, CAPRI, PUNT, CAMERA PONTOON TO BE READY ON LOC. BY 08.00

DAVID BLAGDEN  TO STAND BY IN DORY FOR ASSISTANCE

PROPS:        TORCH, COMPASS, WHISTLE, CHART, BLANKETS, PROVISIONS, ENVELOPE

ELECTRICAL:   PRACTICAL TORCH

ART           ENVELOPE WITH AMAZON'S MESSAGE
----------------------------------------------------------------------------
SET 2 EXT. LAKE  SC.NOS. 149, 151 NIGHT
```

SIMON WEST	JOHN	from above	
SUZANNA HAMILTON	SUSAN	"	
STEPHEN GRENDON	ROGER	"	

```
ACTION BOAT   SWALLOW

WORK BOATS    2 DORYS, CAPRI, PUNT, CAMERA PONTOON, from above

DAVID BLAGDEN  TO STAND BY IN DORY

PROPS:        COMPASS, WHISTLE, CHART, TORCH, BLANKETS, PROVISIONS

ELECTRICAL:   PRACTICAL TORCH required
----------------------------------------------------------------------------
SET 3 EXT. LANDING PLACE SC.NO. 157, 159, 161 NIGHT
```

SIMON WEST	JOHN	from above	
SUZANNA HAMILTON	SUSAN	"	
STEPHEN GRENDON	ROGER	"	

```
ACTION BOAT   SWALLOW

WORK BOATS    2 DORYS, CAPRI, PUNT, CAMERA PONTOON from above

PROPS:        COMPASS, WHISTLE, CHART, TORCH, BLANKETS, PROVISIONS

ELECTRICAL:   PRACTICAL TORCH required
----------------------------------------------------------------------------
DAVID BLAGDEN to be at location by 08.00
CHAPERONES: Jane Grendon & Daphne Neville to leave Oaklands at 08.00 SHARP
TUITION Margaret Causey to be at loc. by 09.00
NURSE:  To stand by on set from 08.30
MAKE UP/HAIR/WARDROBE    On location
RUSHES: At Kirkstone Foot Hotel - time to be advised
CATERING: EARLY TEA, AM & PM BREAKS, LUNCH for approx 70 persons
TRANSPORT: 1)Unit car to be at Kirkstone Foot Hotel by 07.45 to p.up Mr. Whatham,
Mr. Lewiston and Mr. Bracknell and proceed to location
2. Unit Minibus to be at Compston Rd.car park by 07.30 and work to Asst.Dir's instructions
3. Children's minibus to be at Oaklands by 08.00 for children & chaperones - to location
4. 5 seater car to be at Kirkstone Foot by 07.45 and work to Asst.Dir's instructions

NOTE: NICK NEWBY WORK BOATS to be at Brown Howe by 08.00 ready for ferrying

HAPPY DERBY DAY!                                        DAVID BRACKNELL
                                                       ASST.DIRECTOR
```

One of our call sheets.

prop men returned from Bowness with a long ladder in the lorry and ice creams for us all.

As children, we loved the props. I treasured the few items that Bobby made on the set and gave me at the end of the filming, such as his prototype flags. I don't think he mislaid anything, despite all the rushing around in boats, but Mum says that we shot one scene wearing the wrong costumes. We are not sure which one this was, but Terry was in hot water.

Camera boats (foreground), original boathouses beyond *Swallow*.

Thursday 7th June – Twenty-first day of filming

In Arthur Ransome's book, Titty is left keeping watch on an island so small it is little more than a rock, while the Swallows sail into Rio Bay in search of the Amazons. Luckily for me, this is not so in the film.

'They must be making for Rio,' says Susan. The scene then cuts to a brass band playing in the municipal park at Bowness-on-Windermere. John rows into the bay, pretty sure that the Amazons have given him the slip, Susan suggests that we could explore Rio, and I happily declare, 'We could buy rope for the lighthouse tree!'

And that is what we did – leaving the boy Roger in charge of *Swallow*.

> We woke up and went off to Bowness. All the Extras were changed and having their hair done, to suit the 1929 style. There was a pony and trap, old cars, motorbikes, bicycles and boats. Daddy, Perry and Tamzin were Extras. Gareth was an

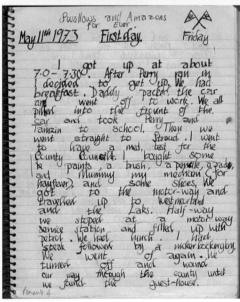

On the diary page:

Swallows and Amazons for Ever

May 11th 1973   First day.   Friday

7.0 - 7.30. I got up at about 7.0 - 7.30. After Perry ran in I decided to get up. We had breakfast. Daddy packed the car and went off to work. We all piled into the front of the car and took Perry and Tamzin to school. Then we went straight to Stroud. I went to have a med. test for the county council. I bought some paints, a brush, a palette, a pad, and Mummy my medicion (for hayfever) and some shoes. We got to the motor-way and travelled up to Westmorland and the Lakes. Half-way we stoped at a motor way service station and filled up with petrol. We had lunch. I had speak followed by a nicker lockerglory. We went of again. We turned off and wound our way through the county until we found the guest-house.

Top: Suzanna, Lesley, me (holding a copy of the Puffin edition of *Swallows and Amazons*), Kit and Simon before our hair was cut. Sten was having a short back and sides at the time.
Above left: The first page of my 1973 diary.
Above right: Director Claude Whatham by Coniston Water.

Above: Me with my mother, Daphne Neville. *Swallow* is in the background being towed by a dory.

Below: Me with Peter Robb-King, Ronnie Cogan, Kit, Lesley and Terry Smith, as the Amazons learn to shoot in the field behind the double-decker buses.

Opposite top: Simon, Sten, Suzanna and me in the yellow taxi.

Opposite bottom: Simon, me and Suzanna reading the famous telegram.

Top: On the camera pontoon out on Derwentwater wearing my BOAC life jacket.
Bottom: Sten, me and Simon at Derwentwater.

Top: Eddie Collins, Bobby Stilwell, Denis Lewiston and Claude Whatham with the 35mm Panavision set on the Landing Place on Peel Island to film the first swimming scene in May. Bottom: *Amazon* lashed to the camera pontoon on Derwentwater. *Swallow* can be seen alongside her.

Top: Virginia McKenna by the boathouses at Bank Ground, with Kerry Darbishire waiting beyond.
Bottom: On a makeshift jetty on Derwentwater fishing with Ronald Fraser.

> Extra too, yet he still came for us for our first scene and all the others. The first scene was coming into Rio, looking for the Amazons.
>
> We had lunch which included ice cream for pudding. After lunch we did school work. Roger did a scene with Mr Price. I did art: a tram and a pram.

Simon Holland had transformed busy Bowness into a Lakeland town of the 1920s. To do this he must have had a huge number of fibreglass boats removed. These were replaced by beautiful wooden launches and skiffs.

In the film, you see my father in white flannel trousers, his dark hair cut short, standing on the jetty in front of the lovely old boathouses that overlooked the bay back then. He is talking to the owner of the launch with the green and white striped awning. Much of the first part of this sequence was filmed from the grey punt, which Claude used as a camera boat. Simon was actually towing this for the shot in which he rowed up to the jetty. It was a hot day and for once we were all feeling the heat. I whipped off my grey cardigan before I leapt out of the boat, no doubt causing havoc later for the film editor.

Although the Swallows spurned the conventional attractions of tripperdom, we children spotted the Stop-Me-and-Buy-One ice cream cart like lightning. I was entranced by the old vehicles, and the number of people dressed to populate Rio. They were organised and directed by Terry Needham, the second assistant director. To our delight we found Gareth, the third assistant director, was dressed in period costume, too, his Motorola

Jane Grendon in costume at Bowness-on-Windermere.

hidden under a stripey blazer, so that he could cue the supporting artists and keep back the general public without having to worry about appearing in vision himself. To his dismay, this entailed having his hair cut, although he wasn't exactly shorn. We all thought it a distinct improvement. He looked so handsome. I'm not sure if you can spot Gareth in the distance when we are climbing out of *Swallow*, but I know that he was playing tennis with my father.

Jane looked fabulous in her 1929 outfit. It was the one and only time I saw her in a dress. Being in costume enabled her to keep an eye on all the children playing on the beach. The first assistant director, David Bracknell, knew she would keep them going and maintain safety, as they flung pebbles into the water or rushed about with the donkeys that were giving rides along the shore. No one wore riding helmets, of course.

You can just see my sisters walking towards the town at this point with Pandora Doyle, our publicist's daughter, who was in a pale blue, short-sleeved cotton dress. Perry was in yellow and Tamzin in pink, their hair plaited. Another excitement of the day was that Claude had given the landlord of our guest house, Mr Price, the part of the native who says, 'That's a nice little ship you've got there.' Mum said that Kit, Suzanna and Lesley had already spied him, pacing his garden at Oaklands, trying out every possible way of saying this line: 'That's a *nice* little ship you've got there,' then, 'That's a nice little ship *you've* got there,' leaving the girls in fits of giggles.

My sister Perry is on the left. Tamzin is facing us on the right.
She became an international event rider.

In the scene after we march out of the general stores, me clutching bottles of grog, you can see Tamzin with her pink dress and straight back riding a chocolate-coloured donkey along the beach, while Dad is pushing out a rowing skiff with a long oar. Roger looks on from the jetty to see Perry riding another donkey while Tamzin walks by in the opposite direction with none other than Mr Price, in his striped blazer, who is walking along towards the boathouses holding a little boy's hand. I am quite sure it was one of his own children, but it looks a bit dodgy, because while Roger watches my sisters and Pandora throwing stones into the lake from the beach where the skiffs are pulled up, Mr Price suddenly comes walking along the jetty and delivers his line: '*That's* a nice little ship you've got there.' It's shot in rather a creepy way, and has since been cut from the television broadcast version in the UK.

A moment later Pandora and my sisters are surrounding the ice cream man while John, Susan and Titty return, striding along the jetty like the three wise men, carrying rope, buns and bottles of grog.

My father's all-time passion in the form of a very graceful steam launch passes, almost silently, in the foreground. This was the *SL Elisabeth* skippered by George Pattinson, the man who established the Steamboat Museum on Windermere. Dad said: 'The Bowness skiffs were not like the Thames version. The outriggers caught the oars and allowed a fisherman to let go of the grip. If, and when, he caught an Arctic char, the Windermere fish, the oars were retained. A heavy boat. The rope for the Lighthouse Tree was huge, fat and unsuitable,' he went on. 'Daphne was not around as she had to go south to present *Women Only* for HTV. She was devastated to miss the donkey scene.' Mum had always loved donkeys. She kept a pair of her own for years, breeding spotty foals.

> We were called out again to do the scene coming back with the stores we bought. Gareth, Terry and Graham had great fun chasing old ladies back into the loos and shooing them up hills. We went in the town to do the scene in the cake shop but didn't get it done. Instead we filmed walking down the street.

Not filming inside the bun shop was a great shame as it had looked glorious. The chasing of ladies referred to some real-life ladies, with garish 1973 garments and bouffant hairdos, who had come scooting out of the public conveniences in the middle of a shot, forcing Claude to re-do the scene.

It had been a happy, happy day. What none of us knew was that it was nearly our last day on earth. The same supporting artists, including my father, had been booked again for the next morning. They were witnesses to what could have been the most hideous accident.

Returning to *Swallow* with our purchases.

Friday 8th June – Twenty-second day of filming

It was a glorious day on Windermere. Conditions were perfect. My father had been asked to appear in the scene in which the crew of *Swallow* narrowly miss colliding with native shipping on their first voyage to the island. He was the tall dark savage wearing a suave blazer and white flannels aboard the very elegant Lakeland steamer *MV Tern*, that has transported holiday-makers up and down the lake since 1891. He was also acting as my official chaperone as my mother was working in Bristol.

Simon, Suzanna, Sten and I were in the *Swallow*, which at the start of the day was attached to the camera pontoon so that Claude could capture the dialogue on film. In the script Roger is down to say: 'Steamship on the port bow.' What came out was: 'Look John! Over there – steamer ahead!' At this point Captain John called out: 'Ready about!' *Swallow* was meant to turn and continue on her way, while Titty grumbled about the natives.

Suzanna's diary is fairly explicit about what actually happened:

> Today was frightening and exciting . . . we filmed (tied onto the pontoon) almost bumping into a steamer. It was a bit frightening as we were 15 yards away from it. But then we really had to sail by it on our own. We were 9 inches away from the steamer going v. fast . . . we didn't have life-jackets on. It was the most frightening thing in my life – and I'm not just saying it – we all would have been killed if the boat turned over.

My father Martin Neville aboard *MV Tern* on Windermere.

My father knew exactly what could have happened. He was standing on the deck just above us, beside the camera, clutching the rail. You can see him clearly in the film. I asked Dad about it recently.

'Claude had no understanding of boats,' he said. 'The older, experienced skipper of the *Tern* had just handed over to a younger helmsman. She was going flat out – doing about twelve knots. I don't think he could alter how fast they were going because she had a notch-speed, rather than a throttle. It was only the steamer's bow wave that pushed *Swallow* off. I was ten feet above you, looking down.'

What happened was that the *Tern* took *Swallow*'s wind, and with no wind we could not turn. There was nothing we could do to sail away from her. My father thought that Simon had wanted to go about earlier, but he was waiting for Roger to yell 'Steamer ahead!' and Sten, being Sten, took his time. However, Simon told me that he was waiting for the cue to come over the Motorola that was tucked under his seat. It came too late.

I'd been in *Swallow*, wondering if I could reach out and fend her off – only the steamer was going too fast. Could we have hit her? What would have happened if we had? We were fully laden with camping gear – tangled things like tents with ropes, the hurricane lantern, biscuit tins and baskets, but did not even have hidden buoyancy on board.

'I looked astern and David Blagden's safety boat seemed a long, long way away,' my father said. 'I expect the skipper could have thrown the *Tern* into reverse, but it would not have been able to stop easily.'

Sten could not swim properly, and presumably there would have been some downward suction caused by the propellers. I'm told that small boats do tend to bounce away from large ferries but have seen dramatic footage of sailing boats hit by large vessels off Cowes. I'm glad we didn't plop into the water. My father still shudders at the memory of how close we came to an accident that morning. Luckily there was a bar open on the *Tern*. Ronnie Cogan bought him a glass of whisky.

I don't think I was quite as troubled as he was. I wrote my diary in the same matter-of-fact way as usual, avoiding any mention of my feelings:

> We went out on the pontoon. The steamer was a little way up the lake with Daddy and the other Extras on her. We filmed near colliding with the steamer once or twice with the pontoon. Then they filmed us from the pontoon. The crew then climbed aboard the steamer and filmed from there. They set us free and we sailed for the steamer. We got close and went along parallel with it. The steamer moved steadily on. *Swallow* was going very slowly. We were meant to tack but we didn't go fast enough. As the steamship bulge came towards us we were no more than a foot away from her. We were so lucky, so few inches further and we would have been under the steamer. Anyone could have been killed, Roger easily. We went home for lunch. After lunch I did art all afternoon. I lay in the sun. The others were filming. Perry and Tamzin had their hair cut. We went home and had supper. I went to sleep with my exams in my mind.

Saturday 9th June – Fourth weekend

> We woke up and played until breakfast. I helped Suzanna find bugs for her slow-worm. Everybody else went shopping. I started my exams: geography, science and maths. I left all the others for next week.
>
> After lunch Daddy, Perry, Tamzin and I went for a walk up to Loughrigg. On the way back we went into a super cave. It was very big and a half full of water. We went on and found a much smaller cave. We came to the car and drove home. We had supper. Gareth took us to see *Carry On Matron*, which was very funny and good. We went home and got to bed.

... *Carry On Matron*! I wonder what near-disasters they had on that film.

Chapter Six
Rain, Smoke and Dangerous Wild Animals

Sunday 10th June – Twenty-third day of filming

The mini-bus took us to Elterwater. We played around until break. We were taken down to the location and Gareth taught us how to fish. We were doing the fishing scene all morning.

My lines were –

Titty: How far down is your hook?

Susan: Nearly as deep as my rod will let me.

Titty: Mine is only about 3ft. down.

Of all the days we spent filming *Swallows & Amazons*, the fishing scene, shot in a reedy bay on Elterwater, was the one I enjoyed most. It was a cold, rather wet morning but we were soon absorbed in a way that Arthur Ransome would have understood well.

The only problem we had that day was keeping the fish alive. A chap in waders had brought along a number of perch. Bob Hedges, Simon Holland and Ian Whittaker, the set dresser, took it upon themselves to keep the fish as happy as they could, until they were – very carefully – attached to our hooks. Titty doesn't catch one but John does. In spite of everyone's best efforts it wasn't a very lively perch.

A bigger challenge was Roger's great fish – a massive pike that was meant to be snapping and ferocious. I've been told that it ended up being resuscitated in Keswick Intensive Care Unit. Sten remembers that it was Claude who was really tugging on his line, not the fish. Roger Altounyan said that he caught a pike when he was only aged about seven. He was alone in a boat on the lake and was quite terrified by it.

Ian Whittaker struck me as being rather different from everyone else on the crew. He was very nice looking and a gentleman of the old school.

Ian Whittaker, Simon Holland and Gareth Tandy guarding the fish.

I remember him telling me that he'd originally set out to be an actor but had found it so difficult to get work that he became a set dresser or designer's assistant. He found he rather enjoyed it, and stuck to the job, although his family did not consider it much of a career. That morning Ian spent his time just building little stone walls in the lake to keep the perch alive on our set, but he was a country sort of person and enjoyed the fishing scene as much as I did.

> We fished until lunch. Just after lunch we played in the reeds. We went on with the fishing scene until about three to four. We met Brenda Bruce. Kit, Lesley and Sten went back to Oaklands. The rest of us went to Windermere to a ship's chandlers to do the shopping scene.

It was quite late that afternoon when we left to shoot one of the few interior scenes of the film, the general store in Rio, where we bought the rope for the lighthouse tree and four bottles of grog. It wasn't a real shop.

Filming the fishing scene from the grey punt on Elterwater.

It had been made out of someone's garage. Ian had dressed it with boxes of wooden dolly pegs and other things you'd buy in brown paper bags. A wonderful 1920s radio set and two purring cats made the scene come alive, especially since, being in reticent explorer mode, we were a bit gruff in our communications with the native shopkeeper, a Mr Turner, who we left standing in a perplexed state.

Monday 11ᵗʰ June – Twenty-fourth day of filming

I woke up, dressed, ate and drove off with the others to Dixon's farm.

My mother was very excited about meeting the actress Brenda Bruce, who had been engaged to play Mrs Dixon. She'd arrived the day before when we were still at Elterwater, where she found Claude keeping up our morale by wearing my mother's ridiculous Donny Osmond hat. He probably needed it for warmth. I'd been worried that Brenda Bruce would be chilly as she was only wearing a blouse and flip-flops. Now I understand that she was 'of a certain age' and didn't feel the cold quite so much as skinny twelve-year-olds with opinions.

Brenda had actually worked for Claude quite a bit and he trusted her to play a small part well. She looked wonderful in the film and very comfortable in her nice clean dairy. I had no idea that Brenda Bruce was so well known, or that she'd won the BAFTA for Best Actress in 1963.

'Yes, you do!' Mum said. 'She was the White Queen in *Alice Through the Looking Glass*.'

When I look back on *Swallows & Amazons*, I can see that Claude made sure it didn't become chocolate-boxy. You can tell by glancing at the costume Mike Pratt wore to play Mr Dixon, the provider of worms for our fishing bait. The lovely Lakeland colours of his garments contrast somehow with the harsh blues and reds of our 1970s clothes.

Mike Pratt insisted that he couldn't have his hair cut as he was in the middle of filming a television series, *The Adventures of Black Beauty*, which was set in the Victorian era. He was wigglier than the worms. Kit looked at me, rolling her eyes. We could all tell this was just a good excuse to avoid being shorn. His hair had to be pinned up under a flat cap, which looked terrible on the big screen. You could see the kirby grips.

Geraint Lewis of The Arthur Ransome Trust found out the details of the location we used for Mrs Dixon's dairy: 'I had a long conversation once with Lucy Batty about her recollections of filming at Bank Ground in the house and barn. She confirmed that they used the buildings shown on maps as Tent Lodge Cottages for Dixon's Farm.

Hairstylist Ronnie Cogan seeing to my hair.

That certainly seems to fit from the view of the lake and shoreline trees in the background.' Perhaps you might be able to find the exact locations yourself.

> After lunch we moved to where we were yesterday. The first scene was climbing up a bank. We went down the road and filmed by a waterfall. My lines were:
>> *Titty:* It must be Niagara, we could get a barrel and bounce
>>> down it.
>> *Susan:* Not today.
>
> From there we climbed up the hill to where a funny tree grew straight out of the rock. We filmed the following scene. My lines were:
>> *Titty:* A jungle almost.
>> *Roger:* It's almost as good as a monkey.
>> *Titty:* If only there were some parrots. Jays, they'll do.
>>> They're savage parrots. They're saying Pretty Polly in
>>> savage language.
>
> All these scenes were going to the charcoal burners. We went home quite early. On the way back we dropped Lesley off at the Kirkstone Foot to have her hair done.

Crossing 'Niagara'.

What Richard and Claude certainly wanted to make the most of was the Westmorland scenery. In many ways they were making a landscape movie. Indeed the document of 'Production Intent' declared, 'The film should be shot with the lakes and mountains continually acting as a back cloth to the action.' I think what they most enjoyed was finding all the locations to put together the imaginary lake, as depicted in the end pages of the Jonathan Cape editions of the book. I am often asked where the waterfall is.

'It must be Niagara!'

'No, Sophie,' I can hear my mother saying. 'It's somewhere near Elterwater.'

I was sent suggestions from Cumbria, with photos that made me feel pretty sure that the actual waterfall is Skelwith Force, but I am not certain. It was certainly a force to be reckoned with. The carpenter had to bring up a scaffold plank to make a bridge so that we could get into position on the other side. They held up a rope for us to use as a hand rail and David Bracknell led us over one by one. Sten found it all a bit scary.

Tuesday 12th June – Twenty-fifth day of filming

'Here we are, intrepid explorers making our way into uncharted waters. What mysteries will they hold for us? What dark secrets shall be revealed?'

The dark secret was that the inky black night scenes had to be shot in Mrs Batty's barn at Bank Ground Farm during the day. The design team strung up thick, light-proof drapes and made the tall, dusty outbuilding into a studio. Claude had no choice. We had quickly run out of interior scenes, and the weather was so bad that we could do little else.

'While the rest of England melted in a heat wave, the Lakes seemed wrapped in mist and rain,' Richard remembers in his book. I have a press cutting from *The Guardian* dated 7th July 1973, which opens with the words:

The weather report follows in half a minute. Richard Pilbrow is obsessed with the weather. Every morning he wakes around 4 o'clock and crosses his room at the Kirkstone Foot Hotel to cock a weather eye at the sky above Wansfell Pike. Most mornings it is the same story . . . Pilbrow looks out of the window. Raining.

What a worry that rain was. When we arrived to start filming at Derwentwater on 12th June, it was so blustery that no one could consider taking a 35mm movie camera out on the water, as my diary entry attests:

We were meant to do the scenes of Cormorant Island but it was too windy to even go on the lake. We did a little school work and were then taken up to do the journey to the charcoal burners. My single line was:
Titty: What's that?
We did this big scene until lunchtime. After lunch we moved back to Holly Howe, where in a barn, the camp was set up for night filming. They did the scenes where I was by myself and going to sleep.

I loved filming in the barn. Gareth led me through the high wooden doors and into a magical version of our camp on Peel Island, beautifully recreated by Ian Whittaker. A real camp fire was burning. Blankets (goatskins, in Titty's imagination) and pillows from our tents had been laid out so I could be 'shrouded in my cloak' while I was waiting up for the Swallows to return from the Amazon River. The scene was beautifully lit with branches clamped in stands placed in front of the lights, while a gentle wind was produced by the prop men wafting a board to lift my hair at the right moment.

I don't think there was an owl hoot for me to hear. I had to imagine that so they could add a real owl call later. I'm afraid I never learned how to make an answering hoot. I tried and tried. I still can't. Simon could do it but Claude asked us all to just pretend, as he needed to lay the sound on afterwards.

They say that films made when everything runs smoothly somehow lack the edge gained when made against the odds, or by a director who is utterly foul and yells at everyone. Despite or perhaps because of the weather, what we gained was a camaraderie that formed the foundation to the movie that, after all, was about becoming resilient. We had to be stoic and get on with filming, regardless of getting cold and wet.

Rain doesn't show up on-screen unless it is pelting down. You can see the effects – wet hair and soggy costumes – but you actually have to use rain machines if you want to show rain in a drama. We could film our trek up the hill to visit the charcoal burners without a problem, but going out on the lake was impossible. You'd have seen the raindrops falling on the water and, besides, it was too windy. As it was, Denis used what natural light he had to capture that limpid quality you find in the Lakes, so quintessentially English. It draws you in, rewinding back to childhood days when you had time to make camps and rush about in the woods.

The rain did deter my mother from taking photographs. She didn't have a flash cube to use in the barn, but she took many the following day, when we experienced very different problems – caused, this time, by smoke. . . .

Wednesday 13*th* June – Twenty-sixth day of filming

I got up and dressed into my costume. We had breakfast and drove off. We drove through a forest area until we arrived at our location. Our school bus had broken down on the way. In the dining bus we sorted out our books and did a little school work. We went down to the charcoal burners' hut, which was

```
                          T.P. FILMS LIMITED

CALL SHEET no. 27                    DATE: THURSDAY JUNE 14th 1973

PRODUCTION: SWALLOWS AND AMAZONS     UNIT CALL: 07.30 leave Compston Rd.Car Park
                                               07.15 ferry from Kirkstone Foot
                                                                         Hotel
SETS:                       SC.NOS.            LOCATION
1.  EXT.CHARCOAL BURNERS' WIGWAM   110 comp. DAY    ICKENTHWAITE FOREST
2.  INT.CHARCOAL BURNERS' WIGWAM   109 DAY          "
3.  EXT. DARIEN                    12 DAY           BANK GROUND FARM (Mrs.Batty)

DIRECTOR:  CLAUDE WHATHAM
```

ARTISTE	CHARACTER	LEAVE HOTEL	MAKE UP	ON SET

```
SET 1.  EXT. CHARCOAL BURNERS' WIGWAM SC.110 COMP. DAY

JACK WOOLGAR             OLD BILLY                        07.00     09.00
JOHN FRANKLYN-ROBBINS    YOUNG BILLY                      07.30     09.00
SIMON WEST               JOHN            08.00                      09.00
ZANNA HAMILTON           SUSAN             "                          "
STEPHEN GRENDON          ROGER             "                          "
SOPHIE NEVILLE           TITTY             "                          "

PROPS:  WHISTLE, COMPASS, ROGER'S SWAG STICK, SUSAN'S BASKET, CIGAR BOX, SPADES,
ANIMALS: ADDER (to be called by ART DEPT.)          SMOKE STICKS
ART/DRESSING:  PRACTICAL FIRES
-------------------------------------------------------------------------------
SET 2.  INT. CHARCOAL BURNERS' WIGWAM SC.109 DAY

JACK WOOLGAR             OLD BILLY                               from above
SIMON WEST               JOHN                                         "
ZANNA HAMILTON           SUSAN                                        "
SOPHIE NEVILLE           TITTY                                        "
STEPHEN GRENDON          ROGER                                        "

PROPS:  WHISTLE, COMPASS, ROGER'S SWAG STICK, SUSAN'S BASKET, CIGAR BOX,SMOKE STICKS
ART/DRESSING:  DRESSING FOR INT. CHARCOAL BURNERS' HUT
CONSTRUCTION:  TO STAND BY TO REMOVE SECTION OF HUT
-------------------------------------------------------------------------------
SET 3.  EXT. DARIEN FIELDS  SC.NO. 12 DAY

SIMON WEST               JOHN                                    from above
ZANNA HAMILTON           SUSAN                                        "
SOPHIE NEVILLE           TITTY                                        "
STEPHEN GRENDON          ROGER                                        "

PROPS:  ALL PICNIC EQUIPMENT, TELEGRAM

CHAPERONES:   Jane Grendon and Daphne Neville to leave Oaklands at 08.00 SHARP
TUITION:      Mrs. Causey to be at loc. by 09.00
HAIR/MAKE UP  at Kirkstone Foot Hotel
WARDROBE:     Mr. Woolgar and Mr. Franklyn-Robbins at hotel,Children on location
RUSHES:       At Kirkstone Foot Hotel, on completion of shooting
CATERING:     EARLY TEA, AM & PM BREAKS, LUNCH for approx. 70 persons
TRANSPORT:
1.  Robert Wakeling to pick up Mr. Whatham, Mr. Lewiston and Mr. Bracknell at
        07.45 and proceed to location
2.  Unit bus to be at Car Park by 07.30 and work to Asst. Director's instructions
3.  Children's Minibus to be at Oaklands by 08.00 SHARP and proceed to location
4.  5 seater car (Browns) to be at Kirkstone Foot Hotel by 08.00 and work to
                            Asst.Director's instructions
5.  1 extra car (Browns) to stand by from midday at loc. for Artistes' return
            to Kirkstone Foot Hotel.
```

The call sheet for our scene with the charcoal burners.

made of wooden poles, reeds and bracken. At one end there was a stone fireplace. There were bracken windbreaks and a big mound of earth, which was the charcoal burners' fire. We did the first scene coming down the hill to the charcoal burners' hut and meeting them. My line was –

Titty: May we?

'Let's just run though our lines, shall we?' old Jack Woolgar said, in a gentle Lancashire accent.

We were waiting around for some reason, so we did just that, sitting by a woodstack. Titty had a lot to say in the scene where we went to see the charcoal burners, but the dialogue was straight out of the book, so it was easy. Or it appeared to be, until I heard Old Billy saying, 'Ehh, then you'll be climbing into that minibus and off back to Ambleside, I expect.'

'That's not in *Swallows and Amazons*! That's real life,' I thought.

'Eee, lass! You forgot to come in on your cue.'

It was true. I was so entranced by Old Billy, so lulled by the music of his voice, that I'd simply gone on listening to him.

Although it grew to be a bright sunny day, the weather was grey and cold at first, with a gale blowing so hard that it was knocking the tops of the trees about and making life difficult for the sound recordist. This felt a bit awkward. It was meant to be 'a dead calm' in the story.

'It's blowing up a bit,' Old Billy put in.

I don't think anyone watching would have noticed if we'd left it at that, but our hair was blowing about so madly that Young Billy had a few savage-like words with John about why we weren't sailing. These are not in the book.

When I watch this scene in the film I notice one technical bit about acting that is never talked about much. You have to hit your mark, without it being obvious. No looking down. Your mark is the exact position established when the shot is lined up. The camera focus, certainly back then, required actors to be consistent and hit the same position in each take as was established in the rehearsal. If you look carefully at the opening shot, captured by the photograph in the colour plates section, you can see it is carefully composed – a nice triangle, with all of our faces in vision. The important bit – Roger holding my hand – is not masked. Do I spoil the magic if I say we are standing on our marks?

If feet couldn't be seen, a piece of camera tape was usually placed on the floor in front of our toes. Sometimes a box would be placed on the ground so we could feel it and not have to look down. Tape didn't stick to

Molly Friedel watching the scene from behind a reflector board, while
Robin Gregory plants a microphone at our feet.

most of our locations so we used sticks or tree bark, taking quite a pride
in disguising them when our feet were in vision. This didn't work at the
charcoal burners'. We all came out of their dark wigwam blinking in the
bright sunlight, shuffling onto our secret marks. Suzanna glanced down
quickly to check she was on hers.

> My lines were:
> *Titty:* If you're burning why not let it burn?
> (Others speak)
> *Titty:* The man on the houseboat?
> (Others speak)
> *Titty:* But they can't, they're at war with him.
> *Titty:* Thank you so much for letting us see your lovely
> serpent. Goodbye.

Was the charcoal heap a real one? You can tell, since that hole had to start
smoking on cue, that it was constructed for us. Terry Wells was inside
with a smoke gun. I know he suffered from getting too much smoke in
his eyes and had to be treated by the nurse.

There was certainly a great deal of smoke around, which looked
atmospheric. In fact the smoke guns would be one of the few items
classified as 'visual effects' in the film. You would normally include the

firework and cannon-fire, but I have a feeling they were real, like the Amazons' arrows, and not visual effects at all. I'm not sure this would be legal these days.

Now we had a 'Dangerous Wild Animal' on set, an adder with a venomous bite. Suzanna, who loves snakes with a passion, got very close to touching it. She was disappointed that you can't see this in the film. I was a bit scared. Arthur Ransome had added that frisson of danger for us to experience. Robin, the sound recordist, wanted to hear the adder hissing. He actually buried a microphone at our feet.

Jean Woodhouse wrote to me from Westmorland:

'I came to watch *Swallows and Amazons* being filmed. We walked down from our village Primary School (Satterthwaite) but the scene was actually just down the road from where I lived . . . we were all terrified of the snake. Because I used to go up and down through the wood each day, I knew the real charcoal burners who worked there and so that scene in the film has always felt quite special to me.' She was ten years old.

One of the most magical things for my mother was meeting the real charcoal burners. They looked exactly like the actors playing the Billies, except that they had lived and worked in the woods most of their lives.

Thursday 14th June – Twenty-seventh day of filming

The real charcoal burner.

I had thought that the older charcoal burner was Jack Allonby, a well-known local character who lived at Spark Bridge, although I have been told that it is Norman Allonby, Jack's brother, who lived at Bandrake Head.

The real Young Billy was almost indistinguishable from John Franklyn-Robbins, the actor playing the part. He seemed to take a wry interest in the filming, but what he thought of us and the crew, I dread to think. We were aliens on his planet, and terribly bossy ones. It was our polystyrene coffee cups that looked so out of place. They certainly weren't authentic for the period. The call sheet for the day scheduled Scene 110 with the adder, but I recorded in my diary that we had completed that on the previous day. I must have meant my part in it. Claude was probably using the time to pick up the shots of Young Billy working with his dampened fire.

Sten with Jack Woolgar.

The interior of the hut would have been tricky and time-consuming to light. We had a proper fire burning in the stone grate and Claude was keen for the scene to be atmospherically smoky. The wood smoke itself was fine, but the crew kept working with smoke guns, since they were more directional and considered more controllable. The acrid fumes produced by their oil canisters choked me, but Jack Woolgar was absolutely solid and kept our attention. I enjoyed drawing with the charcoal. I wish I had drawn him. Apart from the amount of smoke, we loved being inside the mossy wigwam. I could have stayed there quite happily. It was nice and warm.

Much later, I asked Claude what made a good director. 'You need to use your time well,' he said.

Although this skill probably makes you an employable director, Claude had other assets. We all adored him, and would do anything for him. He'd explained early on that he wanted us to keep going, no matter what happened during a take. Suzanna really did leave her basket behind with the charcoal burners. When Old Billy called her, she was honestly taken aback and sweetly ran to collect it. It is something that rings true, a natural quality that was brought to the scene. Claude loved it.

After lunch, we moved to Bank Ground Farm to film the receiving of despatches. The problem here was that Claude had no Peak of Darien and no pine trees as vividly portrayed by Arthur Ransome. But he did have buttercups and daisies, the meadow flowers so evocative of childhood summers spent in the English countryside. 'Daisies are our silver, buttercups our gold,' was the hymn we sang at my rural village school. 'This is all the treasure we can have or hold.'

The excavations in the meadow at Bank Ground Farm.

The field that runs down to Coniston Water looked glorious on that sunny day. It was glowing. We arrived to find that a huge hole had been dug in the meadow for the camera, with a picnic for us spread the other side of it. We thought the hole very exciting and wanted to jump in it. Mum had to physically restrain Sten. I'm not sure whether Lucy Batty felt quite the same way about the excavations in her field.

I was sad that we didn't have a fire with a kettle, as they do in the book, but that was kept as a feature of island life yet to come. It would be too spoiling to have everything at once.

> After lunch we moved location to Holly Howe. When we arrived we did the scene receiving the telegram from father, which said:
>
> ### BETTER DROWNED THAN DUFFERS
> ### IF NOT DUFFERS WONT DROWN
>
> *Titty:* No you're wrong. It says, if we were Duffers we might as well be drowned. Then it stops, and starts again to say: If we're not Duffers we won't drown.

Roger came sailing down clutching the despatches from our father, reaching out to deliver the piece of paper over the hole. I understand

11.   Contd.   11.

> ROGER
>
> So it is, it's dead aft. I'll be a schooner
> and go goosewinged. Hoorah!

He spreads out his arms for sails and runs, whooping with
excitement, straight down the field.

12.   EXT. DARIEN. DAY   12.

JOHN, SUSAN and TITTY sit gazing out at the lake, picnicking.
They hear ROGER running.

> JOHN
>
> Dispatches?

> ROGER
> (calls)
> It's yes, and for me too, so it must
> be yes for Titty.

They all scramble up.

> SUSAN
>
> Read it.

> JOHN
>
> Better drowned than duffers if not
> duffers then won't drown. Hurray
> for daddy.

> SUSAN
>
> What does it mean?

> JOHN
>
> It means that daddy thinks we won't
> get drowned but if we do, good
> riddance.

> SUSAN
>
> But what are duffers, if not duffers?

> TITTY
>
> No you're wrong. It says if we were
> duffers we might as well be drowned.
> Then it stops and starts again. As
> we aren't duffers we shan't be drowned.

> ROGER
> (lost)
> Why didn't he just say yes?

A page from David Wood's original screenplay.

that this was based on the cryptic telegrams that Ernest Altounyan often sent his children. It has become the contrarian's response to Health and Safety ever since.

What we ended up saying altered slightly from David Wood's original screenplay. John referred to Daddy as 'Father'. I'm not sure why. He did so in his letter. It is 'Daddy' in the book and in the script, but perhaps Claude considered 'Father' as having more of a period feel. Perhaps Simon did. I stuck more to Ransome's dialogue, as you can see if you compare the film script with my diary entry. This was only because I knew his book so well, and never saw the script. The acting credit must go to Simon, who sat holding the telegram, graciously absorbing my bossiness, as I grappled with the words.

Back in 1973, it was the job of Continuity to take notes on any changes made to the screenplay. Sue Merry, ever present in her dark coat, took on this role. Today she would probably be known as a script supervisor but her aviator sunglasses and black polo-necked jersey would still be the height of fashion. She would type up her notes on location, using a portable typewriter that was sometimes set up for her on a spindly picnic table. This method of working was different from the BBC, where the production assistants would type up their notes at the end of each day. The method had evolved so that one copy of her notes, typed on triplicate paper, could be sent to the laboratory with the exposed film. It also meant that her

evenings were free. Sue also took technical notes for the film editor and director, indicating which takes were favoured and which had been spoilt, and giving the reason. In those days we had no monitors. The camera lens would be unscrewed after each take and checked carefully. If any fluff was found, the camera assistant would call out:

'Hair in the gate!'

Sue would quietly note this down and David, the first assistant director, would declare:

'Set up to go again.'

Sue was also responsible for the overall continuity, and would take numerous Polaroid

Sue Merry typing up her continuity notes on location.

photographs as an aide-memoire. This scene followed the one of Mother giving Roger the telegram, which had not yet been shot. Virginia McKenna hadn't arrived back in Westmorland.

Looking back, this seems a huge gamble. Would they ever get another sunny day while the buttercups were still blooming, a day to match – exactly – the weather of 14th June?

Friday 15th June – Twenty-eighth day of filming

Roger and Titty rowing to Cormorant Island.

'Pull harder, Roger!'

Hardly a line from Shakespeare, but one that has lodged deep in my memory. Titty was even bossier in the books:

'You keep time with me, Boy,' said the able-seaman.
'All right.' Titty lifted her oar from the water. Roger gave one pull. 'Boy,' said the able-seaman, 'you mustn't say "All right".'
'Aye, aye, sir,' said the boy.

When we auditioned for *Swallows & Amazons*, the emphasis was on sailing. In fact I needed to be good at rowing. Titty and Roger row back

Sten and I rowing *Swallow* while attached to the camera pontoon.

from the charcoal burners, I rowed the *Amazon* out of Secret Harbour, and now here we were rowing across Derwentwater to Cormorant Island. This was more difficult than normal, as *Swallow* was wired to the camera pontoon.

I cringe whenever I watch the 16mm footage my father took of me rowing at home before we left to film in the Lake District. My blades were high above the water, hitting the surface with terrible splashes, but I seemed to achieve my objective and brought my Thames skiff in to the jetty without crashing. I managed to fit an improvised mast to her forward thwart and even made my own sail out of a dark green dust sheet. It didn't look great, but it worked.

Luckily for us, *Swallow* was a much easier boat to row. She has two rowing positions and Sten and I made it to the island without screaming at each other. Simon and Suzanna joined us for the scene when the Swallows lower the Jolly Roger and start to sail the captured *Amazon* back to Wild Cat Island. I changed my costume in the Capri, which was the only support boat with a cabin.

I know the scene was shot with two cameras on different boats, as the grey camera punt was also used. It was not a large vessel but somehow managed to accommodate Denis Lewiston, the 35mm Panavision and quite a few crew members, while Richard remained on the camera pontoon with Eddie Collins operating the 16mm camera. 'We carried on with the scene, pulling up anchor and sailing off.'

This was difficult to achieve in terms of sailing. After hauling up the anchor, Suzanna and I battled to turn. We thought it unsporting to wiggle the rudder and jeopardise her pins – and yet so much was at stake. I remember Simon calling advice over the water. He stalled and we caught up, trying to get close together for the shot. *Amazon* caught a gust of wind coming down from the high fells, and we found ourselves zooming along at an exhilarating pace.

Soon the camera was in *Swallow*, capturing close-ups of a triumphant Captain John. My diary entry for the day went on to note: 'We went back for lunch, but were soon off sailing again. We did a lot of filming, "going to the island".'

It must have been a productive day out on the water at long last. The sequences captured were among the most inspiring for sailors and it felt as if we were able to capture something filmically unique.

Saturday 16th June – A day off

It was Saturday morning. Instead of resting, Claude took us, his *artistes*, as he insisted on calling us, to Blackpool, the famous holiday destination of the north west. None of us had ever been before. It was a great treat and hugely exciting. I carefully chose the clothes I would wear, putting on a long shell necklace Daddy had brought back from Africa.

Jean, Jane, Sten, Kit, me, Claude, Simon, Lesley, Suzanna and Ronnie in Blackpool.

A complete contrast to camping and sailing in the wilds of the Lake District, this proved a day trip to remember. It must have taken nearly two hours to travel from Ambleside to the Blackpool promenade in those days. Jean McGill, our friend and driver, drove us down in the unit minibus. We were joined for the day by Ronnie Cogan, and of course Mum and Jane. I'm pretty sure Ronnie smoked the whole way there and back, but we were thrilled that he wanted to come too.

> When we arrived we parked the mini-bus and walked to the promenade. We walked a little way along and then took a tram to the funfair.
>
> It was surprisingly uncrowded. We walked in. I do not know why but I went on the big dipper. It was very frightening. The more I screamed the more frightened I became.
>
> When we got off we went on the bumper cars. We were the only people on and had double goes. The next thing was the ghost train. We met up with Nancy, Claude and Lesley, and bought some hats. We went back to the tower in a pony and trap. We found the restaurant and had a big lunch.

Claude must have loved funfairs. Before *Swallows & Amazons* he directed *That'll Be the Day*, a rock-and-roll movie produced by David Puttman, set at a funfair of the 1950s. It starred David Essex and Ringo Starr, with Big Bopper singing *Chantilly Lace*, and The Everly Brothers with *Wake Up Little Susie*. Claude gave me the LP of the film soundtrack, which I played again and again.

We did it all. I was most impressed – and terrified out of my wits – by the Big Dipper, but have always loved going in a pony and trap, and racing donkeys.

> The circus was next on the list. It was indoors. The first on was a girl with eight ponies. Then came the man and a girl with the big pole. Next was a man on a tight rope. And then the clowns. High up the acrobats did their act. After the interval came a dogs' football match, more clowns and acrobats. It ended with snakes and crocodiles, in water with fountains and a flooded ring. In the middle were gold statues, which came to life.
>
> We came out of the circus and went to the beach where we had super fast donkey rides. We went back to the funfair. I had another go on the bumper cars and the ghost train. I bought some rock and had a go on the moving floor house. The journey back seemed quicker.

Claude, Sten, Mum and Lesley.

Looking back, it seems we took a number of risks. What EMI's insurance company would have said, I do not know. Falling off a donkey could have cost quite a few expensive filming days, but then EMI did own the circus we visited. There we saw true artistes, along with a number of reptiles.

We were exhilarated by the whole experience, 'Dangerous Wild Animals' and all. It was tiring, but it energised us, bringing us together as a family, all looking up to Claude as our father figure. He had two children of his own. Paul Whatham had been perhaps sixteen years old when we made *Cider with Rosie* in Gloucestershire. Mum remembers him as a curly-haired

Lesley and Claude in Blackpool.

boy talking to his father about the casting. He sadly died in a motorcycle accident, driving home from Oxford Polytechnic when he was only about nineteen. Claude didn't want a fuss made, but he never got over it. I weep for him, even now.

Chapter Seven
Robinson Crusoe and Man Friday

Sunday 17th June – Twenty-ninth day of filming

I hadn't known that Virginia McKenna was back in Westmorland, or that she had come up with her husband Bill Travers. I certainly didn't know that we would spend that Sunday cooking on the campfire.

> As soon as I woke up I was told I was to be working all day with Virginia and the others could stay at Oaklands. After driving off and arriving at Peel Island I went to the top of our double-decker bus and dressed. I met Virginia and her husband and played around until I was called. The first scene done was cooking supper.

There was a hushed reverence when Virginia McKenna was on set. Gone were the saucepan jokes, which was funny, as it was a frying pan scene. The pemmican potato cakes were delicious, and very hot. As always, I noted my lines in my diary:

> *Titty:* Man Friday oughtn't to know about them.
> *Mother:* Very well, but what are you doing all by yourself?
> *Titty:* Well properly I'm in charge of the camp. But while they're not here it won't matter if I'm Robinson Crusoe instead. Man Friday? Would you mind telling me about a bit of your life before you came to this island?
> *Mother:* I was caught by some very savage savages. They put me in a huge stewpot and chanted strange songs.
> *Titty:* Then what?
> *Mother:* They lit a fire under the stewpot and started dancing all around me.
> *Titty:* What did you do?

> *Mother:* I waited till no one was looking and jumped out of
>   the pot and escaped.
> *Titty:* Were you scalded badly?
> *Mother:* Badly, but I buttered the places that hurt most.

We had lunch. Afterwards we did close-ups. The next
scene we shot was me eating cake just before she arrived.
My line was:

> *Titty:* Man Friday! (and hugged Virginia)

After that I sat up a tree doing a scene after seeing a
ravenous animal.

> *Titty:* I'm not afraid of ravenous beasts anyway.

Working with Virginia and Arthur Ransome's dialogue was altogether an
exercise in charm, or managing charm. I hope I didn't overcook it. I was
rather preoccupied by a wobbly tooth but it was good to work on a scene
with just one other actor.

I still don't know how Lee Electric managed to get so many lights working
out on Peel Island. I don't remember having them there before. They must
have had the generator on the bank and run cables under the water on that
dark day. It was wonderful having the flood lights. They kept us warm.

Suddenly Virginia was gone and I was a saucepan once more, a
saucepan with a very wiggly tooth. No more lights. I was sitting up a tree
above Coniston Water in my navy-blue knickers, and descended feeling
a bit like Pooh Bear in search of honey.

Filming with Virginia McKenna on Peel Island.

...

Monday 18ᵗʰ June – Thirtieth day of filming

Losing a milk tooth when you are nearly thirteen years old is rather embarrassing. In my situation it was disastrous.

> I woke up toothless. I had pulled my tooth out that night because it had hurt so much. I had breakfast and nobody noticed it until I told them. When we got to the location Claude told me they might get away with it.

Not only was the gap sore, but since it was an upper tooth at the front of my mouth the continuity of the whole movie was blown. Today they would fit a bridge, but Claude decided he would just have to live with the problem. I spent the next few days trying not to let my teeth show, but even today, all these years later, those who know the film will comment on the fact that I lost an eye tooth.

As it was, I had to concentrate on pushing the hideously heavy Holly Howe rowing boat from the Landing Place in the scene when I bid farewell to Man Friday.

> I did the scene in which Virginia left me alone.
> *Titty:* They'll be back soon.
> *Mother:* I hope so, it'll be fairly dark soon. Wouldn't you like to come home with me? Just for tonight. We could leave a note for John.
> *Titty:* No thank you, I'd rather stay here.
> *Mother:* Goodbye then Robinson Crusoe.
> *Titty:* Goodbye Man Friday.
> *Titty:* Duffer. That's for looking too hard. Try the other eye.

Virginia McKenna

The sequence was more tricky than might be assumed, as the massive camera, the cameraman and sound recordist were in the boat with Virginia. The water was cold, the rocks rather slippy. And I had the telescope in one hand. This was in order to deliver

Arthur Ransome's immortal line, 'Duffer. That's with looking too hard. Try the other eye,' while lowering the telescope to wipe away a tear. I'm afraid that what came out was, 'That's for looking too hard.' I was busy thinking of terribly sad things, all geared up to produce the tears, when glycerine was produced and carefully blown into my eyes. The most enormous tears, far more difficult to contain than real ones, gushed forth. And Terry must have forgotten about a hanky. You can tell that the square of white cotton I had tucked in my knickers is just a frayed piece of cloth.   ·

> We had lunch. The education officer came but never saw us.
> I did a little school, and then filmed a big scene in the camp
> pretending to be Robinson Crusoe. I had a lot of lines with a
> short break in between.

Daniel Defoe's hero, Robinson Crusoe, has been portrayed on the big screen by Douglas Fairbanks, Dan O'Herlihy – who earned an Oscar nomination for his role in the 1952 version – Aidan Quinn, Pierce Brosnan, and me. Or rather, me playing Titty being Robinson Crusoe. Oh dear, oh dear.

The scene opens with Titty sitting on a biscuit tin, reading from her log. 'Twenty-five years ago this day, I, Robinson Crusoe, was wreck-ed on this desolate place.' The fact that I had missed the -ed from wrecked was genuine. I hadn't written the word down properly in Titty's log book. At this point I flung myself to the ground and dragged my exhausted body into the camp, grasping my throat so as to portray the fact that Robinson Crusoe was virtually dying of thirst.

I hauled myself to my feet by grabbing the forked stick by the fire. What I didn't know was that Robin Gregory, our sound recordist, had hidden his microphone there. You can still hear the crunch as I grasp the crossbar that held the kettle. He was a perfectionist and was rather annoyed about it.

'Make a good place for a camp,' Titty declares heartily, standing up and looking around. 'I'll build my hut here out of branches and moss.' So continued my solo performance. 'Can't have two tents for one ship-wrecked mariner.'

My mother, who went to RADA, is very theatrical. In her eyes this was my great soliloquy. The most embarrassing thing I have to admit, is that for ages after the film, during my sensitive teenage years, Mum would insist that I used this scene as my audition piece. Can you imagine? It was dotty. Instead of something appropriate for a young woman, like a scene from a play like *I Capture the Castle*, which Virginia had been in, or even something from *Romeo and Juliet*, I would fling myself to the floor of the audition space and re-enact Titty playing a bearded man. Even now I blush as I remember doing all this in front of five amazed executives, who had never seen *Swallows & Amazons*. They were looking for nothing more than a normal girl to be in an advertisement for Parker Knoll armchairs.

Have you ever set eyes on Daniel Defoe's book? Although Arthur Ransome read it at the age of four, I don't think many nine-year-olds would manage it today. Regardless of the impression given by various film posters, there are no women in it. It's about slavery, cannibals, and rearing goats.

The Adventures of Robinson Crusoe was released as a movie in 1922 and in 1929, but Douglas Fairbanks' film was first shown in 1932, too late for Titty. I wonder if Arthur Ransome ever saw the earlier versions? I have to say that if there is ever a Hollywood line-up of actors who have played the part, I want to be included in it. It might make up for the ignominy I've suffered.

Tuesday 19*th* June – Thirty-first day of filming

I woke up and dressed. It was raining heavily. At breakfast we received a telephone call from Terry to say that we were to leave for the Kirkstone Foot hotel at 08:30. We arrived shortly after and went into the sittingroom. There, with Claude and Virginia, we recorded the conversation in the train. Also done were the songs, 'Away to Rio' and 'Farewell and Adieu to You Fair Spanish Ladies'.

Arthur Ransome must have done much to revive the songs of the sea:

Farewell and adieu to you, fair Spanish ladies,
Farewell and adieu to you, ladies of Spain;
For we're under orders for to sail for old England,
And we may never see you fair ladies again.

We never got as far as the ranting and roaring bit. No one really knows the age of this naval song but it was included in the logbook of *The Nellie of 1796* long before shanties became established as a genre. Titty was still singing it in Arthur Ransome's book *Peter Duck* when the song became quite useful for navigating the English Channel:

The first land we sighted was called the Dodman,
Next Rame Head off Plymouth, Start, Portland and Wight;

We sailed by Beachy, by Fairlight and Dover,
And then we bore up for the South Foreland light.

By this stage in the filming Claude only had one rain-cover option. We were kept busy recording sea shanties with Virginia on reel-to-reel tape at the unit hotel, while Denis Lewiston and the Sparks set up another lighting rig at Bank Ground Farm.

Walking into Mrs Batty's barn that day was hugely exciting. Simon Holland had mounted *Swallow* on a cradle so that she could be rocked, as if by water, while the scenes of her sailing at night were shot. It was brilliant, she could even go-about. Moonlight wasn't a problem. Richard can correct me, but I think it was produced by a lamp called a 'tall blonde'. We didn't have a wind machine. The prop men just used a large sheet of cardboard to produce a breeze.

> 'Wouldn't Titty have liked this?'
>   'Liked what?'
>   'Sailing like this in the dark.'
>   '57, 58, 59, 60, 61 . . .'
>   'What's the matter?'
>   'Can't you hear it? The wind in the trees? We must be near
> the bank. Quick, Susan, lower the sail! Roger, catch the yard
> as it comes down!'

Then there is a crunch as the Swallows hit a landing stage – all of it mocked up and quite fun.

What about Titty?

> **Lesley and I were doing our tapestries. After lunch I did
> another two hours of lessons. Mrs Causey left and I did a
> short scene in the barn of sleeping in *Amazon*.**

While I buttoned my grey cardigan, the *Amazon* was placed on the same mounting. I climbed aboard and started wrapping myself up in her white sail.

Children always love the irony of John's line:

> 'What about Titty?'

Susan replies:

> 'She's at the camp. She'll be all right. She's got a tent.'

Then the shot cuts to me looking damp and uncomfortable about sleeping in the Blacketts' boat, anchored out on the water with violent men on the rampage. Later, I wake up and emerge from under the sail to hear the burglars heaving Captain Flint's trunk across Cormorant Island.

All in all, we achieved quite a bit on that wet day in Westmorland. Much safer and easier than being out on the water. Because the cradle was at waist height Claude was able to get lower angle shots than when on the camera pontoon. Simon did well. Every time I watch the film, I am convinced he is actually sailing.

Back at our guest house in Ambleside a real drama was being played out. Simon Price had gone missing. He was the small boy last seen on the beach at Rio, having his shorts pulled up by his elder sister. The police were called. But as in a lot of real-life situations, things were sorted out – his sister found him under his bed. We returned to the mundane world of maths lessons. I was tutored by Helen, one of the students at the Charlotte Mason College of Education who was also lodging at Oaklands. Mrs Causey couldn't cope with modern maths.

Wednesday 20th June – Thirty-second day of filming

> While I was having my make-up put on I met Ronnie Fraser. I did a little school work. Then we went to Wild Cat Island. We did the scene when Captain Flint made friends with us and declared war upon us.
>
> *Titty:* Was it a very heavy one?
> *Captain Flint:* It was rather.
> *Titty:* Was it full of gold ingots?
> *Captain Flint:* 'Fraid not. Typewriter, diaries, old log books, and worst of all the book I've been writing all summer.
> *Titty:* About your Pirate past?
> *Captain Flint:* Well. . . .
> *Titty:* Was it a very good book?
> *Captain Flint:* I doubt it. And now I may just as well have not written it.

Ronald Fraser! The veteran of World War II movies, who had won a prestigious award for playing Basil Allenby-Johnson in *The Misfits*, had arrived on the shore of Coniston Water.

Curiously, so had two stand-ins. A short lady for me, with dark hair, and a lady with blonde hair for Suzanna. I have fair hair and Suzanna is dark, but that is how it was. Ronnie Fraser explained that lots of film stars had stand-ins and cameramen liked it if they were pretty. The other four actors didn't have stand-ins, which seemed odd. Simon and Sten, the two boys, were younger than us, so that seemed even odder. And we were some way into the filming. However, the ladies were very excited about coming over to Peel Island. They sat in our positions and read our lines back to Ronald Fraser while the scene at the campsite was lit, and returned to stand in for us later when his close-ups were shot. Somehow they managed to do this in scanty summer clothing despite a brewing storm.

Our stand-ins got a great deal of help from the crew as they went from boat to shore. We didn't really, but then we were used to it and had to wear life-jackets. Mummy didn't wear a life-jacket, but she has always been surprisingly good at getting in and out of boats unaided. Her comment on the whole matter of my stand-in is concise. 'I don't think she was invited. She just turned up. Most unsuitable for a children's film.'

The recording of our scene with Captain Flint on Peel Island went well, and Claude was happy with the result, but my diary reports how a Force 8 gale came in. The call sheet for 20th June documents how truly unpredictable the weather was. We had a 'Fine Weather Call', an 'Alternative Dull Weather Call', 'Rain Cover' in the houseboat cabin and a pencilled-in end-plan entitled 'Peel Island'. It was so difficult to plan ahead that Richard had a 1970s embroidered patch sewn to his jeans, which read:

THE DECISION IS MAYBE AND THAT'S FINAL

Claude, Bobby Stilwell, Suzanna and Ronald Fraser on Peel Island.

At the end of the book of *Swallows and Amazons,* there is a dramatic storm with lashing rain. We were rather disappointed that it was not included in the film. It could easily have been shot that afternoon, but this was not to be. 'You can't have everything,' I can remember Mum saying.

The most enjoyable part was that we were all acting together. Kit and Lesley had been so patient, waiting day after day for the scenes with their Uncle Jim to come up. They'd just been stuck in the bus having lessons, endless dictation about Beatrix Potter. The fact that they were on stand-by must have been hugely helpful to the production manager, who had to wrestle with the film schedule, but it was boring for them.

As it was, the storm blew hard but cleared the heavy grey clouds, and the next day was glorious, one to remember forever. . . .

SWALLOWS AND AMAZONS

CALL SHEET no. 33   DATE: THURSDAY JUNE 20th 1973

LOCATION: BANK GROUND FARM   UNIT CALL: 07.30 leave Compston Rd.Car Park
                                        07.15 ferry from Kirkstone Foot
                                        Hotel

FINE WEATHER CALL   ALTERNATIVE DULL WEATHER CALL

                                 LOCATION: A. ELTERWATER _Peel Island_
                                          B. SKELWITH FOLD CARAVAN PARK

1. EXT. HOLLY HOWE   11 DAY,8 EVE.   SETS: 1. EXT. AMAZON RIVER 133 comp,EVE.Loc.A
2. EXT. BOATHOUSE   22 MORNING   2. EXT.OCTOPUS LAGOON 141 NIGHT Loc.D
3. EXT.HOLLY HOWE BOATHOUSE 7 EVE.   3. EXT.OCTOPUS LAGOON 143 NIGHT Loc.B
4. INT. TAXI   6 DAY

                                   WEATHER COVER CALL

DIRECTOR: CLAUDE WHATHAM   LOCATION: DERWENTWATER
                                   SET: INT.HOUSEBOAT CABIN. 140 Night,
                                               75,77,184 DAY

ARTISTE	CHARACTER	LEAVE HOTEL	MAKE UP	ON SET
SET 1. EXT. HOLLY HOWE 11 DAY, 8 EVE				
VIRGINIA McKENNA	MOTHER		07.00	09.00
STEPHEN GRENDON	ROGER	08.00		09.00
SIMON WEST	JOHN	"		"
ZANNA HAMILTON	SUSAN	"		"
SOPHIE NEVILLE	TITTY	"		"
PROPS: TELEGRAM				

SET 2. EXT. BOATHOUSE HOLLY HOWE SC.22 MORNING

ARTISTE	CHARACTER	LEAVE HOTEL	MAKE UP	ON SET
VIRGINIA McKENNA	MOTHER		from above	
SIMON WEST	JOHN		"	
ZANNA HAMILTON	SUSAN		"	
SOPHIE NEVILLE	TITTY		"	
STEPHEN GRENDON	ROGER		"	

EXTRAS:
Nurse   to stand by until called
Baby Vicky   "
ACTION BOAT   SWALLOW
PROPS: ALL EQUIPMENT FOR TRIP TO ISLAND,TINS OF CLOTHING,TENT,PACKET OF MATCHES

SET 3. EXT. HOLLY HOWE BOATHOUSE SC.NO.7 EVE

ARTISTE	CHARACTER	LEAVE HOTEL	MAKE UP	ON SET
VIRGINIA McKENNA	MOTHER		from above	
SIMON WEST	JOHN		"	
ZANNA HAMILTON	SUSAN		"	
SOPHIE NEVILLE	TITTY		"	
STEPHEN GRENDON	ROGER		"	

EXTRAS:
Mr. Jackson   to stand by until called
Mrs. Jackson   "
Nurse   "
Baby Vicky   "
Taxi driver   "
ACTION VEHICLE: TAXI to be called by Art Dept.
PROPS: LUGGAGE FOR TAXI, HAND LUGGAGE

SET 4. INT. TAXI SC.NO. 6 DAY

ARTISTE	CHARACTER	LEAVE HOTEL	MAKE UP	ON SET
VIRGINA McKENNA	MOTHER		from above	
SIMON WEST	JOHN		"	
ZANNA HAMILTON	SUSAN		"	
SOPHIE NEVILLE	TITTY		"	
STEPHEN GRENDON	ROGER		"	
EXTRAS				

The unit call sheet for the Holly Howe scenes.

Chapter Eight
Days to Remember

Thursday 21ˢᵗ June – Thirty-third day of filming

A day of days – the sunshiny day that we had all been waiting for. The buttercups and daisies were still out in the field that flows from Holly Howe to the lake. Roger was able to 'tack up' the meadow to receive the despatches from Mother, just as described in the opening pages of the book: 'Each crossing of the field brought him nearer to the farm. The wind was against him, and he was tacking up against it to the farm, where at the gate his patient mother was awaiting him.'

Virginia McKenna with Ronnie Cogan at Bank Ground.

Art Director Simon Holland painting pemmican labels.

I don't think you can tell that this section of the scene was recorded seven whole days later than the sequence that runs directly on from this, when the Boy Roger delivers the very same telegram to Captain John. The hole that had been dug for the camera alongside our picnic had been filled in and turfed over. We went down to the field below the farm to be in the background. You can see this from Mother's perspective, when I was milling about near the lake looking towards an island that I couldn't actually see. Poor Sten had to keep running up the slope on what proved to be our hottest day ever, in a woolly sleeveless pullover. Jean McGill administered cold drinks and a flannel soaked in cool eau de cologne to make sure he did not get dehydrated. We all wanted a go with the refreshing cloth on the back of our necks at lunchtime.

> In the hot lunch hour, Jean cooled us down, for it was a summer day! In the afternoon we filmed the scenes sailing away. My lines to Mother were:
>> *Titty:* Here comes Good Queen Bess to see us off on our voyage to the Pacific.
>> *Mother:* Captain Drake, pull the boom down. That'll take those cross wrinkles out of the sail.
>> *Titty:* I wonder whether the real Queen Elizabeth knew much about ships.

It was good to escape the heat by getting out on the water. We shot the scene set on the old stone jetty at the boathouses below the farm when Titty leads Queen Bess down to the harbour to inspect her ship. I didn't know she had a large box of matches with her. Virginia kept it a surprise. I was excited to find out later that Simon Holland hand-painted the branded packet himself.

As the call sheet specifies, our dinghy *Swallow* had been loaded with all the tents and camping equipment that had been on Peel Island the day before. We children didn't realise quite how often the design team had struck camp and made it up again. I just sat on top of the equipment singing rather badly, as we sailed out onto Coniston Water, waving goodbye to our queen, baby Vicky, and her nurse, who had all somehow turned into Spanish Ladies.

We filmed one other scene in the field that afternoon. The clue is in the buttercups. See if you can notice it in the film. It was the shot when Robinson Crusoe says, 'Still a very Susan-ish tent,' and removes a jam jar of wildflowers – meadow flowers you'd never find on the island. I was terribly careful about opening the tent flap when I put the jar of buttercups outside but you can see the sunny field for a second. I was meant to be on Peel Island when I declared, 'I'll have to sleep up a tree for fear of ravenous beasts,' but I was actually at the farm. Denis found that he needed bright sunlight shining through the canvas to light the shot.

Sten, me and Simon with Brian Robey Jones as Mr Jackson.

Kerry Darbishire as Nurse and Tiffany Smith as Baby Vicky outside Holly Howe.

> This scene went on till late in the afternoon, yet as the sun
> was still out, they decided to film coming out of the taxi and
> running down the field, arriving at Holly Howe.

I am sure that we had already recorded something of the Walker family's arrival at Holly Howe, but Claude decided to take advantage of the golden light and shoot it again. This was a good decision. It had been a long day and we were tired but the excitement of our arrival is tangible. The girls who had been taken on as our stand-ins the day before did not seem to be around to help limit the hours we spent on set, but perhaps I am muddled. They could have been working at night.

My mother thought that Mr and Mrs Jackson and Vicky's Nurse, who are listed as extras on the call sheet, were particularly well-cast. It must have been a long day for the ship's baby. It was a long hot day for all of us, but a happy one.

What I did not know, was that Mrs Batty, who held the lease on Bank Ground Farm, had locked out the crew. She explained that when she was originally asked if we could film on her property she did not quite calculate the scale of operations and so had only asked for – or accepted – a location fee of £75. The arrival of our generator and the loo truck towing the make-up caravan rather daunted her and disrupted life on the working farm, as did the furniture-moving activities involved at the

Me with Lucy Batty.

start of the filming, not to mention the goings-on in her barn. Having the crew in her upstairs bedrooms must have felt pretty intrusive. She said that she decided that £75 was not enough, padlocked her front gate and wouldn't let them back in until they agreed to pay her £1,000. It was a lot of money, more than double the fee I received.

Simon West recently sent me his scrapbook, in which he had collected the local Lakeland newspaper reports published in 1973. In one of them, *The News*, Brenda Colton wrote:

When Mrs Lucy Batty was asked if her house could be used for the setting of the film *Swallows & Amazons*, with guest star Virginia McKenna, she was delighted. After all, her home, Bank Ground Farm on the east side of Coniston Water, near Brantwood, was the setting chosen by Arthur Ransome for his children's book *Swallows and Amazons*. Mrs Batty thought it a good idea that the story should be filmed in an authentic location, and she felt she should be able to put up with a few cameras and film men for a while. But she just did not realise the scale of a 'medium budget' film like this one, or what the production staff could do to her house.

It was not the two double-decker buses coming down the path and parking on the farm that she minded, nor the numerous vans, lorries, cars and caravans. It was not even the difficulty of having 80 men and women wandering round the farmhouse carrying equipment here, there and everywhere. But when art director Simon Holland started tearing up her lino and carpet in the kitchen to get to the bare stone floor, she did get a little annoyed. Especially when he removed all the electric sockets, lights and switches, pushed all the kitchen furniture into the larder and whitewashed the newly papered walls.

'Have you seen the kitchen?' Mrs Batty said to me. 'The larder is piled high with my furniture; and you would not believe the tip my lounge is in. But they are a funny lot. I asked if I could wash the beams in the kitchen for them, and they said 'Oh no, we want them to look old.' I have even had to hunt out a lot of old pottery from the cellar for them. But I have given up now. I have just left them to it.'

Friday 22nd June – Thirty-fourth day of filming

What a day! We were taken out to Lingholme Island on Derwentwater, sometimes called One Tree Island, which was the location chosen as Cormorant Island in the story. The tree is so much bigger now. It looks rather different from in the film. Beyond it you can see Rampsholme, representing Wild Cat Island. Arthur Ransome said that he had envisaged Silver Holme on Windermere as Cormorant Island with Blake Holme in the distance, but in 1973 Richard found the tree there had been felled and the cormorants shot.

> I woke up, dressed, fed, travelled and arrived at Derwentwater. First of all Roger and I went over to Cormorant Island but only for a short time. We went back and did ten minutes' school work. We were again taken back to Cormorant Island but this time for filming. We landed and started looking for the treasure. Roger cut his knee. I bandaged it up with a hankie.
>
> *Titty:* Which knee is it?
> *Roger:* The one that wasn't scraped before.
> Titty: Here. (Knee is bandaged with hanky)
> *Roger:* Look, bones.
> *Titty:* Real ones?
>
> After that and resting a while they filmed me looking around the rocks. Then I discovered a pipe.
>
> *Titty:* Roger!
>
> The camera was replaced and we went on. Roger came running in and scrambled over a tree trunk. The old trunk went up as a shower of stones fell down. Under the stones was the lost treasure.
>
> *Titty:* We've found it.
>
> There was then a pick-up shot when I found the pipe.
>
> *Titty:* Look, the treasure must be here. I found this. One of
>   the pirates must have dropped it.

I wore what was my favourite costume, not only because I had the option of wearing a vest beneath the blouse, but the navy blue divided skirt was not liable to fly up around my ears. I went to such an old-fashioned

Finding buried treasure on Lingholme Island.

school that I had a pair of grey flannel culottes myself, to wear on the games field, and thought them very much the sort of thing Titty would have worn. Roger, meanwhile, was in long shorts – or knickerbockers as the Walker children would have called them – held up with a snake-buckle belt. As I mentioned before, his even longer woollen underwear was an item requested by Claude who, being born in the 1920s himself, had worn exactly the same sort of underpants as a child.

As the day warmed up, Claude stripped down to a pair of navy-blue tailored shorts and sailing shoes. It was sunny and felt as if we were on a desert island at last.

The hunt for the treasure is slightly different in the book, where Captain Flint's trunk lies buried under rocks. I wasn't expecting the set-up with the tree trunk, although it works well and looks good, giving movement to the sequence. The only hesitation was that Claude didn't want me to get hit by the jumble of slate as it slid off. This was a pity, as I would have jumped aside.

Being obliged to cram together in a confined space becomes difficult to endure after a while, not least when the space is a pontoon on a lake with not much to sit on. You can imagine how long it took to set up shots while totally exposed to the elements. It was quite a stable raft, but when we went for a take it was vital that everyone kept completely still, or there would have been camera wobble. Small boys tend to muck about and become annoying when they are bored. The time had come when someone was going to crack – and they did.

> We were soon out on the pontoon again. Roger was fooling about and one of the camera boys dropped him in up to his waist.

The result was absolute silence. A sobering moment. And one very wet pair of knickerbockers.

> I was put into *Amazon*. It was the scene in which the Swallows find me in her. She was full of water and I had to lie down.

I am not sure why the *Amazon* had not been bailed out. I had to lie in the bilge water, which proved cold and uncomfortable. Perhaps it gave my performance an edge. Titty would have been cold and stiff after a night wrapped in the sail.

In *Amazon* on Derwentwater.

> *Titty:* I've got her!
> After that I was so tired I couldn't stand up.

Great grey clouds were gathering by the time we shot this scene and we were all getting tired. In the end three of us went home in wet underwear. 'Gareth was pushed right in and went back wet, in his boots. I had a quick bath and went to bed, very, very, very tired.'

Saturday 23rd June – Sixth Weekend

> I woke up late but feeling much better than the other night. I wished Kit a Happy Birthday and went down to Breakfast. Kit opened all her presents. I collected all my things – for I

have five exams to do. The others left for Grasmere by bus, where they went swimming and up to the big cave we had visited. I started off with French. I had a break and did History. Another break and Divinity. Then I breaked until lunch. The others came back and had lunch with me, except Suzanna who had lunch with her father. I did my two English papers while the others went shopping.

Why did they make me take summer exams? None of the other actors had them. My school friends later wrote to assure me that they were quite easy, but I was learning different lessons that, as it happened, would be tested over years to come.

The letters I received, little notes scrawled by friends at school, were a huge support. Some girls even wrote to me as Titty. The nickname touched me, as did the fact that they were thinking of me that long summer term.

Suzanna had a blast of a day. Her diary is, as ever, quite different from mine:

For a treat Kit asked if we may go and swim in Bridle Water (a lake) and all the streams around it – it was really good and not at all cold. When we got home Dad was there with a scooter, so we went out for a lovely lunch at the 'Porthole' in Bowness, a near town. After lunch we went and bought a knife. Then we came back to Ambleside and went up Stockgill falls with the scooter. When we came back Daddy stayed for the party.

One of the secrets of the film is that Lesley was actually older than Kit, who played her elder sister. I'd met Kit's twin sister, who had also auditioned for a part. It must have been difficult being separated, especially when you share a birthday.

I changed for Kit's Birthday party. Ronnie arrived. Gareth, Claude and Ronald Fraser came as well. We had a super tea. After that we watched television. Mummy went to watch Macbeth with Claude. I went to bed and sleep.

Suzanna noted that Ronald Fraser was still a little bit drunk by the time that he came to Kit's tea party. This could only mean he'd been drinking all day. It was a sign of things to come.

Meanwhile I had more letters to reply to. My friends were wonderful, but it was up to me to keep my relationships in the best possible order.

KESWICK

PEAK of DARIEN

FRIAR'S CRAG

LINGHOLME

LORD'S ISLAND

RAMPSHOLME
ISLAND

DERWENT
WATER

BORROWDALE

N
W E
S

CHART · SOPHIE NEVILLE

Chapter Nine
In Houseboat Bay

Sunday 24th June – Thirty-fifth day of filming

My diary entry for that day is not exactly revealing. As it was raining steadily in the Lake District, I was given a second day off. 'We had a quiet morning,' I wrote. I am sure I needed one. Legally we were meant to have two days off a week. This had not always been possible for me.

My mother must have been exhausted but she was on set, as was a newspaper journalist, so I can tell you exactly what happened. I can even tell you what the location caterers from Pinewood cooked that Sunday: melon, followed by roast beef with Yorkshire pudding, boiled or roast potatoes, peas and carrots, with apple crumble or tinned peaches served with custard or evaporated milk.

The crew were back on Derwentwater.

'The houseboat has been converted from a pleasure steamer,' wrote Michael McNay in the Features section of *The Guardian*. 'The whole of the superstructure fore faked up by props, the cabin aft converted into a retired colonist's sittingroom – African rug, flowery curtains, assegais on the walls, an ebony elephant with silver howdah and trappings, a walnut wireless cabinet, tall brass oil lamps, a pile of 78rpm records, a silver mounted cricket ball (presented to G. Gumbleton, 1899, for the highest individual score of the season), a chest, a writing desk and an ancient upright Imperial.'

'Ronald Fraser, alias Uncle Jim, is tapping away at a book,' Michael continues. 'Last minute panic: who can type out quickly a folio of copy to leave nonchalantly in the roller?'

The first scene was the one in which Uncle Jim is typing with the green parrot on his shoulder when a firework goes off on his cabin roof. I wonder if Arthur Ransome had ever been disturbed by anyone in such a way? He certainly used an Imperial typewriter.

Ronnie Fraser and Terry Smith beside *The Lady Derwentwater.*

'By now, the houseboat has been moved and moored to the western shore just off a promontory that is being faked up as one end of Wild Cat Island.' We think that this was Brandlehow Bay. The houseboat, like a movie star in her own right, was being played by *The Lady Derwentwater*, a fifty-six-foot motor launch, owned by the Keswick Launch Company since 1935.

'The rain has stopped, the mist is lifting from the 1,500 foot ridge of Cat Bells. Fraser climbs gingerly aboard, awkward in co-respondent's brown and white shoes, rosy make-up and moves into the aft cabin,' McNay continues. He was describing the main scene to be shot that day. 'John, alias Simon West, is in a rowing boat 15 feet away. . . . The problem this time is that the rowing boat has to remain anchored but look as though Simon is pulling steadily in towards the houseboat and the anchor rope has to remain hidden.' This must have been so that *Swallow* could be lined up accurately and remain in focus for the camera.

'Simon shows Claude Whatham how he'll manage it. Quick rehearsal inside the cabin. Ronald Fraser on his knees by the chest folding a white pullover, catches sight of approaching boat, mimes angry surprise. Told not to jerk head so far back. Instead jerks eyebrows up. The cabin is no more than eight foot by ten and contains besides Fraser and the props, four men on a camera, one on lights, and the continuity girl.'

McNay had not included Claude, who I know would have squeezed in, since these were the days before live monitors off the camera feed. Besides, he was skinny. Robin, the sound recordist, was bigger, but could have just planted a microphone on the desk.

The article goes on to describe the filming:

> On the small aft deck Pilbrow is for the next few minutes going to be redundant. He is a mild, inoffensive looking man producing his first film. He is 40 . . . looks like your friendly local antiques dealer. He and Whatham are a good team: Whatham is slight, energetic and calm. He has time, even as a sequence is being set up, to ask the Press if they can see enough of what's going on from the cramped aft deck of the houseboat. It's a cheerful crew; [*the Director of Photography is*] watching clouds overhead with benign suspicion, taking light meter readings inside and outside the cabin every 30 seconds.
>
> 'Stand-by Simon.'
>
> 'Action,' said quietly into the cabin.
>
> 'ACTION,' across the lake to Simon. The clapperboard shows 461 take 1. Fraser folds the pullover, looks up, jerks eyebrows in angry surprise, camera swings round to follow Fraser's gaze through the window, Simon pulls on left oar, keeps the rope hidden.
>
> 'CUT.'
>
> Pause.
>
> 'Stand by. Quiet everybody. Action. ACTION (461 take 2) . . . CUT.'
>
> 'Once more please. Stand by. Action. ACTION (461 take 3) . . . CUT.'
>
> There's a consensus that the third take was best. Ten minute break while the succeeding sequence is prepared: Fraser rushes out on deck and tells Simon to clear off. That too is filmed in triplicate. The time is 12.45. They started work at 6.30, began filming at 12.25 and they've got maybe 45 seconds in the can. Everybody seems pleased.

Ronald Fraser had a driver from Ambleside called David Stott. 'I had just finished my three years at college and was at a loose end before I started my working life.' He was nineteen. 'In the morning Ronnie was reasonably sober and for this reason the director Claude Whatham would try and get most of the shooting with Ronnie in the can before the lunch hour came around when I would be summoned to take him to the nearest hostelry. Ronnie would then order his own concoction 'The

Fraser'. I cannot for the life of me remember what it consisted of, but believe you me these disappeared at a rapid rate of knots down Captain Flint's throat. By the time the liquid lunch came to an end I would have to bundle him into the back of the car and deposit him back on set, much to the dismay of the producer.' Jean McGill, the Unit Nurse confirmed this. She was the one who had to try to sober him up. David remembered that, 'Afternoon shooting was often a disaster when Ronnie was involved and I'm sure he frightened the children from time to time.' He was more scared of the parrot.

'The first day that I had to collect the parrot the old lady who owned him travelled with him to the location on Derwent Water. However she soon became bored with all the hanging around and after that she entrusted me with the parrot. Now birds are not really my thing and I really did not like handling him. He would travel to the location in an old shopping bag with a zipper, where l would hand him over and he would be placed in his cage. This was all well and good, then came the day that was so wet they did not use him, but instead he stayed in the production office at the Kirkstone Foot Hotel where the crew were hanging out. I was told he was in the bathroom. I expected him to be in his travel bag, but no, he was sat on the edge of the bathtub looking at me. By this time he hated being put in the bag it took me all my time with a towel to catch him. Finally, after being scratched and bitten I got him home to his Mum, Mrs. Proctor. She lived in a cottage in one of the old yards in Kendal.'

David had much preferred driving Virginia McKenna. 'I was rather star struck,' he admitted. 'On one occasion I had to drive her from the farmhouse on Coniston to Grange railway station. She was telling me all about filming *Born Free* with the lions and I drove a bit slowly as l was enjoying her company. We arrived rather late and l had to throw her and her luggage onto the train just as it was leaving.'

Monday 25ᵗʰ June – Thirty-sixth day of filming

Do all children dream of living on a houseboat? One with a cannon on deck? Going out for tea in Captain Flint's cabin was a highlight for us – a true celebration. It was such a lavish feast – I suppose it was prepared by Ian Whittaker and Bobby Props. We hadn't actually seen Captain Flint walk the plank at this point, but we could all imagine it. It was a pirate banquet, and one they had kept as a complete surprise for us. Suzanna recorded our mood: 'This was nice as we all could eat chocolate eclairs and ice-cream. Titty had a parrot on her shoulder.'

The green parrot was called Beauty. He had very sharp claws. If my eyes are watering in this scene it is because they were digging into my shoulder. Someone found a piece of foam rubber to slip under my blouse but it didn't do much good. He wasn't a very tame parrot and had to have a chain around one leg in case he took flight. I was rather worried he would twist my ear off but ploughed on with the dialogue. If this is convincing it was because I needed to get through my close-ups before I lost part of my face. Although this was a concern, I did rather want a parrot of my own – a tame one.

In real life, it was Arthur Ransome's sister Joyce who had had a green parrot. Arthur used the feathers to clean his pipe. I am often asked if Captain Flint's parrot really did speak. He could certainly talk. I remember something along the lines of, 'Who's a pretty boy, then?' delivered in a broad Lancashire accent. 'Pieces of Eight' was beyond his natural vocabulary and was dubbed on later, along with music from the accordion. Ronald Fraser couldn't actually play one. His driver, a local lad of nineteen called David Stott, arranged for him to have lessons in Ambleside with Mrs Dora Capstick. Having said that, all music from instruments played on screen is added later, so that the sound runs seamlessly no matter how the editor cuts the shots together. The accordion had been carefully muted by Terry Wells. He was also in charge of muting the parrot.

Tuesday 26ᵗʰ June – Thirty-seventh day of filming

Suzanna recorded in her diary that Ronald Fraser 'was quite nice but v. fussy'. It seems to me that he loved three things – ladies, laughter and liquor. Although he had a small mouth, Ronnie's capacity for alcohol of almost any kind was legendary. Funnily enough this was the day that we all had a drink on set. The clapperboard or slate had snapped shut on the 500ᵗʰ shot of the movie and, in line with tradition, a bottle of champagne was cracked open. Somehow I managed to end up with the dregs. I thought them utterly delicious.

> I did the scenes done yesterday because of our background – sky. We went back and did more school work. We had lunch. Simon was given a super fishing rod by Claude. We filmed after lunch. We carried on with the scene.
> *Titty:* Really?
> *Captain Flint:* Really.
> *Titty:* Oh thank you so much.

Celebrating with Claude, Ronnie and Denis.

(Captain Flint speaks)
Titty: Won't you be lonely?
(Others speak)
Titty: He's not so very old.
We went back to school again. In the tea break I caught a perch. We did some more filming and we danced around the room singing. After that we had a false fight with Captain Flint for the press.

The fishing rod was such an excitement. Simon was very generous and let us all catch fish with it. Arthur Ransome would have been proud of him. Suzanna added another story:

Everyone was celebrating today as it was the 500th take. Also it was Mick the painter's birthday and a beautiful cake was made. All the unit stood around and sang happy birthday and at the end this lovely cake was thrown all over him – it was v. funny!

Suzanna refers to the 500th take, but she was mistaken. We rarely took more than three takes of each shot. It was the 500th slate.

In this scene, after we started to clap and sing 'What shall we do with the drunken sailor?' Claude shouted:

'Go round!'

Not once, but twice. If you listen very carefully you can just hear him the second time.

He wanted us to dance around the room. I knew this but couldn't move much with the parrot, so went up and down. Kit was absolutely boiling in her red bobble hat and no one else could move much for fear of knocking into the furniture. It was left to Suzanna to dance about – a tricky thing to do without seeming self-conscious. All in all, we needed a glass of champagne by the end of that particular afternoon.

Wednesday 27th June – Thirty-eighth day of filming

'It was quite a nice day weather-wise,' Suzanna wrote, but obviously not the solid sunshine needed for the big scenes yet to be shot out on the lakes. However, David Blagden, the sailing director, was already back with us in order to appear as Sammy the Policeman, a part he played beautifully. He looked rather distant and confused at the campsite on Wild Cat Island. He was so desolate about having had his hair cut short that he took off his helmet during the scene to prove that he had been shorn.

We were excited that David was on the set, in costume. He'd always been behind the camera before. But he made a very serious policeman and didn't let the persona of his character fall while he was in uniform.

Gareth Tandy, Suzanna's stand-in and Claude (in Mum's hat),
with the 35mm Panavision camera and crew.

What works best in the film is the edit. 'No more trouble of any kind,' Virginia McKenna insists – and the shot cuts to the boots of a policeman arriving in camp. It looks as if this was one sequence – but the section where the content of Uncle Jim's book was discussed, while we sipped tea, had been shot a week previously when Ronald Fraser first arrived in the Lake District.

It was a long day. The secret that made itself apparent occurred in the short scene when John declares 'a dead calm' as he looks over the mirror-like lake, before deciding to visit the charcoal burners. Out on the rocks it became embarrassingly clear that I had grown taller than my elder brother. A box was provided for Simon to stand on so that I looked shorter when I ran into shot. Even though it was fairly complicated, the shot was recorded in one take. Everyone was amazed that we moved on so quickly. We needed to.

I have a copy of the Daily Progress Report for 27th June. It states that Kit, Lesley, Zanna and Sten arrived on location at 9.00am and left at 4.30pm. This was not true. The unit was dismissed at 6.50pm, which was probably when we left. Simon and I weren't mentioned. If Mum called this 'cooking the books' they were now roasted. Under additional remarks, Neville typed:

1. Dark weather a.m. caused original call for EXT. HOUSEBOAT to be changed to the above.
2. Slight delay on arrival at island due to vandalism during our absence, which meant certain rigging etc. had to be replaced.
3. Location catering 26th – 68 people; 27th – 69 people

His preoccupation was that, since the bad weather had caused delays, we still had an awful lot to film. The report states that we were five days overschedule with only three remaining days. Four scenes had been shot that day. We still had fifty-one to shoot.

Thursday 28th June – Thirty-ninth day of filming

If you ever see a cormorant you must sing out: 'They've got India-rubber necks!' Then, if you are on a long journey, you can add: 'Cormorants. We must be near the coast of China. The Chinese have cormorants. They train them to catch fish for them. Daddy sent me a picture.'

If you ever get lost, or the journey is a very long one, you can say: 'Here we are, intrepid explorers making the first ever voyage into uncharted waters. What mysteries will they hold for us? What dark secrets will be revealed?'

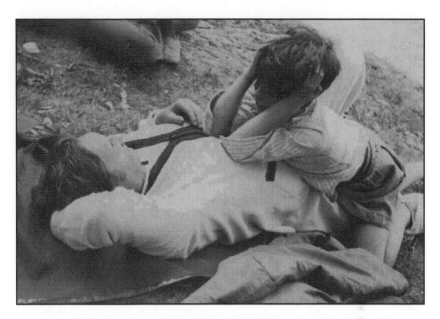

Sten with Ronnie Fraser.

They were most complicated speeches to deliver afloat, ones I had to learn. In the end the second part was heard OOV – out of vision. I could have read the lines. But then they wouldn't have stayed in my head forever.

If, on your journey, you happen to see a man sitting in a chair writing notes, you score high and can say, 'What's that man doing? He's probably a retired pirate working on his devilish crimes.' I'm a bit hesitant about that one, because my Aunt Hermione really was approached by pirates when she was sailing round the world. The *Daily Mail* published her diary chronicling the adventure: a double-page spread with photographs, no less. Rather sadly they ran the headline 'Intrepid Pensioners'. What a swizz. She should have lied about her age and said she was twenty-seven instead of sixty. Well, perhaps fifty-seven, as they took quite large photos. At least she was intrepid.

The scene behind the camera that day on Derwentwater was rather different from the scene in front of it:

> My first scene was setting anchor and hearing the robbers. After this I did some school work, while the next scene was set up. The next scene was sailing past Darien on the voyage to the island. We sang 'Adieu and Farewell'.

This was a mistake. I should have sung 'Farewell and Adieu'. 'On this shot we were going along on the pontoon when we went aground. There was an awful jolt and Cedric (camera assistant) went overboard.'

Although I was chilly, it was a glorious sunny day when shots were taken for the montage of our voyage to the island that captured the excitement of sailing with a fair wind. It was as if Peter Pan and Wendy were flying off to Neverland with John and Michael, espying Captain Hook on the way. We achieved a huge amount, even if Cedric fell in. Some of the boatmen and crew were wearing life-jackets, others were not – including my mother. *Swallow* is a safe little boat – her keel ensured we didn't capsize if we happened to jibe, and we never fell in. The pontoon was rather more dangerous, being a raft with no gunwale or railing. Anyone could have misjudged their step and plopped overboard. Fortunately, we were not stifled by Health and Safety legislation in those days.

I'm sure that we had already recorded the first two scenes of the day when I was in *Amazon*, setting the anchor and later hearing the robbers. I expect Claude needed to re-shoot for technical reasons. Day-for-Night filming was tricky, as was keeping shots on the water horizontal with only a spirit-level for a guide.

I have some of my mother's 8mm ciné footage showing us at around this stage in the filming. It shows us waiting around on the shores of Derwentwater one minute and rushing off across the lake in motor boats the next, no doubt to finish filming before Claude lost the light. You see the pontoon and a safety boat towing *Swallow*, me snapping bossily at Roger to get a move on, which was unforgivable even though I was four years older than him and irritated to distraction. Another shot shows David Blagden splicing rope and *Swallow* rigged and ready to sail while mallard ducklings shuffle about at the water's edge. The weather looks idyllic. It was quite different the next day.

Friday 29ᵗʰ June – Fortieth day of filming

The rain poured down.

Ambleside was covered in cloud, the Lake District dark and dismal. We were way behind schedule, Lesley was ill in bed, and we had run out of 'rain cover'.

There was one sequence left that could be recorded in dull weather. Today was the day Claude shot the haunting scenes of Octopus Lagoon. After finishing our school work, Kit and I sat watching the filming from the sloping field above a beautiful but rather smelly lily pond.

The location chosen was on private property above Skelwith Fold Caravan Park. The Arthur Ransome expert Roger Wardale cites Octopus

Lagoon as originally being Allan Tarn, a short distance up the River Crake at the southern end of Coniston Water, near High Nibthwaite. You need a shallow-bottomed boat to get there. This is the place Ransome had in mind. He went there with his brother and sisters as a child, when they spent their summer holidays staying at Swainson's Farm nearby. His father enjoyed the fishing.

The lily pond we used was in a high-sided dip, which made it appropriately dark and gloomy. It was also more accessible for the film crew and captured the conundrum faced by Captain John, while he was stuck in the waterlilies as night drew in.

Terry Needham, Neville Thompson and Graham Ford were responsible for the film schedule, putting together the whole logistical jigsaw puzzle posed by factors such as the availability of leading actors and locations with the movement of vehicles and boats, including the massive camera pontoon. It was Graham, the production manager, who took the stress of problems caused by wet weather. I guess that he also took on the responsibilities of managing the locations, negotiating with owners and the Lake District National Park, something that authors such as Arthur Ransome would not have had to face. Although young, Graham was pretty experienced. He had previously worked as an assistant director on such classic films as *Steptoe and Son* and had been the unit manager on *The Devils* with Neville Thompson.

Terry Needham, Neville Thompson and Graham Ford on a sunnier day.

The following day was a scheduled 'Unit Day Off' but I expect that Graham was trying to work out how we could possibly record the huge number of scenes that remained. Claude was desperately behind schedule and yet, like the Swallows in the waterlilies, he was thwarted whichever way he turned.

Ronnie had not been on set that day but I heard he had been enjoying his time in town. Peter Walker, who now lives in Kendal, told me that he literally bumped into him in a pub. 'In 1973 I worked for Post Office Telecommunications (now BT) as a local maintenance engineer and had been given the job of repairing a fault on the payphone in the White Lion Hotel in the centre of Ambleside. As I pushed open the door to the bar it slipped out of my hand. The handle caught a customer in the back who happened to be taking delivery of a large drink. I apologised, but he said, 'No damage done, my boy, haven't spilt a drop!' I said I was referring to his back, 'Don't worry,' he insisted, 'being stabbed in the back is normal in my line of business!' It was Ronnie, through and through.

'He was a total lush,' one of his friends claimed, 'but charming, funny and scandalous. His fund of acting stories was endless. I'm surprised he made it through *Swallows and Amazons*.' Claude must have been slightly worried whether or not he would.

'You children persuaded me to go out to dinner with Ronnie Fraser!' Jean McGill told me forty-three years after the event. 'Why I went, I haven't the foggiest. He was a rough character - very coarse. I used to have to drive him to the local hotel in the mornings and order champagne to sober him up.'

'How would champagne have helped to sober him?'

'I don't know. He told me it would.'

'I think he'd been divorced for a while.'

'I wouldn't have married him in the first place,' Jean assured me.

Saturday 30th June – Fame in the Express

After breakfast we went to the newsagent and bought an *Express* in which was a big photograph of Ronnie Fraser, one of us, and an article about Ronnie.

The secret was out: 'The ice tinkles quite merrily as a counterpoint to his anecdotes which are many, outrageous, and largely unrepeatable.' Ice in a tall glass, accompanied by a large amount of vodka and 'a kiss of lime'. While we had been busy filming on the stinky lily pond, the 'joker's joker' had been languishing in the bar of the unit hotel saying that 'he was a lousy lover but loved to practise'. Oh, deary me. Worse was to come. 'Baby, you've got to be a bit dotty' to be an actor, he said. At least we were described as 'very bright and very active'.

'Mr Ronald Fraser,' wrote Geoffrey Mather, 'that distinguished actor of stage, screen and cocktail bar, possessor of an accent all fruity with well-modulated vowels, is dressed in what appears to be cricket gear [*his costume*]. . . . He is not, he says, a great drinker. He sometimes pretends to be one. The lure of a bar, such as it is, concerns the interplay of personality and anecdote. Close friends can, he says, find this need in him irritating.'

Luckily, we were not around to add comment on this. David Blagden had previously had a small part playing a prison officer in the movie *Kidnapped*, which was being shown at the local cinema that afternoon. 'Mummy and Jane took us to see it.' The film starred Michael Caine, Trevor Howard and Lawrence Douglas, with Jack Hawkins, Donald Pleasence and Gordon Jackson, but sadly not Ronald Fraser. He was still in the bar.

Suzanna Hamilton's perspective on the day was written confidently in purple crayon: 'We had to have medicals as our licenses were going to run overtime.'

Sten referred to this as going to 'the docters for a examination'. I was fine – 'I had put on 5lbs.' Luckily the insurance company didn't want to test Ronnie, in spite of caustic suggestions published that day in the national press:

> And you know what Mr Fraser has to do now to pursue his career? He has to go in that water – SPLASH. Pushed in by those bright and vigorous kids. It hardly seems fair to do that to such a splendid gentleman. Especially one who had his fill of water when the violins went . . . BOING.

Did the insurance brokers miss this on purpose?

What no one could deny was that our medical tests were a sign that the movie was under the weather and over-stressed, with nothing much anyone could do about it but keep going. We still had to capture the houseboat – and make that splendid gentleman walk the plank.

Chapter Ten
Going to War

Sunday 1ˢᵗ July – Forty-first day of filming

'It would make a superb lighthouse,' but not for a good few years yet. The Scots pine planted by The Arthur Ransome Society on the northern end of Peel Island was growing well when I last paid it homage. I hope I don't spoil the magic if I explain that the pine used in the film of *Swallows & Amazons* is on a promontory above Derwentwater.

If you can avoid being distracted by David Bracknell's trendy two-tone trousers, you can see in the photo below a bit more of the lighthouse tree location with the lake beyond. I've been told it is on Friar's Crag.

The lookout point was a promontory by Houseboat Bay. They spent a long time setting the scene up. While this was going on I had makeup on and did a lot of tapestry. The first scene was when John climbed to the top of the lighthouse tree and gave me my orders. My lines were –

Titty: Take care.
(Others speak)
Titty: Except me. I'll be staying here.
Susan: Are you sure you'll manage by yourself?
Titty: Of course. I'd love to stay.
(Others speak)
Titty: Aye aye, Sir!

We had a super lunch of melon, cold roast beef and salad – strawberries. Work came again, working on the same scene. After tea they did the scene of me lighting the candle. They also did a scene with the Amazons sailing past the houseboat. On the way back, in the middle of the lake, our Dory broke down. It was mended soon and we went back to Oaklands.

As a child reading *Swallows and Amazons* I was always deeply impressed that Captain John managed to climb the pine tree in Arthur Ransome's drawing. Simon was able to use branches but he did climb quite high. The cameraman had a scaffold tower.

Suzanna wrote: 'In the late afternoon the Amazons were filming on the pontoon. Kit wasn't feeling well.' Lesley was feeling a bit better, but there was an influenza-like bug going around.

> Kit had a small temperature and went to bed. Simon was feeling funny too. The doctor came.

Would we ever finish the film?

Simon climbing the
Lighthouse Tree.

Monday 2ⁿᵈ July – Forty-second day of filming

I was often asked by journalists about my future career in acting. I was even asked about it by the film crew as we climbed in and out of boats.

'Are you going to be another Bette Davis?' (I gathered I looked vaguely like her, but didn't know her films.)

'You might get stuck as a child actress like Shirley Temple.' (I didn't really know who she was either.)

There was much speculation. The truth was that I was always more interested in what was happening behind the camera, and how the story was told, than I was in our performances. I had empathy for the men who had to keep changing carefully made arrangements when the clouds rolled in. I loved aiding and abetting Terry Needham, the second assistant, with whom we naturally spent a great deal of time. That 2ⁿᵈ July must have been a busy day for him, a maddening day, but I found working with a pine tree was quite fun. 'It would make a good lighthouse. If any of us were sailing home after dark we could hoist a lantern up.'

While I was in front of the camera, delivering the line that foreshadows the adventurous section of the story, Terry would have been planning who would go out in which boat and when. It was just as important.

Having a go with the 35mm Panavision camera.

When we were filming out on the lakes, *Swallows & Amazons* was far more complicated than most movies to stage manage. Terry needed to have his *artistes* standing-by, ready on set, when the set was a boat moored out in a lake. This meant that Ronald Fraser had to wait around on the houseboat with Costume, Make-up and Props as the sun tried to decide whether to come out or not.

Terry, ever straightforward and prosaic, also had to make provision for a number of extra people who wanted to try and watch the action, notably Albert Clarke, the stills photographer, and Brian Doyle, who was often looking after journalists. We were making a movie that needed to be well publicised if it was to succeed.

What made Terry's job even more demanding than usual, was that legally the children were only meant to spend three hours a day on set. In reality this didn't happen, but they did try to keep our hours down in any way possible. This meant that, unlike Ronnie Fraser, we had to be collected from our red bus and taken over the water to our set at the last possible moment when the camera and crew were ready to roll, our set often being a clinker-built dinghy, of course.

Me with Terry Needham.

Terry Needham resting on the houseboat.

Terry also had to take into consideration the numbers of people licensed to be in each support boat. Although a period film, our clothes were simple, so we didn't need the contingent of dressers and make-up artists typically demanded by costume dramas; we just had Terry Smith. However, wherever we went, a legal chaperone had to come too. Since Mum stayed at our guest house in Ambleside with Kit, who was ill with 'flu that day, Jane Grendon came out on the lake with us. I don't know how it started or who the main culprit was, but everyone was mucking about so much that Suzanna fell in whilst she was wearing her costume. Poor Jane was also pushed in fully clothed, and her son Sten walked off the jetty into the water. What a nightmare for the Terrys.

Things were to get worse.

'We were driving back from Derwentwater,' David Stott told me, 'when a cow jumped off a bank and landed on the bonnet, causing quite a lot of damage.' He was driving Richard Pilbrow. Luckily no one was hurt but David remembered how much he dreaded, 'going back to Browns Motors and telling Alan Faulkener, the owner, what had happened'.

Tuesday 3ʳᵈ July – Forty-third day of filming

When *Swallows & Amazons* was first shown on British television in 1977, a trailer was made by ITV to advertise it. This started abruptly with the shot of me exclaiming, 'They're pirates!'

People loved that trailer. Everyone was going around crying 'They're pirates!' Perhaps the film should have begun at that point. If it was my best performance, the reason was that I had been lying on a red ants' nest – and they were biting. Another little-known fact is that this lighthouse tree was not a tree. Not one that was growing, anyway. It was a long log that Bobby Props had planted in the ground, making the ants very angry indeed.

This was the second location for 'Lookout Point on Wild Cat Island'. Brandlehow Point overlooks the bay where the houseboat was moored on Derwentwater. From here one could clearly see Captain Flint stamping out the firework on his cabin roof. There were bushes, but sadly no big pine trees. Having a fake one meant that Claude could get what is called a two-shot of the Swallows watching Nancy sail past the houseboat, while Peggy raises the skull and crossbones to the top of their mast. As we were keeping low, the height of the lighthouse tree was not an issue. So, the secret of Wild Cat Island is that it was filmed in three different places, as well as being depicted in the opening titles as Rampsholme, on Derwentwater. I am sure this is faithful, in that Ransome indicated, by using annotated postcards, that he wanted the fells you can see from Castle Hill above Keswick as a backdrop for his story.

Just prior to this scene, when we spot the Amazons for the first time, I was working on the chart while Susan was sewing a button onto Roger's shirt. The needle stuck into him as he flung himself down on the grass beneath the lighthouse tree. Since needles are small you can hardly see what is happening but it is a detail that Arthur Ransome would have appreciated. I wonder if the same sort of thing had happened to him as a child? He used his memories of Annie Swainson throwing him across her lap to darn his knickerbockers while he was still wearing them, just as the fictional Mary Swainson frequently has to darn Roger's shorts after sliding down the Knickerbockerbreaker rockface in *Swallowdale*.

Suzanna's diary entry was succinct. 'Today I feel depressed.' That was it. I don't know why she felt depressed. Perhaps it was the ants. She was on more of them than me. Like the Amazons stranded on Wild Cat Island, they were not waving. They were very angry.

Wednesday 4ᵗʰ July – Forty-fourth day of filming

Graham had kindly scheduled the second of our swimming scenes as late in the summer as possible. The water was warmer – we'd elected to go bathing in a river up near Rydal Water on our day off – but, perhaps because Coniston Water is exceptionally deep, we all felt the cold. 'Not half so cold as last time but still icy.'

We tried to acclimatise by dancing around in our swimming costumes. The crew were still in their thick coats. My mother took it upon herself to film behind-the-scenes preparations for this. Someone on the crew shouted, 'Quiet please, for the second unit!' as she lifted what looked like a grey and white plastic toy to her face. We had bought her 8mm ciné camera by saving up Green Shield stamps collected from petrol stations. Coping with reams of these coupons was an experience of the early 1970s, which left my generation with taste-buds annihilated from sticking the stamps into books, before they could be exchanged for objects of desire.

Since her ciné camera was a bit noisy, Mum was unable to record during a take. You only see us before and after the swimming sequences, but her footage is interesting, as it shows quite a few of the members of the crew. They were all smoking away, even when they were trying to warm us up after we emerged from the lake. Jean was popping Dextrose into our mouths and giving us hot drinks, while a cigarette hung from her mouth, and she was an experienced nurse!

The camera pontoon must have been left up on Derwentwater. Claude was obliged to shoot these scenes from the camera punt, which was smaller but quite useful. Richard sent me a picture. The three Lakeland boatmen all look like pirates – real ones.

David Bracknell, David Whatham, David Cadwallader, Denis Lewiston and the Lakeland boatmen on the camera punt.

Goodness knows what a health and safety inspector would say about that punt today. Denis Lewiston managed to get two sizeable electric lights, on stands, into a boat already overloaded with personnel and expensive equipment. These 'Filler' lights must have been powered by portable batteries, as the Lee Electric generator was on the shore. I was in the water, busy being a cormorant.

At one point that afternoon we had the camera with us in *Swallow*. I was given the honour of clapping the clapperboard and calling out 'Shot 600, Take one!' for a close-up of Suzanna.

> Denis came into Roger's place and filmed us and a close-up on Susan. Susan and I clapped the board for slate 600 to 603.
>
> We were dropped off at the island for tea. It was crowded with the worst kinds of natives.
>
> We were called back again to film going round the island. It was filmed from the land. We changed costume and also filmed a shot of chasing Amazon. We went home to a supper of strawberries & cream.

Tourists were beginning to arrive en masse for their summer holidays, and yet we still had quite a bit more to film.

Thursday 5th July – Forty-fifth day of filming

Sunlight on the water tells the story of my life. At last the skies cleared and the fine weather we had hoped and prayed for settled over Derwentwater. It enabled us to film the climax of our adventure on the high seas of Westmorland. It was the day we went to war.

Simon, Sten and me by Derwentwater.

'"There won't be a leeside to him," said Captain John. "The houseboat'll be lying head to wind. Our plan will be to reach into the bay, and then come head to wind one on each side of him,"' Arthur Ransome wrote in the novel. '"If you'll lay yourself aboard his starboard side, I'll bring *Swallow* up on his port."'

There were war cries from everyone. To my everlasting regret, while some of the others managed to yell 'Swallows and Amazons Forever!' my battle cry was 'Kill, kill!' The script was pretty sketchy. I have the original and the re-writes, not that I saw either on the day. I was up on the roof of the houseboat with the Siamese flag.

I wrote later:

> There was another take with Nancy dropping from the roof onto Captain Flint and onto us, shot from a moving boat. We made Captain Flint surrender while Peggy then lowered the white elephant flag.

We loved capturing Ronald Fraser and of course making him walk the plank. He was very good about it.

Filming on the foredeck of the houseboat.

> We bandaged his eyes, untied him and made him walk. The
> scene was cut and the cameras changed position. Captain Flint
> walked. He went in with a big splash. He started panicking and
> was rescued. After coming out he went in again so they could
> cut and wouldn't have to dry him. My first lines for the day
> were, 'Perhaps he can't swim. Never thought of that.'

Actually filming all this was tricky. The entire film crew with all their
equipment, including two cameras, two huge reflector boards and a
second costume for Ronald Fraser, had to be accommodated either on
the houseboat or other craft. It was a squash. The good thing was that
by now we were all pretty experienced with the procedure of getting out
to what amounted to an inaccessible location with no lavatories – and
certainly no room for tea urns.

My mother recorded quite a
bit of 8mm ciné footage that day,
showing life behind the scenes.
She captured Simon Holland
rowing *Swallow* without his shirt.
Richard was hanging onto the
side of the houseboat and Terry,
the wardrobe master, was busy
drying off Ronald Fraser's wet
costume on the aft deck. The

All of us with Mum in the Capri.

white pith helmet was being touched up by the unit painter. Trade unions
must have been strict back then.

The cabin of the houseboat was soon turned into a dressing room for
Ronnie Fraser. Mum even managed to film a scraggy-looking man with
one front tooth, paddling alone in a fibreglass boat. He was the chap who
drove the mobile lavatories from one location to another, and yet managed
to persuade the girls of Ambleside that he was producing the film.

Claude was making the most of the glorious but rare weather to
complete the scene on the foredeck. Everyone, including Ronnie
Fraser, who was dripping wet, waited patiently while I delivered Titty's
triumphant line, 'Captain Flint – we've got a surprise for you.' Not quite
the same as in Arthur Ransome's book, but it worked well.

> The others stepped back revealing the chest. It was now nearly
> 7 o'clock and we broke up and went back to the mainland after
> the great battle. Many people got pushed in, but tomorrow
> would be the great day for that. We had heard that we would
> be staying on until Tuesday to do a very special helicopter shot.

Production Manager
Graham Ford.

Molly Friedel, who'd been busy keeping an eye on the script, seemed satisfied. It had been a productive day; a battle well fought, the treasure returned. I don't think there had been any room for Graham Ford. He'd been looking after the base camp.

Friday 6th July – Forty-sixth day of filming

Before Jean arrived at the Oaklands guest house in Ambleside to transport us to the location, a letter arrived. It was from Daddy, who somehow must have found time to post a quick note after taking my sisters to school. We were all looking forward to the wrap party to be held that evening. There was much to do before it started. Twelve scenes are listed on the unit call sheet and it was pouring with rain.

The day proved difficult and wet, but everyone was in high spirits. It was the last day for most.

> Just before tea the chipper-painter-props etc. started playing with buckets of water. Pete Sparks was running about on top of the buses trying to avoid a soaking. But he got one. The others came back and the water fight went on. It was still raining and everything was wet. Albert

Mum loves
Hope you have
a good party!.
Not too good
tho!.
love M.

was taking a photograph of Mummy and me when a bucket of water came flying over a car onto us. We got soaked. I changed, all the others were in the lake. Mummy got another two buckets. We all went home wet except Lesley who never went in because she got so cold.

It was a great wrap party, held at the unit hotel. Suzanna noted that it didn't start until ten o'clock. 10pm! This was very grown-up. It must have been the talk of Ambleside. Mum took off her Donny Osmond hat and wore a long, high-collared dress in pink gingham. I wore a brown and black velvet pinafore dress Mummy and Daddy had bought me in Carnaby Street when we went up to London for my first interview with Claude. Everyone was kind and jolly, and for a while the party revolved around us. We enjoyed the dancing so much that we didn't want to leave, but it was evident that the adults wanted to have their play-time. As you can imagine, no one could persuade us to go to bed.

Jean McGill saved the evening by organising a conga. Having led a sheltered life, I had never danced the conga before and thought it the greatest fun. Luckily the Carnaby Street dress was well designed for the job. We conga-ed around the hotel with the entire crew. Somehow we ended up conga-ing into her minibus, and were whisked back to Oaklands before midnight.

Jean McGill helping me operate the Motorola.

Saturday 7th July – The Last Weekend

Mummy had lost Lesley's friendship ring. It was a gold ring. Since it would not have been appropriate for a Blackett girl, Lesley couldn't wear it with her costume. Mum had slid it onto her little finger to keep it safe for her. It slid off. It must have been something to do with all the buckets of water being flung about after yesterday's filming. We looked and looked, but couldn't find it anywhere.What with all the nocturnal pushings-in, Graham Ford had broken his ankle. Although we were up and about, it became clear that the entire film crew were comatose after the wrap party. There was certainly no sign of the director. 'We rang up to find that everybody was still in bed.' Since it was raining, an unexpected day off from filming was called. Instead of heading for Derwentwater, we went exploring the Lake District.

We split up into two groups for the afternoon, which is how I came to explore Rio with the Amazon pirates. While Suzanna, Jane and the boys went on 'a native walk', as Mate Susan put it, I made a discovery about the origin of the town's name. I could see exactly why Arthur Ransome thought of Rio as the native settlement on Titty's chart. He must have been to a Rushbearing Festival. It was just like a colourful Rio carnival.

The Price family at the Rushbearing Festival.

Crowds came out to watch as the procession came down the hill, with arches of reeds and flowers held high. Drums were beaten in true native style together with a brass band, and it seemed that everyone was wearing colourful clothes, as they walked down to a service at St Mary's Church.

Traditionally the children of Ambleside are given a piece of homemade gingerbread if they have carried one of the rushes. We hadn't done this but we did join in with the hymn. Our kind neighbours, who lived next door to the guest house, gave us some gingerbread for tea.

The Rushbearing Festival procession.

We had met up with the Price family at the festival. The two girls were both carrying dressed reeds. Mrs Price must have worked so hard when we were staying with them. She had three children and was accommodating a number of students while cooking our breakfast and high tea. I expect the demands of the filming, what with drivers coming and going, was a little more that she had originally imagined. We never knew what would be happening next.

Although most of the crew were leaving – going away from Rio – we knew we had to be back on location the next day.

I wonder what happened to my pendant with the cross? It would be the height of fashion now. Gareth Tandy sweetly gave them to us as going-away presents. Jean also wanted to give us a little bit of the Lake District to take home. This came in the form of a bedside lamp made out of a chunk of slate. Mine had a pink shade on top. I used it for years.

Kit and Lesley with me in Ambleside.

Chapter Eleven
Last Days on the Lakes

Sunday 8th July – Forty-seventh day of filming

I am sure that as children we could be intensely irritating, especially when we were hanging around with not enough to do. Although we had found our lessons tiresome, at least they'd kept us occupied and out of mischief. It was now a Sunday, right at the end of the summer term, and the red double-decker school bus was no longer with us. Neither was the large camera box that the crew put Sten in to keep him quiet.

Although the day was full of essential activity there was no major scene to focus on. It was the last day Ronnie Fraser was available. Claude must have had vital shots to pick up so that the scenes set in the houseboat would cut together. It was probably just as well there was no dialogue to record. Ronnie, it has to be said, was a little the worse for wear. Although he managed to play the accordion as we sailed into the distance, Uncle Jim was still drunk from the party two days before. We were all waiting in the cabin of the houseboat, which was in a bit of a mess.

> Now and again Captain Flint played his accordion to camera. They told us to lie on the floor. Ronald Fraser started throwing books at Sten. Four out of six missed him and hit me. One hit me in the face and the cover fell off. The others he hit. Then he threw all the parrot's food over us. Plus the tin.

My father was not pleased to hear that Ronnie Fraser had flung books around the cabin, hitting me in the face. 'They were valuable first editions!' Perhaps I ought to explain that when the parrot's cage was lowered into *Swallow*, there was no parrot inside. Instead there were four children finding parrot seed that had made its way inside their costumes.

Denis Lewiston operating the 16mm Arriflex.

Our little ship still had much work to do. David Blagden was with us, making plans with Claude and Denis to film more shots of us sailing in what we hoped would be sunny weather.

Claude was also desperate to get the shot of us arriving for the first time at the Peak of Darien – Friar's Crag on Derwentwater. He wanted to capture this just before the sun went down. Peter Robb-King, the make-up artist, was insistent that the sun-tans we had naturally gained over the summer should be toned down, and had to do something about the fact that Sten's lip had been split open by flying books. He had no help or preparation time. Dabbing the four of us with a tiny sponge took ages. I don't know why he bothered with my legs, as I hadn't changed colour, but he was a perfectionist. Mum kept saying that it was getting so dark that no one would ever notice.

"Who's going to be looking at your legs?" as Nancy Mitford's nanny would have said. I was a stickler for continuity by then and contradicted her. By the time we were ready the sun had set. Claude missed the chance to film this vital scene. Again. It was the second time we had arrived too late for it to be captured.

Did we feel silly travelling back to Ambleside in full costume? We were cheeky and full of beans one minute, shy the next. It is difficult to find the balance between becoming confident and being over-confident when you are twelve years old, but we were learning, and we learned a great deal.

Monday 9ᵗʰ July – Forty-eighth day of filming

Monday morning, and we had no lessons. The Westmorland schools had broken up for the summer holidays so we were free to play, or as free as you can be when you are wearing a costume that can not under any circumstances get wet or dirty.

Although Claude was operating with a skeleton crew, Terry Smith was still getting us into the right kit for each scene. One of the secrets of filming *Swallows & Amazons* is that, on this day, Terry adapted Ronald Fraser's costume and white colonial sun helmet for Bob Hedges to wear. It was he that fired the cannon on the houseboat.

> After lunch our make-up was changed for sailing away to the island. The wind and the sun had both come up a lot. It was a force ~~eight~~ six. We sailed from one end to the other altogether. Denis came in the boat and filmed in the dory going alongside.

A number of local boatmen worked on the support crew. They were certainly busy once the wind got up on this particular day, when Claude handed over the direction of the montage sequence for *Swallow*'s first voyage to the island to David Blagden. At last we had the sun and wind for it – if not too much wind. By now we were pretty experienced, but the little ship was challenged to the full as wind gusted down from Cat Bells.

Suzanna Hamilton wrote in her diary: 'it was very rough. We thought we were going to do a Chinese jibe but it was OK. We sailed the whole length of the lake.'

What must have been tricky for Simon was that he had Denis Lewiston on board with a 16mm Arriflex, as well as all our clumsy camping gear. You can see me heaving the crockery basket past the camera in one shot. The result was probably the most exciting sequence in the film, or so my father later declared. I wrote in my diary:

> We heeled a lot and 'nose dipped' as the ballast went into the water. Jean said to Sten, who had wet shorts, 'Get some dry ones on or you'll get a rusty whatnot.'

In the evening, Molly, Richard and his assistant Liz Lomax came up to show us the ciné footage they took on the sailing weekend back in March that had served as the final audition. The conditions had been pretty rough back then. I remember telling Claude that we 'helmed like anything'. I felt terribly embarrassed later when I realised that 'helmed' was not exactly what I had meant to say, but I don't think he was familiar with sailing terminology. He would simply have picked up on my enthusiasm.

Bob Hedges on the houseboat with *Swallow* alongside.

Richard may correct me on this, but the theory is that he acquired *Swallow* that weekend. She was twelve feet long, with a keel running the length of the hull rather than a centreboard, which provided her with stability. Originally an all-purpose run-around dinghy, she was built in the 1930s by and for William King & Sons' Boatyard at the great sailing town of Burnham-on-Crouch, in the Maldon District of Essex. She has the initials WK carved on her transom. *Swallow* is described in the books as thirteen feet long, her hull painted white with a chocolate-brown interior, as would have been typical in 1929.

Up in the Lake District, they found the gaff-rigged dinghy with a white sail and centreboard that had been used as *Amazon* for the black-and-white 1960s BBC drama serial, and re-cast her in the same role. Captain Flint's tender and the Holly Howe rowing boat were also sourced locally with the help of Nick Newby. I'm afraid it was in keeping with the stripped-pine fad of the 1970s that most of the boats featured in the film were varnished rather than painted to protect the wood.

Tuesday 10th July – Forty-ninth day of filming

When Zanna brought me the diary she kept during that far-off summer, we had time to reflect on the seven weeks we spent together as sisters.

'We were beautifully looked after,' she said. 'I mean, we were really well cared for. Look – Jane took me fell walking.'

Suzanna was right. My mother and Jane worked day and night with very little time to themselves. They had both left younger children at home in Gloucestershire with their husbands, which can't have been easy. Mum told me that she wrote an article for *Woman* magazine saying that being a chaperone was 'Fascinating, Fattening and Fun' but it must have been demanding. It would have been quite a trial preventing us from getting sunburnt, let alone keeping us entertained.

As I've mentioned, whenever we had to do anything scary or unpleasant during the filming, Claude would assuage any moans by awarding us 'Danger Money'. It was a huge encouragement. He gave me £2 for being good about diving into the chilly water for the swimming scenes. It was a lot of money back then. My mother would make a careful note of it while we were still in costume.

On Derwentwater.

We spent our gains in Ambleside buying presents to take back for the stay-at-homes. We received a little more than £2 each after *Swallow* was nearly mown down by the Windermere steamer, but, a bramble scratch was worth 50p, which stretched quite far in those days.

After all the rushing about in boats, the risks taken clambering from one vessel to another and inevitable dangers that we faced out on the water, it was the boredom involved in filming that proved most dangerous: children's games that went terribly wrong.

> In the morning all the others twisted the swing right up to the top and let it go. It went so fast that I couldn't pull my legs in and had to hang on very tight because of falling back. It went on winding up and they helped it go higher than before. I was so giddy at the top I couldn't hold on and gave out a yell and burst into tears. I was put in the caravan for a long time after, to recover.

The swing in question was strung from a tree on the shores of Coniston Water opposite Peel Island, where a couple were living in a wooden caravan. The make-up caravan, which had previously been used as a dressing room for Virginia McKenna, was parked beside it. I was sent to lie down there, and rest properly.

> Before lunch we all played baseball with Molly and the 'boys'.
> Proper teams were picked and a proper game was started.
> I was in the first batting team. The game suddenly stopped
> when a girlfriend was hit in the eye. She went to Jean who
> cleared up a nasty nose bleed and a black eye.

It was a shame that the baseball game ended so abruptly. We longed to keep playing, but Molly could appreciate that it could so easily have been one of us who ended up with an injury.

At one stage during the filming we'd all got into whittling wood. Bob Hedges made a number of props on location. Different versions of the Amazons' bows and arrows were made from hazel saplings gathered nearby. He also made forked uprights for the fireplace and various stakes for the charcoal burners' scene. Suzanna bought a penknife with her Danger Money and became quite a keen carver until the knife slipped. Jean treated the cut finger, adding such a massive bandage that Claude put a firm stop to any future whittling. It had been the one thing that kept us quiet. We were active children, but were not allowed to climb trees or get wet. Instead Lesley plucked away at a tapestry and I painted pictures.

Richard and Claude still had a few vital scenes to record and yet the weather forecast remained bleak. We spent the later part of the afternoon back at the hotel, looking at the black-and-white stills Albert had taken. We all looked so serious in them. Was it going to be a gloomy film?

Richard Pilbrow and Neville C. Thompson.

Wednesday 11th July – Fiftieth day of filming

This photograph of Richard and Neville (opposite), sitting on the deck of the houseboat in the pouring rain, must epitomise the struggles they went through to bring the film in on budget.

It was Claude's dream to end the movie with an aerial shot of *Swallow* and *Amazon* sailing away from the houseboat. He had a helicopter pilot standing-by with a special cameraman, but it wasn't to be. He needed bright sunshine for the shot to cut with our farewell sequence after the battle. We waited for this for three days. The weather was too grey and wet to film anything useful. In retrospect, I'm glad. Claude ended up freezing the simple end shot that captures the book completely. It was later used on the front of one of the first VHS copies of the movie.

Since our location caterers had returned to Pinewood Studios, we were taken to the hotel for lunch where I'm afraid we hung about getting bored and precocious, or so the evidence of my diary suggests:

> We had a buffet lunch. Sten and I hid under some tables and heard a waiter say: 'They're right little bastards if you ask me.'
> We nearly split our sides with laughter.

I spent the afternoon with a tube of Copydex – or 'rubber solution glue', as they called it on *Blue Peter* – sticking the tiny contact photographs Albert had given us into scrapbooks that I had been keeping. Richard kindly let us choose 10" x 8" versions of the photographs, which we were able to take home.

> After waiting around picking out photographs until 3 o'clock, we went swimming in a river, we dived in. I decided to swim across as it was very wide. I stubbed my toe and started to swim very shallow, because I thought it was a stump. Suddenly I stood up. I found that it came up to my waist and was very cross.
> On the way home we went to Jean's old house and picked roses. We all dressed up. Claude took us to the cinema to a queer film before we had supper at the Kirkstone Foot.

I can't believe that we went 'wild swimming', as it would now be termed, after making such a fuss about recording the swimming scenes at Wild Cat Island. Even if it was raining, the water must have been fairly warm. I don't suppose we were in for that long. I'm now rather shocked to read in my diary that we dried our hair by sticking our heads out of the windows of the minibus. We could have been decapitated.

Thursday 12th July – Fifty-first day of filming

While Claude was busy looking at the sky, still hoping to record the shot of us spying the island from the Peak of Darien, I spent the whole day industriously cutting out tiny photographs and pasting them in my scrapbook. Mum usually had her 35mm camera films developed by 'Tripleprint'. A long, fat envelope had arrived at Oaklands in the post, containing the 'one large, two small' style colour prints so that she had some to give away. Two of these tiny photographs show us sitting in the Grizedale Forest with Wilfred Josephs, who had composed the music for *Swallows & Amazons*. He had visited us on location when we were shooting the charcoal burners' scenes.

Wilfred had written a canon with the idea that he could do something musical with our voices. Our efforts were recorded by Robin Gregory and his assistant. The words went in a round, like this –

> Swallows: 'Swallows sail the ocean-wide, Natives we cannot abide.' (Sung in a high register.)
> Amazons: 'We are the Amazons.' (Sung beneath us in a low register.)

Wilfred Josephs sitting below the microphone next to me.

What Wilfred soon discovered was that, apart from Lesley, we were all pretty useless at carrying a tune. Whatever was recorded on that day near the charcoal burners' hut never made it to the final soundtrack, or even the LP that EMI brought out to accompany the movie.

Mum was thrilled to meet Wilfred Josephs. He was fantastically talented, with a huge list of credits to his name, including the lilting theme music for *Cider with Rosie*. He became famous for his *Requiem in Memory of the Jews Lost to the Holocaust* and composed a number of ballets, operas, symphonies and concertos as well as film scores.

Neville told us that we would be going home tomorrow unless the weather was good. I stuck in nearly all the photographs into my two stuffed scrapbooks. We had supper. I went to bed but not for long. Mummy had gone out with Claude. The others burst in saying that I must join in the fun. We jumped around on the beds and ran around the block in sheets. We all made tents. I shared one with Lesley. They started throwing water and I got locked in the loo for a long time. I got wet. We finally went to sleep. Lesley was very uncomfortable to sleep with.

Friday 13th July – Going home

In the morning I woke up next to Lesley dreaming I had a snake around my neck. We cleared up the mess from our 'orgy'. We packed all morning. Everything was ready. We went to the Waterhead for lunch.

Back home in
Gloucestershire.

We'd had the most amazing seven weeks but the end had drawn in with the clouds. It was time to go home.

After lunch we said goodbye to everyone. It was very sad. The journey back was long. We dropped things off at Jane's house.

Since we lived in the Cotswolds it was an endless drive south. I'm not sure how Jane and Sten got back as I don't think Jane drove, but we must have delivered their luggage on our way past their village.

> When we arrived everything was lovely and fresh and many
> new things. Daddy gave us a super supper. I had a bath and
> went to bed for the first time in my bed for seven weeks.

I can remember seeing my little sisters again and walking around the
garden in the afternoon sunshine, looking at all that had changed. We'd
left in early May, now it was full summer.

'Shall we go and put flowers on Lupy's grave?' Perry asked.

I hadn't heard that our dear old dog, the sheep dog I had known all my
life, had died while we were away.

I was inconsolable. Mum explained that they hadn't wanted to tell me
when it happened as we were filming – she thought that the sadness on my
face would have come through on camera. I understood this but was still
desolate and rather upset that she had kept the news from me. Having had
to cope with the grief of losing Lupy, on top of the heartbreak of leaving
everyone I had grown so close to in Ambleside, I was not in a good way.

Being back at home for the
summer holidays was lovely, but,
adjusting to real life when articles
kept appearing in *Woman's Realm*
was tricky. Everyone seemed
to be reading about me in their
dentist's surgery.

'What was it like?' I was often
asked.

How could I begin to describe
the way we had lived?

'Did you have lots of lines to
learn?'

How could I explain that this
was not how we worked on the
dialogue?

'What were the others like?'

How could I tell people about

Chatting to Terry Smith in Bowness.

the crew, that I had developed working friendships with so many adults?

Technical questions were much easier to answer than 'How did you
feel?' No one wanted to know that most of the time I felt cold.

'Did you have to wear make-up?'

This was a difficult one, as we didn't wear conventional make-up, but
my legs were regularly coated in a layer of foundation so as not to appear
shockingly white. Suzanna was amusing about this in her diary. She

hated being sponged down with a matt base and sunbathed whenever she could, so as to avoid it in the near future.

'What did you wear?'

Suzanna drew pictures of the two dresses she wore at Bank Ground Farm. I always rather liked her blue gingham one.

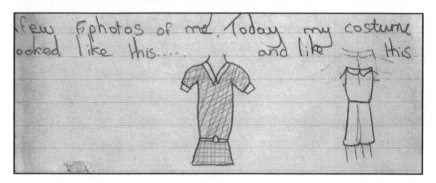

I have never worn a yellow dress, apart from the sleeveless one I had to climb into to play Titty. I always wished it had more shape.

'How did they film you sailing?'

'Did you really sleep in tents?'

'What was Virginia McKenna like?'

This was easy. 'She was lovely.'

Virginia with us at Bank Ground Farm.

One of the most treasured things that I had returned with – apart from the lump of slate Jean had given me – was a hardback copy of *Swallows and Amazons*, signed by the entire cast and crew (overleaf).

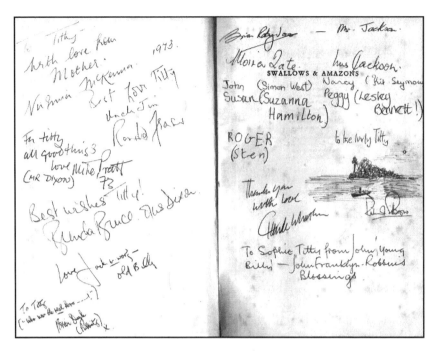

It is interesting that all the children signed their character names, with their real names in brackets. We had grown to think of ourselves as Walkers and Blacketts.

Claude wrote 'Thank you with love', and Richard enchanted me by drawing a picture of Wild Cat Island at night.

The only other signature on the first page was from Brian Doyle, Mum's friend the publicity manager, who encouraged us to collect the autographs.

I have a signature from Kerry Darbishire, who played Vicky's Nurse. Like the actors who played the Jacksons, she was not credited in the movie, although I have included all of their names in this book.

At the back of the book David Blagden drew me a picture of what must have been a vision of himself, sailing into the sunset in his little yacht *Willing Griffin*.

Gareth Tandy signed himself 'the whipcracker', which bemused me. I never saw any whips.

Peter Robb-King wrote 'Make-up for the Stars', while Simon Holland drew me a wonderful set of crossed flags that were also paint brushes – a logo for my life.

Chapter Twelve
Swallows in Egham

While I had been at home with my family, Claude had been busy in the editing suite putting *Swallows & Amazons* together with Michael Bradsell, his film editor from *That'll Be The Day*. Sue Merry and Neville Thompson must have known Michael too, as he'd edited Ken Russell's film *The Boyfriend*.

Richard had been told 'three hard months of editing are ahead', but I'm not sure it took quite that long. Claude had me acting in a Weetabix commercial he shot that August at harvest time. Maybe he was given a few days off.

What Michael confirmed was that they definitely needed the sequence when the Walker children run up to the Peak at Darien and see Wild Cat

Simon, Sten, Suzanna and me in Runnymede.

Island for the very first time. It is the scene that heralds the start of the adventure and indeed the opening titles of the movie.

Richard must have somehow found the money to mount a pick-up shoot at Runnymede near Egham in Surrey one Saturday at the beginning of September. We were told that King John signed the Magna Carta there.

We loved the idea of meeting up again. Claude said he made an effort to get as many members of the same crew together as possible so it wouldn't seem strange for us. Neville Thompson had even managed to book the same make-up caravan. The one thing that was striking was how much our hair had grown. We all needed a trim. Sten needed a full haircut. Luckily, Ronnie Cogan was free. Our summer tans were toned down in an effort to match the skins of the pale Walker children who'd been sitting in the railway compartment at the start of the film.

Claude (wearing my hat) lining us up for a take under the oak tree.

There was no cliff-top peninsular at the farm in Surrey, but a field had been found where we could run up an incline to an oak tree. It was Claude's intention to cut to a mid-shot of our faces from the wide shot of us running down the buttercup meadow at Bank Ground Farm. We just had to pretend we were looking out over the lake.

Instead of King John we met Denis setting up a 16mm Arriflex camera on 'short legs' under the oak tree. Although we look a bit hot and stiff when we were lining up the shots, the movie was probably made by this scene. We had learned how to deliver decent performances by this stage.

Kissing Claude goodbye.

If you watch the finished film our faces can be seen glowing with excitement. This was also partly because we were happy to be together again, on a sunny day in a lovely place.

The image of Titty, clutching her school hat as she looks out over an entirely imaginary lake, was the last actual shot recorded. Soon my close-up was 'in the can' and 'a wrap' was called. It had been labelled 'Slate 1003'. We celebrated with tins of Fanta rather than champagne.

I cannot help thinking that the photograph below is symbolic of the futures we were to step into. Sten is holding an apple, Suzanna seems to have a framed photograph, and I'd been given a roll of camera tape. What Simon is holding is something of a mystery, but it is tightly clasped. 'Whatever happened to the Swallows and the Amazons?' has been the question asked most frequently even though we'd really rather like to keep it a secret.

Mum, Sten, Suzanna, me, Jane and Simon.

Chapter Thirteen
Studio Secrets

The process of editing a film can be terrifying for a director. There is always the prospect of finding a sequence that will not cut together. But working with a good film editor is hugely creative and fulfilling. Richard said he was completely captivated by the process: 'Moving a few frames from here to there could change the whole emphasis of a scene.' Editing is an exciting, yet more relaxing time for the director than having to lead a massive crew out on location. And the actors are never around. Sadly, I didn't meet our film editor, Michael Bradsell. Oh, but to think that he hauled my image over his Steenbeck, razor blade and sticky tape poised.

Once Michael and Claude had finished editing we were called to work on the sound, summoned to the EMI-MGM Elstree Studios in Hertfordshire. It is not usual for actors to enter such territory, but our adventure was to continue.

I met Ian Fuller, the sound editor, and Bill Rowe the dubbing mixer with the other Swallows, but I don't think we saw anyone else in the cast. Suzanna came along with a nine-year-old cousin called Seymour – a very bright boy who was wearing stripy canvas trousers like a deck chair. Mummy had bought me a smart new halter-neck dress that was the height of fashion. Looking at the photograph, I rather wish she hadn't bothered.

At Elstree Studios.

We were led into a huge dubbing theatre hung with long black drapes around a high white screen. Claude explained that he needed to re-record our dialogue for various sequences. This was because the original soundtrack had been spoilt by the sound of motorboats, car horns, or simply the wind. At first we were handed dubbing scripts, but it was difficult to look at them as well as the screen. We soon found we didn't need them. Instead, we stood in front of microphones that hung from the ceiling and sung out the words we knew, as sections of the film were projected. To help us, a thick black cue-line would pass across the scene. When it hit one side it was time to start speaking. This was to ensure that our voices would be in sync with our lips. It could help. It could be off-putting. In the end we just went for it naturally. After each 'take' the film would be rewound and we would go again. There is a scene at the *Amazon* boathouse when John scrunches up Peggy's message and throws it in the water. It amused us hugely to see this played in reverse.

The one line that I simply could not replicate was the dialogue Titty delivered when saying goodbye to the charcoal burners: 'Thank you so much for letting us see your lovely serpent.' We went over it again and again, but Jack Woolgar wasn't at the dubbing studio and I couldn't do it without looking at him. The charm and sincerity of the moment was not something I could reproduce. In the end Claude said he would just have to use the original and put up with the sound of wind in the trees.

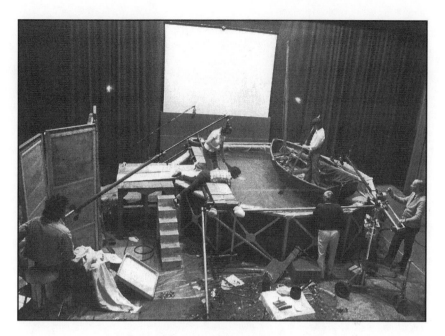

Swallow on the soundstage at Elstree Studios.

We were at the studios for a week. On one tea break we were taken to watch a vampire film being made – *Vampira*, starring David Niven and Teresa Graves. At lunchtimes we were allowed to run around on the back lot. There was a Western cowboy set – an entire street that had been constructed – and a crashed WWII aircraft, in which we were allowed to play. Extracting Sten to return to the sound-stages was near impossible.

It was when we returned from lunch in the studio canteen that we discovered the main reason for post-syncing our film. It is the biggest secret of all. When *My Fair Lady* was made, Audrey Hepburn's singing voice was replaced by that of Marni Nixon. Other film actresses have also had their voices dubbed, such as Andie MacDowell in *Greystoke: Legend of Tarzan, Lord of the Apes*, whose voice was post-synced by Glenn Close in 1984. That day, as we walked back along the corridor we could hear Claude auditioning actresses in the dubbing theatre. An adult actress was reading Nancy's part. She was overacting – crying, weeping hysterically. It sounded awful.

Even Mum was shocked. She reluctantly explained that a decision had been made to dub over Kit's voice throughout the entire film. While I could see why they had chosen to replace her north London accent, at least Kit had sounded laid-back. The ladies being auditioned didn't sound like tomboys at all. I suggested to Claude that he should ask Suzanna's cousin Seymour to read the part. He proved far better than any professional actress, was totally unselfconscious and very quick. He simply repeated what Kit said, exactly as she said it. 'Shiver my timbers!'

We went ahead with Seymour reading the part and finished that day. Isn't it odd that two Seymours ending up playing Nancy?

The post-syncing was also meant to be a chance to improve on our performances and diction. Some time was spent in re-recording our sea shanty, *Spanish Ladies*. I made a mistake that I have always regretted. Instead of singing sweetly I went for volume, which was not only unnecessary, but disastrous. It is acceptable in the film, where you can see that I am singing out on the water, but sounds horrid on the LP.

We had no idea that EMI were going to bring out an album to accompany the movie. It had the shot of John and me bringing *Swallow* into Secret Harbour on the cover, with the story narrated by David Wood. You can still buy one on vinyl, all these years later.

Once, when I was away at school, Mum had an unexpected visitor for tea: Eric Morecambe. He enjoyed fishing and arrived to see if he could catch one of the carp my parents kept in their lake, when it started to rain quite hard. Mum put on the LP of *Swallows & Amazons* to entertain him, while she went into the kitchen. She returned with a plate of biscuits to find him shaking with laughter. Tears were rolling down his face. She couldn't think what was so funny – until he pointed out that she'd put the gramophone on at the wrong speed.

I remember a discussion about the font type for the opening titles. A very fashionable pseudo-Edwardian script as used on the poster of the film was favoured. I said they ought to use the handwritten capitals that Arthur Ransome's illustrator had penned on the map in the opening cover of the book, which Simon Holland copied onto our chart. They agreed.

The squiggly pseudo-Edwardian script had been used in the title sequence of Lionel Jeffries' movie *The Railway Children*, which starred Jenny Agutter and Dinah Sheridan. As a viewer, I felt that this soon seemed dated, while *Swallows & Amazons* sailed onto our television screens in the 1980s and 1990s, and indeed into the 21st century, without being hindered by what became jarring, unfashionable graphics. What was amazing, was that the retro 1970s graphic swung back into fashion at about the same time as a DVD of both the films was launched. They somehow worked well as an EMI double bill.

One thing that worried me was that I saw *Swallow* lying outside the studio. She looked forlorn, a ship out of water. They had needed her for recording, but I was concerned that we would not see her again.

After we left Elstree, sound effects were added to the movie. Richard wrote in his book: 'Bill Rowe was our masterful sound mixer, working magic with birdsong, a rustle of leaves, a broken twig – all the tiniest details that went into making the story spring to life.'

When I watch the film now I so admire the technique of using sound to illustrate the soaring of Titty's imagination. The storm bell on Robinson Crusoe's ship heralds the roaring wind, and lends reality to the scene where I play the shipwrecked sailor, dragging my parched body towards the island campsite. You can even hear parrots and monkeys in the palm trees.

I am sure Arthur Ransome would have supported all this with great enthusiasm.

Chapter Fourteen
A Storm of Publicity

Although we didn't mind our photographs being taken while on location, and were happy to have Mum clicking away with her little Instamatic, we all hated the idea of promotional photographs. They were usually so posed, set up by strangers who had no idea of the story. A prime example would be the shot of us six children and Mother lying in a row in the buttercup meadow (see colour plates). Virginia McKenna tried to make it fun for us, but why were the Amazons at Holly Howe? Why weren't we with any of the boats? It was all terribly hot and difficult to squint into the sunshine. Only Mrs Batty's dog seemed to enjoy the attention, and he didn't appear in the story at all.

Posing for a publicity photo at Haverthwaite Railway Station.

The glare of the flash bulbs had started on day one. As Suzanna said in her diary, it made us feel like 'right twits'. Claude was very good at explaining things to children. Looking back I wish that he had explained why these photographs were so important, but of course this was not his job and he would have been busy setting up the next shot. Certainly once the filming had finished we needed to know how vital it was to promote the film. Richard wanted to make a sequel, particularly an adaptation of Ransome's last book in the series – *Great Northern?* He loved the Outer Hebrides and had a house on Coll. David Wood was commissioned to write the screenplay. We might have been a little keener about publicity shots if we had been told that the outcome would have been spending another summer on the Isle of Lewis.

Journalists were introduced to us by Brian Doyle. Brian had been the publicist on *Straw Dogs* in 1971, the thriller that starred Dustin Hoffman and Susan George. She had of course played Titty – renamed 'Kitty' – in the black-and-white BBC adaptation of *Swallows and Amazons* made in 1962.

By 1973, Susan George was regarded as a glamorous sex symbol in British cinema – setting me a rather daunting example. It was much easier for Brian to publicise her than me. She had a gorgeous figure with beautiful, thick, blonde hair. I had what my sister called 'tendrils' and was skinny with crooked teeth.

Brian kindly turned this around:

> Sophie Neville's friendly grin was by far the most infectious and heartwarming of the entire cast and crew ... with her ever-windswept hair and incredibly slim figure she was perhaps the most distinctive member of the six leading children playing the 'Swallows' and the 'Amazons'.

As soon as Brian's press release arrived on their desks, the journalists flew towards us like seagulls greeting a fishing fleet. It was terrifying.

There was a very trendy women's magazine in the early 1970s called *Over 21*, which the senior girls at school used to read. My mother was thrilled to find that Celia Brayfield had written a double-page *Swallows* feature. I was amazed. I didn't mind her picture of us gutting fish, but started reading with trepidation. I was described as 'an etiolated Tolkien elf-child with huge pale eyes and uneven teeth'. I looked up the word 'etiolated' in the dictionary and burst into tears.

The Lord Mayor's Show – November 1973

Sailing through the streets of London.

One major public appearance was the Lord Mayor's Show. For the first time since the filming we climbed into our costumes and then into a boat that looked like *Swallow.* It had been mounted on a low-loader. Afloat on a float, we made ready to sail through the City of London. It was early November but we tucked our coats under the thwarts. What was fun, if a little odd, was that it was the only time that the Swallows and the Amazons had been in a dinghy together. But did anyone know who we were? The film hadn't yet come out. We were riding on the waves made by Arthur Ransome's books, which were well-loved by the people of our nation.

As we were taken through the streets of London, passersby started to wave at us and we waved back. Soon it was waves all around. Being Titty, I had Swallow's flag to fly. John let Nancy take the tiller. We were stunned to see that huge crowds of people had gathered.. Sten wasn't sure and soon joined my mother on the pavement, wearing the tartan hat that Claude had bought him at Blackpool funfair. Maybe he found it all too overwhelming. Bizarrely, Jeremy Fisher the frog was leaping about in front of us. With him danced other representatives from The Tales of

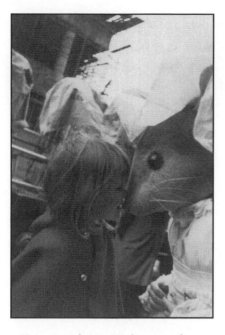

Tamzin with Mrs Tittlemouse from
The Tales of Beatrix Potter.

Beatrix Potter, the Royal Ballet's wonderful feature film brought out that same year.

The float in front of us depicted an EMI film crew, with 2K lights and a camera. We were marking the 35th anniversary of Anglo-EMI, and bringing the Lake District to London Town, which was something I could embrace.

Since we didn't have to talk to anyone, we were able to enjoy being involved in the pageant, which included so many icons of British Life. I hadn't met a Pearly Queen before, but there was a whole clan of them in their glorious suits, lovingly embroidered with mother-of-pearl buttons. I resolved to collect enough to adorn a jacket of my own. My favourite view was of the Queen's Gold State Coach pulled by her lovely white horses, six in hand. It was like something out of fairyland.

Smiling for the crowds.

The Preview and the Premiere

The first time we saw *Swallows & Amazons* was at 'The Preview'. This was held at a small viewing theatre in London, to which newspaper and magazine columnists were invited. It was a special occasion. We met up with various members of the production team who were also seeing the film for the very first time.

We sat deep in our seats during the screening, utterly amazed at how sunny everything looked. Denis Lewiston's insistence that we should wait for clouds to pass had paid off.

It was wonderful to see how the scenes had been put together. We had not known that Claude would add shots of wildlife, which brought so much to the feature film. I loved the scene he included of cattle standing in the shallows of the lake at dawn. We laughed out loud, appreciating the humour. Much of this was generated by the serious expression on Roger's face while he was learning how things worked. He always seemed to be eating at the opening of a scene and made observations that drew the audience into the adventure.

The premiere of the movie was held at the ABC Cinema in Shaftesbury Avenue, London, on 4th April 1974. It was to be a Royal Gala, held in aid of the charity KIDS. Can you imagine the shock of finding a picture of ourselves on the cinema tickets when they arrived in the post? And they were so expensive! £3.50! Normal tickets cost 80p.

I didn't know what to wear. I wished that we'd been able to climb into our costumes, but it was clear that I had to find an appropriate dress. Sadly I had outgrown the trendy one we had bought in Carnaby Street. Nowadays one would be inundated by offers of designer dresses to model on the red carpet. As it was, my mother bought a blue outfit for herself, and a green pinafore dress that I agreed would be appropriate for an afternoon event. I was not so happy about wearing ballet shoes. Please note that these were actual ballet shoes, and I was now thirteen. I would have preferred court shoes with buckles. Ironically, these zoomed out of fashion, while ballet pumps have been loved ever since. My previously bobbed hair was now long again, but Mummy put it in Carmen rollers. I am not sure the result was particularly successful, but I thought it looked grown-up.

My sisters wore velvet with their ballet shoes. The dress from Carnaby Street was slightly large for Perry, but she coped. When I arrived in London, I found that Suzanna had chosen a Laura Ashley pinafore. The Amazons both got away with wearing trousers. They looked far more sophisticated.

There was an awful lot of fuss at home about who should come and who couldn't. Mum had insisted on bringing, not friends of mine, but two of the nuns from my school. I went off to my first premiere accompanied by my headmistress, Sister Ann-Julian, and my house mistress, Sister Allyne; not very cool in a teenager's world. *The Exorcist* was out at the same time. The nuns made no comment. At least they didn't have to worry about what to wear.

Mum and me outside the ABC cinema with Sisters Ann-Julian and Allyne.

In fact, Sister Allyne proved the very best person to take. She had once been Australia's foremost flautist, so knew how daunting it was to stand in the limelight. She must have understood the turmoil in my little head and was undoubtedly praying for me. I would not be surprised to learn that spiritual protection was granted by her presence alone. She could have been an exorcist in her own right – a real one.

Claude defied any plans my mother might have made by taking the six of us in the cast, and only the six of us, out to lunch at a bistro where we were able to order beefburgers, relax and enjoy ourselves. Thankfully there was no red carpet outside the cinema, but rather smart souvenir programmes were being sold in the foyer, one of which is still in my possession.

Arriving at the ABC Shaftesbury Avenue.

Richard had invited an array of special guests. Princess Helena Moutafian arrived with Earl Compton, chairman of KIDS. I had been practising my curtsey. I was interested to hear that she later became patron of the Young ME Sufferers Trust. Sadly Virginia McKenna could not be there, although she sent her daughter Louise and her eldest son Will Travers, now CEO of the Born Free Foundation. Bobby Moore, who'd played soccer for England, came with his family, as did Mrs Spike Milligan, and Nicholas Parsons, who was at the time famous for presenting the ITV show *Sale of the Century*. The Hollywood star and wife of Roald Dahl, Patricia Neal, who had won an Oscar for her leading role in the Paul Newman film *Hud* and had also appeared in *Breakfast at Tiffany's*, brought her sweet little girls. Julie Ege was there – a lovely Norwegian actress, who appeared with Frankie Howerd as a character rather wondrously called Voluptua in the movie of *Up Pompeii*. Richard might have known her, as he had produced the West End version. She was also known as a Bond Girl, since she'd appeared in *On Her Majesty's Secret Service* with Joanna Lumley, when George Lazenby played Bond. We didn't know any of this, but having a Bond Girl at your premiere was quite the thing.

On stage with Ronnie Fraser after the screening.

As the film was being shown I watched my performance for the second time becoming aware of how I came across on the big screen. It was like seeing endless photographs of oneself that were not exactly flattering. I cringed. All Sister Allyne said was how much she enjoyed seeing the owl – a natural history shot that was only added after our toil on the drama.

Ronnie Fraser led us down the sloping side-aisle onto the stage after the screening to be presented to the audience. I felt terribly shy, and glad that I didn't have to say anything.

By the film poster outside the cinema.

I have a few precious posters of the film. The artwork for the colour poster, which hung in the London Underground, is still used for the cover of some DVDs. I quite liked the design, except for the rather jarring colour of my blouse, which for some reason was bright pink. I never wore pink in the film. And no one seemed to be in control of the boat. Far more attractive were the huge sepia posters that hung outside cinemas. They were so large I was unsure what to do with mine. A school friend sent me an advertisement she had found in *Tammy and Sandy,* a teenage magazine we all read. There was a similar one in *The Sunday Times* – both with smaller versions of the poster.

Riding the Waves of Film Critics

Now the film was out, it had to sell itself. Everyone was waiting to hear what critics from within the movie industry felt about it. My mother must have written to Barry Norman, inviting him to bring his daughters to one of the promotional events held at the Commonwealth Institute. He was then presenting BBC Television's *Film '74* and writing a weekly column in *The Guardian* newspaper. He replied straight away:

> Like my daughters I enjoyed 'Swallows and Amazons' a great deal and I'm sure it will be a huge success. It deserves to be.

Barry Norman enjoyed it! I can see from reading his *Radio Times* billing that he was looking at 'films for the family over the Easter holidays'. *Film '74* was shown on BBC2 at 10.15pm and repeated on Fridays even later, so he must have been speaking to grown-ups. Sadly not all the newspapers agreed with him. Films were not given review stars in those days but the critics could be merciless.

My mother subscribed to a press clippings agency called Durrant's – Durrant's of Herbal Hill, London EC1 – who, for the vast fee of £50, sent her all the articles written about the film. The Prince of Wales told a friend of mine that he never reads the newspapers. I know why. Reading about yourself can be upsetting, especially if the facts are incorrect. My mother didn't mind. She highlighted the bits about me, filling four albums.

After entertaining the *Daily Express* so nicely in Ambleside, a close-up of me was printed on the front page of their newspaper, with the headline 'Kids won't swallow this watery old tale':

> Spring is with us – a time of year that brings the call of the cuckoo and the plaintive cry of the harassed parent that there isn't a film on locally suitable for the kids during the holidays.

As if in answer to the complaint comes a film that would seem
to fill the bill, in that it is made for kids, acted by kids and has
a certificate that will allow kids to watch it. I won't let mine see
it, though, for fear they would leave the cinema long before
it ended in search of an adventure more stimulating than the
one on the screen.

This was written by Ian Christie, the jazz clarinetist, who worked as a theatre
and film critic for the *Daily Express* for twenty-six years. Born in Blackpool and a habitué of Fleet Street pubs, he held fiercely left-wing views.

The same black-and-white photograph of me appeared on the front of
The Daily Telegraph with the title 'One Swallow won't make a Summer'. *The
Scotsman* said, 'The gentle charm of Arthur Ransome's story is appealing
but hardly gripping . . . the youngsters might find it lacking in excitement.'

However, Russell Davies of *The Observer*, another jazz musician
who now presents *Brain of Britain* on BBC Radio 4, saw that the film
of *Swallows & Amazons* had a niche: 'Make the most of an unexpected
chance to see real, intended child-orientated pictures . . . it isn't really
about anything, apart from the joys of camping, so fantasy is given plenty
of room to move.'

Some recognised it as an innocent nostalgia trip, others just loved
it. The critic Rosemary Caink said that her three children 'completely
identified themselves with the children in the story'. It became clear that
journalists who took their own children along appreciated the film.

The *Coventry Evening Post* wrote, 'Claude Whatham's film beautifully
captures the period flavour and keeps closely to the format of the
book. It's refreshingly un-self-conscious and the performances of the
children . . . are nicely unrestrained and free of the gawky camera-shyness
which used to make such a hash of this kind of thing.'

My favourite article wasn't found by Durrant's, but was published in
The Brownie. They recommended it highly.

Newspapers are read one day and used to light fires the next. Back in
1974 they might have been used to wrap up fish and chips. Either way,
an article in the paper is soon forgotten. Not so a feature in a magazine.
They tend to hang around in hotel foyers and doctors' surgeries, waiting
to have their pages turned for months, if not years. The judgement they
cast on our movie was important.

To my surprise I found a four-page feature about how we spent the
summer of 1973 in *Homes and Gardens* magazine. What amazed me was
that the black-and-white photographs taken on the film set had been
colour-tinted. Meanwhile, Elspeth Grant gave us a wonderful write-up

in *Tatler*. She was the journalist also known by her married name of Elspeth Huxley, the author who had written *The Flame Trees of Thika* and so many other books. She wasn't quite right in saying the film was shot entirely on location in the Lake District, but she would not have known about our day at Runnymede.

We were in both *Punch* and the *Sunday People*. My mother saved them all. There seemed to be articles in every periodical imaginable – *The Tablet, Smith's Trade News* (a publishing magazine I hadn't heard of), *What's On,* and even the *News of the World*. We were also in the April edition of the film fan magazine *Photoplay*, which featured Steve McQueen on the cover. It cost 20p in those days.

I was taken with friends to see the film at our local cinema. A child in the row in front of me stood up when the film ended and turned around. He looked up at me, looked at the screen, and looked back at me in disbelief. How could I be sitting behind him? I was meant to be on the houseboat.

Nowadays children's films are released with a multitude of games. Back in the early 1970s, this amounted to four jigsaw puzzles. One had the dreadful promotional photograph of us sitting in the daisy field on the front. I couldn't bear to make it up.

Long after the first showing of the film, I was sent a note:

> I remember going to the Puffin Club exhibition in London around the time of the film release and some of the cast were there with one of the boats. There was a quiz about *Swallows & Amazons* and you could win a copy of the book – which I did! Sophie, were you there? And do you know if the boat was *Swallow* or *Amazon*?

We did indeed go along. *Puffin Post* published a very good article using the black-and-white stills in a better way than any other magazine. We were excited as the publishers brought out a copy of the book with a photograph of the two little ships near Cormorant Island on the cover. You can't see us clearly but it was from the scene after Titty had captured *Amazon*. On the back of the book was a photograph of Nancy and Peggy in their red knitted caps, waiting in the reeds at the mouth of the Amazon River.

Not long after we finished filming, my parents came across a green parrot called Chico who was remarkably friendly, a sweet bird who soon came to live with us. He chatted away in Spanish and was good company. I went everywhere with him – even taking him out rowing on the lake. He was much more affectionate and less of a threat than the parrot who played Polly. One minute he'd be sitting on Tamzin's shoulder, the next, he'd be on mine.

My sister Tamzin scratching Chico's neck.

Once the film was on general release I was often invited to appear on radio or television. This usually entailed going to a studio to appear on current affairs programmes such as *Points West* or *Nationwide*. However, Robin Hellier, who had begun working for the BBC Natural History Unit on *Animal Magic*, was thrilled to hear that I really did have a green parrot, and brought a film crew from Bristol to our house. Although the focus of the item for *Animal Magic* was a profile of my role in *Swallows & Amazons*, the aim must have been to get as many animals on the programme as possible, since they also featured our donkeys having their feet trimmed with the parrot still on my shoulder. He took a shot of me rowing down the lake with Chico. It was used to fill small gaps in the schedules instead of the famous static shot of the BBC Test Card featuring Carole Hersee playing Tic-Tac-Toe with a creepy clown called Bubbles.

Being conscientious, Robin took the trouble to write to let me know when *Animal Magic* was to be broadcast, although I can't remember ever seeing it go out. However, everyone else did. Children's television seemed to be watched by the entire planet in the 1970s. Letters poured in. My mother loved getting them. The volume was such that she had to answer some of them for me. And over the years they kept on coming. My friends at University were amazed to find post arriving addressed to Titty, but it was always charming. I appreciated them more and more as the years went by.

My mother only wrote me one proper letter while I was away at boarding school. It was to tell me that Chico had died. He spent so much time flying free that he caught a virus from wild birds and could not be saved. I wept for days.

One thing that struck me recently when I opened the March 1974 copy of *Films and Filming*, kept by my mother, was that *Swallows & Amazons* has to be one of the most enduring movies to come out at the time. In 1973 Sean Connery opted to appear with Charlotte Rampling in *Zardoz*. I've neither seen nor heard of it. Why couldn't he have played Captain Flint with us?

Reflecting on the performance of *Swallows & Amazons*, Richard Pilbrow concluded: 'We had a success.' *Variety* magazine called it a 'Charming, delightful, beautifully made film'. It was 'not a hit but a reasonable success that continues to play, principally on television, around the world'. He goes on to quantify how it did financially: 'The world of film finance is a distinct mystery. Our production costs were just under £300,000. Over the years, income trickled in from an international market. Curiously the costs inexorably rose to match the income. The costs of marketing the movie always seemed to equal receipts at the box office. In 2004 our film actually recouped. That's why I have the temerity to call it a success.'

Richard Pilbrow with Neville C. Thompson in the Lake District in 1973.

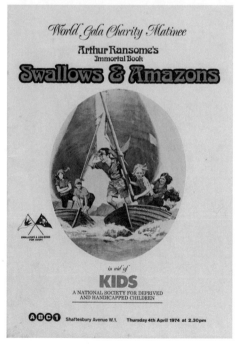

Above: Reluctantly posing for a promotional photograph in the meadow at Bank Ground Farm with Virginia and Mrs Batty's dog. Sadly, the shot made its way into the programme sold at the film premiere.

Left: The programme from the *Swallows & Amazons* premiere.

Right: The Swallows encounter Old Billy the charcoal burner.

Opposite top: Kit and Jane with Tamzin and Perry by the icecream cart in Rio.

Opposite bottom: Suzanna, Simon, Claude, me, Mum, Kit and Jean at Blackpool funfair in our funny hats.

Above top: Robinson Crusoe by the camp fire with Man Friday.

Above bottom: The lights and crew surrounding us as we filmed the scene. Virginia's husband, Bill Travers, is in the foreground with a newspaper.

Above top: The Walker family arriving at Holly Howe.
Above bottom: Ronnie Fraser with me and Mum at Derwentwater.
Opposite top: Fishing on Elterwater.
Opposite bottom: Posing for the native press in Rio.

Top: Filming the very last shot to be recorded, under the oak tree at Runnymede.
Bottom: Reunited with Suzanna Hamilton at Bank Ground Farm in 2003.

Chapter Fifteen
Reflections

It is always wonderful to hear how the film of *Swallows & Amazons* has affected people's lives. Over the last forty years people have written to me saying how much they have treasured the VHS, the DVD, the LP (which was narrated by David Wood) and even the jigsaw puzzles. Some say watching the film was like being in a dream, others consider it an integral part of their childhood. Many viewers have said how much their own children enjoy taking on the roles of the characters, especially when they go to the Lake District.

I received such an interesting e-mail from Christopher Kenworthy in Australia that I asked if I could publish it:

> I became a film-maker largely because of *Swallows & Amazons*. As a nine-year-old, I stumbled across Wild Cat Island just days after seeing the film. I was so thrilled to be standing where the film had been made, and so excited to see how clever use of the camera could exaggerate the feeling of a location and capture the magic of performance, that I set out to discover everything I could about film. It was a life-changing moment.

My daughters (5 and 7) adore Titty, and we are all impressed
by your acting. I've directed my girls in a couple of things, and
I know they gained confidence from having seen you perform.
When Tabitha, my eldest daughter, saw the film for the first
time, she burst into tears at the end. It was a release of pure joy,
and is testament to the quality of the film. When reading your
recent blog post about set dressing at Bank Ground Farm, I
wondered if you'd noticed that the clock on the mantelpiece
is still there. It's on the other mantelpiece, I believe, but it is
still there.

The clock, which you can see in the scene when I am sewing the flag,
must have belonged to Mrs Batty all along.

I wanted Richard and Molly Pilbrow to read some recent reviews of
Swallows & Amazons and found many online, where the movie usually
receives four or five stars. It is clear that second and third generations
of viewers are still able to appreciate the drama, watching it time and
time again.

These days, children are encouraged to post reviews on the internet.
One little boy wrote to say the 'film was excellent' but that he 'was
DISCUSTED when they used dirty water wich had mud in it to drink'.
A girl called Sade wrote: 'I would love to be allowed to be free and go
anywhere without my mum FREAKING out. I like how Amazons were
enemies to Swallows but they became friends and they were a good
group. The character I liked most was Titty because she was the HERO!'
Robbie, aged 12, states: 'I really liked this film because it was fun and
adventurous,' while five-year-old Daniel simply writes: 'I fourt that it was
good.' It was lovely to read nine-year-old Megan's review:

> I thought *Swallows & Amazons* was very wondrous,
> adventurous, inspiring and competitive. They are brilliant
> actors. Even though it was made in 1974 it is mind blowing.
> Sophie is my favourite actor she is very brave and kind but the
> rest are very nice too.

Gracie, aged 11, is clearly impressed:

> What an adventurous movie! This film was awesome!! It's
> really hard to tell what genre it was though, it's like all these
> different things mashed into one movie. The children take a
> boat and find an island in the middle of the lake. I would love
> to go on that island! I would recommend this movie to anyone
> because it's spectacularly amazing!!!!!!!!!!!!!!!!!!!!!!

A young reviewer of a clip from the film on YouTube commented:

> I wish I'd grown up in those times and actually been able to be
> a kid instead of having to be careful and always carry a phone
> and never talk to strangers. The kids in this film are what real
> kids should be like, able to cope by themselves and have fun.

Eleven-year-old Alice was taken with the freedom that the children have
in the film and how she would be much less carefree in their position:

> I think Titty is the bravest of all. I don't think I would've stayed
> on the island on my own if my Mum had visited though. I
> would've asked her to stay with me.

There are some very well-considered reviews relating children's reactions
to the film, appropriately enough, on Amazon. One reviewer, who cites
it as one of her favourite children's films when she was young, 'before
animated space-zombie-machines ruled the earth,' found that her
daughter and son 'thoroughly enjoyed it'. Someone else admits to being
initially concerned that her 8-year-old daughter 'might find it a little old-
fashioned', adding: 'I needn't have worried, as she loved it and watched it
over and over again.' Another reviewer comments: 'I loved this as a kid
and I bought it having read the story to my two boys. It is as good as I
remembered it and I was completely amazed that my two boys love it as
much as I did, if not more. They watch it again and again.'

A reviewer from Germany wondered:

> . . . how children would react to this, brought up as they are
> these days on CGI, *Harry Potter* and all the rest. However,
> my son (9) was gripped from start to finish. I think what is
> appealing is the sheer independence of the children, their
> capability and the good old-fashioned adventures outdoors
> messing about in boats.

What I now find interesting is that, as in Arthur Ransome's books, there
are no scenes in *Swallows & Amazons* (1974) that only feature adults.
Was this the secret to its success?

> your Titty is wonderful ... I always
> liked the way she did sketches and
> maps. the way Susan ran the

Chapter Sixteen
A Journey Back in Time

On a wet but beautiful day in Cumbria in the summer of 2012, I set off on a quest to find some of the locations used in *Swallows & Amazons*. My journey started with a drive down through the streets of Rio (Bowness) and along the east shore of Windermere to Haverthwaite Railway Station at the southern end of the lake (or Antarctica, as Titty labelled the region). It was here that we spent our very first day filming nearly forty years previously. I had not been there since.

I had a chat to the train driver who explained that they now run six journeys a day from Haverthwaite alongside the River Leven to Lakeside Station. Here you can take a native steamer back up to Rio (the Bowness pier) or to the Far North – Ambleside, at the head of the lake where we stayed when filming in that long-ago summer.

While engine number 2073 was used in the movie, I travelled on a steam locomotive built in 1951 that burns about two tons of coal a day. The driver probably uses rather a lot of steam oil too. It's a smell I relish, familiar since childhood days spent on steamboats, particularly a Steam Boat Association rally my father took me to on Windermere. Curiously, Haverthwaite Railway Station looked cleaner and shinier than when we used it as a location. I can only suppose it was still in the process of being restored back then, when Simon Holland cluttered it up with push-bikes and luggage trolleys.

I climbed aboard the train and explored, as Titty would have done, discovering people seated inside from far distant lands. With me was the chairman of the Nancy Blackett Trust, who remarked that, although the train is not included in the book of *Swallows and Amazons*, Arthur Ransome featured locomotives in his later novels, notably *Pigeon Post* and *Coot Club*. He knew the Furness Railway well. We saw the distinctive carriage with the compartment used in the film sitting in a siding as we steamed down the valley.

When we reached the Lakeside Railway Station, I jumped out, wondering how many signs of *Swallows and Amazons* we would find, if we'd see any crossed flags that have become the symbol of the whole series of stories. The first sign was on the lane above Coniston Water, standing at the gate of Bank Ground Farm where I'd come so many times, so long ago. Sadly some of the great trees have gone from around the old gate and the boatsheds by the lake. They must have reached the end of their lives. It is still beautiful. I wanted to run down the field full of buttercups just as I had as a child.

The sign above Bank Ground Farm.

Bank Ground Farm is much smarter now. Lucy Batty is not around but it is still in the family, run by her grandson and his wife. You can either stay in the main house, where there is a lovely corner bedroom with views right down Langdale, or take a cottage since they have been able to convert the barn and stables into places for people to stay. You will have to look for the clock on the mantelpiece and see if the beds we used are still there. The family business has thrived on its connection with the film. I am so glad they've benefited from the publicity, which we so hated.

We went on our way, passing Lanehead, the Collingwoods' house next door, as we drove down the hill. Coniston Old Man or 'Kanchenjunga', as the Walkers and Blacketts called the mountain, was snoozing under a thick blanket of cloud but the challenge of climbing to the summit was for another day. Below the village, mooring up to the jetty at the Bluebird Café, was *Ransome*, the Coniston Launch. As we set off across the lake we could see *Swallow*'s boatshed clearly from the water. It has been renovated and repaired but the old stone jetty is still there, below the huge horse chestnut trees. I remember how icy the water was when we first brought *Swallow* out from the depths of that cobwebby shed.

The Coniston Launch can take you right down the lake to Peel Island. In her novel, *In Aleppo Once*, Taqui Altounyan described it as being 'like a green tuffet, sitting in the water, the trees covering the rocks'. While you can see the remains of our shingle Landing Place, there will not be

Bank Ground Farm.

one stick of firewood on the island. In fact the roots of the trees look exposed, the soil around them eroded over the last forty years, but it remains an inspirational place. You can see the Secret Harbour best from a boat and imagine Titty trying to get *Amazon* out through the rocks on a dark night. The mossy tree, which I climbed for fear of ravenous beasts, is still there. If you look carefully, you can find a young pine tree planted by Taqui on the spot of the Lighthouse Tree, under the auspices of a forestry officer. In his book *Discovering Swallows & Ransomes*, John Berry notes that there was a pine tree at the northern end of Peel Island, but it blew down before World War II.

On the way down to the south of the lake you pass The Heald, a bungalow set in the woods of 'High Greenland' where Ransome wrote *The Picts and the Martyrs*, keeping his dinghy *Coch-y-bonddhu* on the lake below. She played the part of Dick and Dot's boat *Scarab*. The original 'Dogs' Home' can be found in the woods above the house. It was in the Grizedale Forest that we went to see the charcoal burners and met the real men and an adder in the process.

By now the rain was falling on the water so hard that it had hammered the surface flat. Peel Island looked surreal, almost ghostly. No one was about. I tried to imagine how a location catering wagon, let alone two double-decker buses and all our caravans, could have driven down the winding East of Lake road and parked in the fields. The gypsy wagon is still there. Further along the road you can find a large, sturdy jetty with a view of Peel Island.

I gazed out over the water to see Brown Howe, the house that we used as a location for Beckfoot, and shortly after, the Edwardian *Amazon* boathouse. I don't think this was the one Ransome envisaged. The pictures in the book illustrations show a building with a low-pitched roof. His was at the mouth of the Amazon River – a reedy place.

The four Ransome children, Arthur, Joyce, Geoffrey and Cecily, spent their summer holidays on a farm at Nibthwaite, by the southern end of Coniston Water, below Brockbarrow. Their father fished at Allan Tarn – Octopus Lagoon – a little way along the River Crake. You can walk down the path they must have taken to dip their hands in the lake. And there you can find what must be the model for the *Amazon* boathouse at Slate Quay, the 'rough stone-built dock' Ransome refers to in his autobiography. How wise he was to write about the places, the culture and experiences that he knew so well.

The *Amazon* boathouse at Brown Howe.

The boathouse came to be owned by Brigit Sanders, *née* Altounyan, who was the inspiration for the youngest of the Swallows: Vicky, the ship's baby. She lived with her family in the house nearby, teaching her children and grandchildren to sail on Coniston Water in *Mavis*, the original *Amazon*. She was joined by her brother Roger, who, with his passion for fishing, had his five children sailing to Peel Island without life-jackets. Sadly *Mavis* became too leaky to take out on the lake. She has been restored, renamed *Amazon*, and resides at the Ruskin Museum in Coniston much like a great aunt, where she can be visited.

The 'Knickerbockerbreaker' rocks rise above what must be Swainson's Farm at High Nibthwaite, featured in *Swallowdale*, which you can find across the road nearby. I knew that Titty Altounyan ended up living on the western shore near Coniston. Trained by Henry Moore at Chelsea School of Art, she spent much of her time painting. When she died on 3rd July 1998, she was heralded in the obituaries as Arthur Ransome's muse, although she was uncomfortable with the fame in her own lifetime.

A hassock embroidered by Jean Hopkins at St Paul's Church, Rusland, where you can find the Ransomes' gravestones.

I eventually found another representation of the crossed flags. It was embroidered on a kneeler at the church where both the Ransomes lie buried. A tapestry! Lesley could have made one.

As we drove through the gentle countryside south of Coniston Water, we passed Lowick Hall, a house Arthur Ransome once rented. Climbing up past Gummer's How we wiggled down to reach The Mason's Arms, which I gather was one of his favourite pubs. Then, seemingly in the middle of nowhere, we came across the Holy Grail: Low Ludderburn and the erstwhile grey barn where *Swallows and Amazons* was written in a long room on the first floor. Here owls hooted from the yew trees, and the Ransomes kept their Trojan car or 'Rattletrap' in the wooden garage that you can see in front of the building.

You can still go out on our houseboat, the *Lady Derwentwater* owned by the Keswick Launch Company. She returned to real life after the filming, rather like I did, and can carry up to ninety passengers. If you are planning to stay in Coniston, book a trip on the Victorian steam yacht *Gondola*, rebuilt by the National Trust. As an eight-year-old boy, Ransome travelled on the original vessel with its serpent figurehead, and was allowed to take the helm by the captain, whom he considered to be a good friend. To help the illustrator depict Captain Flint's houseboat, he marked his imagined adaptations on a photograph of her, vividly describing her lines, and was furious when the flagpole was forgotten.

The *Gondola* in 1973.

My father took a picture of the *Gondola* as she was in the 1970s, when sadly she was too unseaworthy for the production team to contemplate using. In 2011 we went to see *TSSY Esperance* at the Windermere Steamboat Museum, another Victorian steam yacht envisaged by Ransome as a possible houseboat. It is a beauty but Claude enjoyed a better view of the lake from the large cabin windows of the *Lady Derwentwater*.

I have not been up to Derwentwater for a long time, but Claire Kendall-Price provides a wonderful map showing how you can walk from Keswick to find some of the film locations, in her book *In the Footsteps of the Swallows and Amazons*.

What the people of the Lake District most remember is how Bowness was transformed into Rio. Photographs of the set are still used to publicise local hotels. A member of The Arthur Ransome Society wrote to me: 'You were so lucky the old Victorian boatsheds were still there then, recorded forever more. How on Earth do people sanction such monstrosities as that which replaced them?'

Throughout the summer, rushbearing ceremonies are still held on saints' days at different churches in Cumbria, and are ever popular Christian celebrations. From Bowness you can take the native steamer *MV Tern* back down the 'wide open sea' to the railway station where our voyage of discovery began. Just beware of natives while you are waiting on the jetty.

Chapter Seventeen
Where Are They Now?

The Cast

Ronald Fraser

I have been told that long after the filming, when Ronald Fraser was having a pint with his friends, he was fond of muttering 'Natives!', especially if someone ate the last of his crisps. 'I've been propping up this bar *for yaahs and yaahs*,' he is quoted as having declared. In his era, booze and bars went with the territory.

Ronnie appeared in more than thirty feature films. It has to be said that *Swallows & Amazons*, along with *Wild Geese*, which he made in 1978, are the ones still being broadcast today. When he died in 1997 at the age of sixty-six, his coffin was carried by Sean Connery, Peter O'Toole, Simon Ward and Chris Evans – proving he always had time for people.

Virginia McKenna

I still see Virginia from time to time. She claims not to have done much acting since she played Polly in *The Camomile Lawn* in 1992, but in 2010 she starred with Keith Michell in *Love/ Loss*, appeared opposite Greg Canestrari in *Leona Calderon* in 2013, and was a bank robber called Martha alongside Bernard Hill in *Golden Years*, which is not bad for a great-grandmother.

Ever since meeting George Adamson in 1966 she has been pouring her energy into campaigning for the rights of captive animals. The Born Free Foundation, which she set up with Bill Travers and their son Will thirty years ago, takes her travelling all over the world, on missions to raise awareness and prevent animal suffering, protecting threatened species and keeping wildlife in the wild.

In 2004 Virginia was given an OBE in recognition of her work in the arts and wildlife conservation. She has written a number of books including *The Life in My Years*, in which she admits that the highlight of her acting career was probably spending sixteen months at the London Palladium in *The King and I* with Yul Brynner. She won an Olivier Award for Best Actress in a British Musical for the performance, which I saw in 1979 before working for a few months as her housekeeper, looking after Bill and her youngest son when she was on the stage.

Me and Suzanna.

Suzanna Hamilton

Suzanna did well, enjoying thirty good years as a leading movie actress, along with a variety of interesting roles on television. Photographs of her are stored at the National Portrait Gallery.

Simon and Suzanna.

Claude cast Suzanna as one of Queen Victoria's daughters in his fabulous costume drama *Disraeli*. She wore her lovely silken dresses with attitude and launched her adult career as a beauty of the screen. Soon she was appearing in classic movies such as Roman Polanski's *Tess* and *Brimstone & Treacle* with Sting. She starred as Julia in *1984* with John Hurt and Richard Burton, then appeared alongside Vanessa Redgrave and Tim McInnerny in David Hare's film *Wetherby*, before playing Felicity in Sydney Pollack's Academy Award-winning movie *Out of Africa* opposite Meryl Streep and Robert Redford. Lucky thing. She said that her finest hour has to be appearing in *The Wildcats of St Trinians*, but it is only one of the fourteen feature films and countless television dramas that she has contributed to.

Simon West

Simon had the lead role in a six-part BBC children's television drama called *Sam and the River,* broadcast in 1975, in which he played a teenager who thwarts a gang of diamond smugglers in London's docklands. He used his fees from acting to buy fibreglass sailing dinghies, in which he won the British Optimist Championships. Many people ask if he is the same Simon West, also born in 1961, who is now a Hollywood movie director with an impressive list of credits that include the *Lara Croft: Tomb Raider* movies and *Con Air*. But no, Captain John has an engineering business in England. Married with four children, he often spends his holidays hiking in the Lake District. He looks and sounds completely different from the brother I once knew so well. You'd never recognise him.

Sten Grendon

The last time I saw Jane Grendon was when a herd of cows escaped. She was there, knocking on our front door, looking just the same. She told me that Sten was living in a garden shed.

'He's a hermit.' She went on to say that he did the odd gardening job, but seemed happy to spend most of his time looking at beetles. 'He lives without running water or electricity but then he always has done. Even when he was at Pershore he lived in a bender in the woods.'

Apparently the staff at Pershore College of Horticulture had no idea that he was living in a homemade tent, a bender, in the college grounds. He spent years travelling across Spain, France and Morocco so probably cooked a great many meals over the camp fire. It seemed appropriate that the boy who loved apples became a fruit picker in France. I gather he became fluent in the language.

It was only when planners from the local council noticed that Sten was making his shed look quite nice, and made a fuss about it becoming established as a residential property, that he was served with eviction orders. There was a concern that his place of abode did not meet living standards since he only used water from a spring. There were access issues. The shed measured 13.9 foot by 19 foot with an outside earth closet but the issue went to the High Court. Before he knew it, Sten was in the newspapers again:

'Hermit makes new bid to stay in woodland hut.' None of the papers raised the fact that he had acted as a child. *The Telegraph* finally ran the headline: 'Hermit wins four year battle against eviction from his hut,' while the BBC News website stated: 'Stone hut man wins eviction fight.' He'd won.

When Sten came to supper recently, I found we had an unexpected closeness. This was probably forged during our time spent together in small tents and boats, overcoming adversity.

Kit Seymour

Kit is still sporty and difficult to pin down. 'Just back from camping in Scotland,' she'll report. 'Must be up at 5.30am to go running, as I'm competing in the local half-marathon.' Then she'll be off to Australia for a year. Happily married, hair cut short, Kit can still be seen on a boat.

Suzanna said she was walking down a lane once when a cyclist came towards her. 'I thought, that looks just like Kit, and it was.'

I'd heard she was working as a tree surgeon, but Kit told me that although she's up to felling the odd tree, she's a landscape gardener with an interest in interiors. People are surprised that she didn't go on to make more films but it was never on her agenda, she just loved sailing. Acting was not really her thing. She loathed the publicity.

Lesley Bennett

Lesley went into marketing, working for Unilever on the international launch of Cornetto ice cream. With a love of travelling and meeting people from other cultures, she moved to Holland in the early 1980s, married a Dutchman and now has two grown sons who are doing well. They spent a year in Dubai but are back living in the Netherlands where she works for a university, co-ordinating international research programmes and events. She never tires of discovering new places and learning more about how different people live their lives.

Martin Neville

Of all those who appeared in the film, it was actually my father whose career was launched, albeit inadvertently. He didn't become an actor until years later, after he retired from business at the age of sixty-two, but when he did he needed plenty of credits on his CV to gain an Equity card.

After *Swallows*, Daddy was featured in Claude's Weetabix advertisement. He used his fee of £25 to buy an old Massey Ferguson tractor. Since he looked like an archetypal Englishman, vaguely resembling Richard Briers, Dad ended up with small parts in quite a few movies. Early on, he was given the role of Hugh Lutteridge on a Touchstone-Disney movie shot at Broughton Castle called *Three Men and a Little Lady*, starring Tom Selleck, Steve Guttenberg and Ted Danson. It was a huge box office success. He was then an Ambassador in *An Ideal Husband* for the director Oliver Parker. It featured Rupert Everett, Minnie Driver and Julianne Moore. Opportunities kept coming along. He enjoyed being Queen Victoria's butler at Windsor Castle in *Mrs Brown* with Judi Dench and Billy Connolly – who winked at him whenever things got too serious. Dad was happy to be appointed Prison Governor in *Feast of July* for Merchant Ivory, as Mum was also in it. He later played the vicar in *The Clandestine Marriage*, directed by Christopher Miles. It starred Nigel Hawthorne, Joan Collins and Timothy

Spall. But my father's grandest part was possibly playing a peer of the realm in *Onegin,* starring Ralph Fiennes.

After getting into the swing of playing estate agents, solicitors and postmen who never said very much, Dad had a bit of a shock. He arrived in Edinburgh to appear in a drama called *The Dinosaur Hunters* that was being shot at the Royal College of Surgeons, to find he had to learn sixteen pages of dialogue by the next morning. It was quite complicated, full of Victorian intellectual statements about reptiles and their dentition. The other actors rallied round and kindly helped him to deliver the lines with rather a desperate but genuine sincerity.

Jane Grendon and Dad in Claude's Weetabix commercial.

The Crew

Daphne Neville – Chaperone

My mother relentlessly pursued a career in television. In the early 1980s she worked in the region which had since become Cumbria as a newsreader and continuity announcer for Border Television, which she loved. She became infamous for pronouncing Cockburnspath exactly as it is written during a late night evening bulletin, rather than Coburnspath, as the locals pronounce it. She could never see why anyone found this amusing.

She also had small parts in a number of feature films, including *The Invisible Woman* about the life of Charles Dickens, *The Old Curiosity Shop*, *Amazing Grace* and *Summer in February*, but probably became best-known just for crying a great deal in the television series *Prime Suspect*, starring Helen Mirren. Late in life she became an internet sensation for staggering off to Amsterdam to sample marijuana at a cafe with two friends for a television programme presented by Barry Humphries called *A Granny's Guide to the Modern World*. 'I've had nine million hits,' she told me with pride. 'I'm not sure what kind of hits these are but it is considered impressive.'

Mum went into otter conservation and spent more than thirty-five years lecturing the public on clean water issues. This came about after my sister wanted to hand-rear a little Asian short-clawed otter called Bee. She became exceptionally tame and appeared in a number of films, including *Tarka the Otter*. Other otters we kept appeared in *All Creatures Great and Small*, *The Durrells*, *Down to Earth*, *Scottish Mussel* and natural history programmes including *Velvet Claw* and *A Day in the Life*. Eventually, Sue Tully cast Mum in a role where she handled her own baby otter in *The Chase*, a drama series about a veterinary practice.

Daphne Neville at Border Television.

Ronnie Cogan – Hairdresser

Mum said that she bumped into Ronnie in Oxford Street but heard soon afterwards that he had sadly died. He must be hugely missed. He'd worked on classics such as *The Boys from Brazil* with Sir Laurence Olivier and *A Bridge Too Far* directed by Richard Attenborough. That must have been quite something. *A Bridge Too Far* starred Sean Connery, Michael Caine and Ryan O'Neal, who I am sure would have been pretty concerned about being given standard issue WWII military haircuts. Ronnie also worked for Roland Joffe on *The Killing Fields*, and Kenneth Branagh when he had quite an alarming hair-do, the historical pudding-basin, for his monumental film of Shakespeare's *Henry V*. It is funny how things interconnect. Kenneth Branagh played my great-uncle, A.O. Neville, in *The Rabbit-Proof Fence*.

Peter Robb-King – Make-up

Peter worked with Ronnie Cogan again when he was the chief make-up artist on *Diana: Her True Story*, the biopic based on Andrew Morton's outrageous book. Serena Scott Thomas played Diana Princess of Wales, David Threlfall was Prince Charles, Anthony Calf had the glorious opportunity to play James Hewitt, and my mother was given the role of Diana's nanny, who hit her on the head with a wooden spoon. Having worked on movies such as *Indiana Jones and the Temple of Doom*, *Batman Begins* and *The Dark Knight*, he is still involved with the most glamorous feature films. He recently completed *The Cabin in the Woods* where he was Sigourney Weaver's personal make-up artist – and there you go! He was once mine.

Emma Porteous – Costume Designer

Emma went on to work on many Bond movies, including *Octopussy*, *A View to a Kill* and *The Living Daylights*. She worked on *Aliens*, *Judge Dredd* and, guess what? – the menacing film *1984*, which starred Suzanna Hamilton. This was partly made near my home in Gloucestershire – Mum visited the set at Hullavington. Of all the costumes worn in movies throughout the decades, Zanna wore a classic – a workman's boiler-suit. Not designed by Emma Porteous, of course, but by George Orwell. Nice and comfy for wearing on location, but a difficult garment in which to appear graceful and elegant.

Terry Smith – Wardrobe Master

Terry went on to work on some outstanding costume dramas, including *Chariots of Fire, Lady Jane, Restoration* and *Willow*. He lost his life to cancer in 2012.

Mum's tame otter Bee was auditioned to be in *Willow*. I've written about it in my book *Funnily Enough*. Mum was most indignant because they wanted her otter to wear a tutu. She didn't know that Terry Smith was to be the wardrobe assistant. It might have made a difference. Instead they featured Val Kilmer in dialogue with a possum.

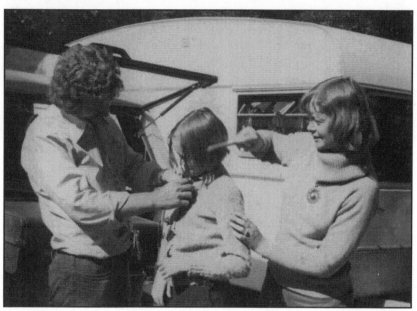

With Mum and Terry Smith.

Albert Clarke – Stills Photographer

Albert was later the stills photographer on *The Hound of the Baskervilles* – where Ian Richardson played Sherlock Holmes – *Return of the Jedi*, and *Porridge*, which starred my all-time hero Ronnie Barker, the man who inspired me to go into television production.

Brian Doyle by the houseboat.

Brian Doyle – Publicist

Brian also died at a relatively young age, collapsing after a heart attack in 2008. His daughter, Pandora, told me that he left a collection of 35,000 books, which she didn't quite know what to do with. Editor of *The Who's Who of Children's Literature* published in 1968, he always adored the Arthur Ransome books. He'd had extraordinary opportunities, going on to work on films such as Ken Russell's *Valentino* with Rudolf Nureyev and Leslie Caron, *Educating Rita* starring Michael Caine and Julie Walters, and the James Bond movie *For Your Eyes Only*, with Roger Moore was in the lead role. Brian even had his name on the credits of one of George Lucas's *Star Wars* films.

Michael Bradsell – Film Editor

Michael went on to edit many great movies: *Local Hero* for David Puttnam; Patsy Kensit's first feature film *Absolute Beginners*; and *Wilde*, which starred Stephen Fry.

Bill Rowe – Dubbing Mixer

I read that Bill Rowe was the director of Post Production and Sound at Elstree Studios until he died at the age of only sixty. He'd worked on over 150 films between 1961 and 1992, winning an Oscar for *The Last Emperor* and BAFTAs for *The Killing Fields, The French Lieutenant's Woman* and *Alien*, with nominations for *Chariots of Fire, A Clockwork Orange, The Mission* and *Batman*. And to think, we had played Hide and Seek behind his sound drapes.

Wilfred Josephs – Composer

Wilfred also composed the theme music for *Enemy at the Door, The Prisoner, Pollyanna*, and, perhaps most memorably of all, the stirring theme for *I, Claudius*. He worked for Claude on the movie score for *All Creatures Great and Small* that starred Simon Ward, as well as the television drama *W. Somerset Maugham* and the serial *Disraeli*. Wilfred was prolific, composing many classical works, including twelve symphonies and twenty-two concertos, as well as the opera *Rebecca* and the ballet *Cyrano de Bergerac*. The Wilfred Josephs Society was founded to promote interest in his music after he died at the age of seventy.

Marcus Dods – Conductor

Marcus, a regular collaborator with Wilfred, died in 1984 after contributing to many memorable film scores, including *Yanks, Watership Down, Murder on the Orient Express, Death on the Nile, Life of Brian, The Great Muppet Caper* and *The Dark Crystal*, as well as David Attenborough's groundbreaking TV documentary series *Life on Earth*.

Simon Holland – Art Director

After leaving Westmorland, Simon progressed onto legendary motion pictures – *Callan* with Edward Woodward, *Equus*, and *Reds* with Warren Beatty. Mum and I met him again on location near Bath, when we took part in *Agatha*, the story about Agatha Christie, starring Dustin Hoffman and Timothy Dalton. By the 1980s Simon was working on huge projects including *The Emerald Forest* with John and Charley Boorman, *Buster* with Phil Collins, and *Scandal* with Joanne Whalley and Bridget Fonda. His last film as production designer was *Tales of the Riverbank*, voiced by Jim Broadbent and Miranda Hart.

Ian Whittaker – Set Dresser

Ian, who spent his time making little stone walls to keep our perch alive, did prove himself to his family. After *Swallows*, he worked on Ridley

Clutching bottles of grog in Woodland Road, Windermere.

Scott's film *Alien*, and was nominated for an Oscar with the others on the design team. Eventually he won the Oscar for Best Art Direction-Set Decoration with the designer Luciana Arrighi for *Howard's End* – the movie of E.M. Forster's book starring Anthony Hopkins, Emma Thompson and Helena Bonham-Carter.

In 1994 Ian was nominated again, this time for Merchant Ivory's *The Remains of the Day*. After that he worked with Emma Thompson again on *Sense and Sensibility*, the 1995 movie of the Jane Austen classic that helped launch Kate Winslet's career, some of which was shot at Montacute in Somerset where my great-grandmother lived. Ian received yet another Oscar nomination for *Anna and the King* in 2000 and a nomination for an Emmy Award for the TV movie *Into the Storm* in 2009.

Bob Hedges – Action Props

Bobby Props later worked with some of the other *Swallows* crew members on *The Rocky Horror Picture Show*, *Julia*, *The Shout* and *Midnight Express*, as well as *Scum*, *Breaking Glass*, *Excalibur*, and *The Wildcats of St Trinians* with Suzanna.

Terry Wells – Stand-by Props

Terry Wells is listed as having been the property master on well-known movies such as *The Mission, Braveheart, Cry Freedom, Quadrophenia, Full Metal Jacket*, and the most recent *Robin Hood* starring Russell Crowe and Cate Blanchett, as well as TV series such as *Holby City* and *The Increasingly Poor Decisions of Todd Margaret*.

Gareth Tandy – Third Assistant Director

If I'm not mistaken, *Swallows & Amazons* was Gareth's first film as an assistant director, but it got his foot in the door. He has many chart-topping movies on his CV – the original *Superman, Indiana Jones and the Last Crusade, The Bourne Identity, Charlie and the Chocolate Factory, Nanny McPhee, Johnny English Reborn*, and was the first assistant director on *A Fantastic Fear of Everything*. I remember Jean McGill making him wear a hat because he suffered from sunstroke.

Terry Needham – Second Assistant Director

Terry survived to have the most prestigious career in film. As well as fulfilling the role of assistant director for Stanley Kubrick on *The Shining*

Bob Hedges and Terry Wells carrying the parrot in his cage.

(would Jack Nicholson have been easier to manage than us lot?), Terry was unit manager on *Empire of the Sun* for Steven Spielberg, which was Christian Bale's first film as a child actor. Then Terry was first assistant director on such classic movies as *Rambo III, The Field, The Golden Compass* and *Clash of the Titans*. I only list a few of his many credits.

He worked for Ridley Scott as associate producer and first assistant on *White Squall, G.I. Jane, Gladiator, Hannibal* and *Black Hawk Down* – all gargantuan tasks – and was the executive producer of *Red Dragon* and *Kingdom of Heaven*, again for Ridley Scott. He is still working on movies. What changes must he have seen? I wonder if he can remember that far-distant summer spent in the Lake District.

David Bracknell – First Assistant Director

David led the crew of more *Carry On* films before working on both *The Sweeney* and *The Professionals*. He wrote and directed *The Chiffy Kids* in the late 1970s, and worked on *Shaka Zulu, Sword of the Valiant: the Legend of Sir Gawain and the Green Knight,* and the London sequences of *Indiana Jones and the Temple of Doom.*

Graham Ford – Production Manager

After *Swallows*, Graham Ford's ankle must have healed well, as he went on to work as the production manager on *S.O.S. Titanic, The Honorary Consul* and *Princess Daisy*, as well as *Time Bandits* and *Brazil* directed by Terry Gilliam. Imagine being Terry Gilliam's right-hand man! He was a location manager for David Lynch on *The Elephant Man* and for Richard Attenborough on *Gandhi* in 1982.

Graham's career progressed. He produced *The Nightmare Years* and *A Connecticut Yankee in King Arthur's Court* in the late 1980s, before working on *Gettysburg*, the massive four-hour-long movie about the American civil war. A life in film. He died in Ontario in 1994, aged only forty-eight.

Neville C. Thompson – Associate Producer

Neville Thompson also worked on *Time Bandits*. It featured Michael Palin, who then co-produced *The Missionary* with him. Films such as *The Mosquito Coast* with Harrison Ford, *Erik the Viking* with Tim Robbins, and TV movies *Sharpe's Rifles* and *Sharpe's Eagle* with Sean Bean, kept Neville busy in the 1980s. He remained great friends with

Richard Pilbrow, who still mourns his passing. Years later, when Richard flew over to visit his widow, he said that *Swallows & Amazons* was being shown on British television. It was somehow a tribute to all his hard work and determination.

Sue Merry – Continuity

Sue, our script supervisor, went on to work with Denis Lewiston and other members of our crew on *The Rocky Horror Picture Show*. Sue also did the continuity for Nicolas Roeg on *The Man Who Fell to Earth*, starring David Bowie, before moving into television to work on *The Professionals* and *The Comic Strip Presents*. . . . All quite high-profile.

David Cadwallader – Grip

David is still working as a grip, recently operating the crane on the 2011 movie of *Jane Eyre*, which starred Mia Wasikowska, Michael Fassbender and Jamie Bell. I'd been reading *Jane Eyre* in May 1973. It was my set book: my set book for school and the book I read on set. I should have been reading *Robinson Crusoe*.

Denis Lewiston – Director of Photography

Denis shot numerous other movies – *The Scarlet Pimpernel* with Anthony Andrews, Jane Seymour, Ian McKellen and Julian Fellowes, *The Country Girls* with Sam Neill, *The Thief of Baghdad* with Roddy McDowall, Terence Stamp and Peter Ustinov, *Heidi* with Patricia Neal and *A Man For All Seasons* with Charlton Heston, Vanessa Redgrave and Sir John Gielgud. I wonder if all those esteemed actors had to wait, shivering, while the clouds passed for him? He died in 2014, soon after approving StudioCanal's remastered 40th Anniversary version of our DVD.

David Blagden – Sailing Director

The huge sadness was that David, so vibrant and good-looking, with so much to live for, lost his life to the sea when he was very young.

After *Swallows & Amazons*, he presented an ITV series broadcast on Sundays called *Plain Sailing*, featuring *Willing Griffin*, the 19' Hunter in which he'd crossed the Atlantic despite horrific weather in 1972. The show also included the survey of a 39' wooden boat he intended to take on another crossing. Apparently he and his girlfriend set off in this yawl

David Blagden.

from Alderney in the Channel Islands in a Force 11 storm, and were never seen again. The harbourmaster had begged him not to go. They found his girlfriend's body and parts of the boat, but there was no trace of David Blagden.

David Wood – Screenplay

When I contacted David, he replied with an email telling me about his further *Swallows*-related activities:

> It was decided that *Great Northern?* should be the follow-up to the *Swallows* film, because it was 'different', being the only book set in Scotland. Also, the villainous birds' egg collector was a strong adult role – Peter Sellers was mentioned. . . . We had great fun looking for locations, swooping around in a helicopter over Harris, Lewis etc.
>
> Word got out that I was working on *Great Northern?* and I had a very firm letter from Mrs Ransome saying that no permission had been granted to work on this title, and that it would not be granted!! No reason was given. Years later, the Ransome autobiography suggested that Mrs R didn't like *Great Northern?* and criticised it to Ransome's face. Also, he

used to sometimes swan off to the Highlands with his friend, Quiller-Couch (the 'Q' so beloved by *84, Charing Cross Road* author Helene Hanff) to fish, leaving Evgenia on her own back in the Lake District. The only communication from him would be the occasional delivery on a horse and cart from the railway station of a salmon, caught in Scotland the day before! Maybe she resented Scotland for luring him away! But she was determined that *Great Northern?* the movie would never see the light of day. . . . I still wrote a complete screenplay!

I did a film treatment for *Winter Holiday* that never got off the ground.

Pigeon Post was to be a six-part serial, presumably for the Beeb. . . . I actually wrote all six episodes! But it didn't happen. Years later an independent TV producer called David asked to read them, but again nothing happened. Maybe they were terrible! But I remember the first time round we got as far as looking for locations.

We Didn't Mean to Go to Sea was also to be a serial. I did a treatment, visited Pin Mill and other locations, and met the man who built one of Ransome's boats, or maybe worked on it with his father.

I kept in touch with Claude. He is the only director for whom I worked as an actor on film (*Sweet William*), television (*Cheri, Disraeli*) and stage (*Voyage Round My Father*), as well as working with him as a writer (*Swallows* and a film that never got made called *The Heyday*).

Claude Whatham must have made the BBC adaptation of Colette's novel *Cheri* just before *Swallows & Amazons*, as it was broadcast in April 1973. Brenda Bruce, who I knew as Mrs Dixon, played Charlotte while David Wood was Desmond, supporting Scott Anthony and Yvonne Mitchell as the lovers Cheri and Lea. David later played Lord Derby in the 1978 BBC costume drama *Disraeli* that Claude directed as well.

David was awarded an OBE for services to Literature and Drama in 2004. His output has been prolific. He has adapted many books for the stage, including Roald Dahl's *The Witches* and *The BFG*, and *The Tiger Who Came to Tea* by Judith Kerr. *The Gingerbread Man*, which he wrote and scored in 1976, is perhaps his most well-known original musical. My mother appeared as Miss Pepper in a production at the Everyman Theatre in Cheltenham a few years later.

In April 2013, David's adaptation of Michelle Magorian's classic book *Goodnight Mister Tom* won the Olivier Award for Best Entertainment and Family and we were interviewed together on the series *Cinemaniacs* by Novel Entertainment for CBBC.

Richard Pilbrow – Producer

Richard Pilbrow never made another film, but in 1977 he produced a star-studded TV series with Neville Thompson, called *All You Need Is Love*. It followed the history of pop music from Liberace and Bo Diddley to The Beatles and The Rolling Stones.

Richard ended up designing theatres all over the world – about 1,700, including the Dolby Theatre where the Oscars were held. In 2011 he was given the Knights of Illumination Lifetime Recognition Award for more than fifty years of work in theatre lighting.

We had a serendipitous day just before Christmas 2012, when he flew over from the States with Molly to be presented with an Honorary Fellowship by the Royal Central School of Speech & Drama at the University of London graduation ceremony held in the Royal Festival Hall. Richard and Molly kindly asked Zanna and me to lunch in Covent Garden the next day. It was nearly forty years since we'd first met at Theatre Projects in the West End. Suzanna had also been a student at the Central School of Speech and Drama, and has since performed at the Royal Festival Hall.

Richard told us that the most difficult task of his life had been persuading Mrs Ransome to give him the film rights for *Swallows and Amazons*. As the waiter came around with coffee we asked Richard what she had thought of the finished film.

'She said that the kettle, packed by Susan at Holly Howe, was of the wrong period.' We laughed. 'She was quite right, of course,' Richard admitted. I later read that she did not think Ronald Fraser an appropriate person to play Captain Flint, but I am sure no one could have replaced her husband, who clearly had written himself into this character in his story.

An amazing thing happened almost straight after lunch. Suzanna was guiding me north, to the bus stop on Shaftesbury Avenue, when we came across a trio of Christmas singers, busking. As we approached them, they were singing, 'Oo-rey and up she rises, oo-rey and up she rises, oo-rey and up she rises early in the morning' – the song we sang on Captain Flint's houseboat at the end of the film. What are the chances of that? We hurried on, only to find ourselves opposite the Odeon cinema which had once been the ABC on Shaftesbury Avenue, where *Swallows & Amazons* was first shown in 1974.

Claude Whatham – Director

I last saw Claude on my wedding day. He died of cancer in 2008, aged eighty. Although he directed a huge number of dramas, *Cider with Rosie*, for which he received a BAFTA nomination, and *Swallows & Amazons* remain his best-known works, with terrific DVD sales. Somehow they never felt dated.

I had no idea how prolific Claude was until I read his obituary. He'd even painted murals for the Queen – or, rather, for Princess Elizabeth. As a young art student he'd been commissioned to paint theatrical scenes in a hall at Windsor Castle in place of portraits that had been removed for safe-keeping during the Blitz. He didn't see this as at all unusual.

Claude's secret was that he had the self-confidence to succeed. Starting his career as a scenic artist at the Oldham Rep, he soon became a production designer at Granada Television in Manchester. By the age of thirty he was directing television programmes, pushing out the boundaries of what could be achieved on screen. Single-minded and determined, yet usually coming across as relaxed, he fulfilled his dream to become a movie director in 1972 at the age of forty-five. David Wood told me that he'd actually been the second director appointed to work on *Swallows*, which stunned me. I would never have appeared in the film if he hadn't been casting it.

Claude was always happy working outdoors on what he called 'a picture' – and by that he meant a feature film – preferably in summertime, wearing nothing but a pair of blue shorts, a big smile and someone else's hat. All his period dramas are marked by a timeless quality. His classic sense of style simply never dated. He once told a reporter called Tom Parkinson that *Swallows & Amazons* was 'the happiest filming I've ever done. I grew very close to the children and even now I feel a responsibility for them. They write to me frequently. Some of them intend to continue in the business and one of them, a girl, has a rare talent.'

Chapter Eighteen
What Sophie Did Next

People ask what effect the feature film has had on my life. There were aspects of being labelled a 'child star' which were not easy to cope with. I survived at school by never talking about filming unless I was specifically asked. This wasn't easy, as I was bubbling over with stories, but I knew that modesty was imperative. Almost anything that I said about filming could have been construed as braggish. I did not care to imagine the consequences of this. As it happened, I didn't have to. My friends were generous and strangers polite. Even today people ask if I mind talking about my role in the film.

It is amazing that people take so much interest in the old film. Initially it felt weird being applauded for something I only spent nine weeks of my life working on. I never once thought that I deserved the attention. People wanted to know if the movie made me money.

'Didn't you earn a packet from residuals?'

I was paid £45 a week during the filming – £7.50 per day. This was on the basis that our legal agreement specified that we were only meant to work for three hours a day. Our film extras earned £5 a day. The parrot accrued a grand total of £25, which his owner spent on a new cage. We received nothing for the soundtrack album, television or video rights, or for the DVD later on. There were no residuals. I was only a child; being paid at all seemed incredible. Sten wanted to buy the biggest Lego set in the world with his pay. My riding teacher tried to persuade me to buy a decent horse, but instead my earnings were tucked into Unit Trusts, which devalued during the inflation years of the late 1970s. In the end I used my fee to buy an air ticket to Australia, where I enjoyed learning to dive on the Great Barrier Reef. This seemed appropriate as Titty loved diving and would have been excited to see real sharks. The place was stiff with them.

When I was fifteen I took the lead in another children's feature film, *The Copter Kids* with Sophie Ward and Vic Armstrong, for which I was paid even less. Donald Alexander wrote to say that his friend Ronnie Fraser, who he remembered as 'a great eccentric, wit, raconteur and heroic imbiber', had put Lesley and me forward for a children's film: 'He was impressed with you ("huge comic potential") and the younger Amazon ("expressive eyes").... However, it had come to nothing through funding problems.'

Instead I appeared in a number of television dramas including the 'Charley Farley and Piggy Malone' serial within *The Two Ronnies*, which was fun. Until then, I hadn't realised that Ronnie Barker both directed and appeared in the series. I put on round glasses, a yashmak, and a Southern American accent borrowed from Molly Friedel for my role, and learned that it was not impossible to make the transition from acting to working behind the camera.

With Ronnie Corbett in *The Two Ronnies: 'Band of Slaves'* in 1981.

Mum kept her letters, my diaries and scrapbooks in what must have been the smart carrier bag from Carnaby Street that had held the expensive velvet dress. What I hadn't recognised, until I started delving through the photographs, was how themes from Arthur Ransome's life seemed to have continued through mine. Odd things floated to the surface. When the time came for me to matriculate I went to Collingwood College at the University of Durham. The name 'Collingwood' resonated when I discovered that W.G. Collingwood's family were connected with

Swallows and Amazons. I had that odd feeling of liquid flowing down my back when I discovered that he was an artist who had studied at the Slade. My grandfather, H.W. Neville, went there in 1892, not that long afterwards.

Arthur Ransome gained a Kitchener Scholarship. Years later one of these rare awards was won by my niece. It took her to the Ruskin School of Art in Oxford. W.G. Collingwood had been John Ruskin's secretary at Brantwood on the banks of Coniston Water. He painted him at his desk there. When Arthur Ransome first lived in London, he had digs in Hollywood Road. When I moved to London I shared flats with friends just up the street.

I don't know if Claude ever remembered me writing, but when the film ended, he kindly sent me an engraved Parker pen and propelling pencil. I loved the pen and wrote all my essays at University with it. Sadly I lost it just before my finals, but I still have the pencil. Somewhere.

After graduating with a BA Honours in Anthropology, I entered the BBC as a researcher. Having spent three months working on the chat show *Russell Harty*, my life came around in a circle: I started casting children for a television serial based on the two Arthur Ransome books set on the Norfolk Broads: *Coot Club* and *The Big Six*. It was not a chance thing: I contacted the producer, Joe Waters, and asked if I could work on the series, but the fact that I'd heard about it was serendipitous as it was made in the year when I was available to join the production team. I would never have been given the job of casting had I not been on the General Trainee Scheme, and if the director had not joined the team unusually late. I discovered that Rosemary Leach was to play the Admiral – Mrs Barrable. One could almost say that Claude launched both our careers, as she had starred, not as Missee Lee, but as Mrs Lee in *Cider with Rosie* all those years before, when I played Eileen Brown.

Since Theatre Projects still owned the rights to the Arthur Ransome books, Richard and Molly came to visit us when we were filming *Coot Club*. They had married, and brought along their baby, Daisy. Although our two stories were set in Norfolk, the series was titled *Swallows and Amazons Forever!* as there were great hopes to adapt as many of the books as possible.

I visited Suzanna's old drama club when I was casting the children. Anna Scher ran the children's theatre in Islington that Suzanna went to after school, along with the young Pauline Quirke and Linda Robson, who as adults starred in the popular BBC sitcom *Birds of a Feather*. Although I didn't find anyone there who could sail, I learned from Anna myself and used her acting exercises when I was auditioning kids in East Anglia.

When *Swallows and Amazons Forever!* was broadcast, a viewer wrote in to ask if 'Sophie Neville, who is credited as a Researcher on the series, is the same Sophie who appeared as Titty in the feature film' – they had noticed. The letter was published in the *Radio Times*.

We were planning to make adaptations of *Swallowdale* and *Pigeon Post*, which are both set in the Lake District. I was hoping to cast the Amazons – if not all the children – from schools in Cumbria. I don't expect Claude had had the time to do that. Joe Waters went on a recce looking for locations with his production associate. They returned with long faces. The series was going to be prohibitively expensive. The National Trust were asking for location fees of £1,000 per day, even for filming on open moorland.

Since BBC Drama Series and Serials had no need for a children's casting director, I was out of a job. Instead, the manager of the department recommended that to gain experience in drama production I should start again as a runner. That is what I did.

The 'hanging around' aspect of filming that had bored and frustrated us as children completely evaporated once I became a third assistant director. Any time I was able to relax on set was treasured, absolutely relished. When doing Gareth Tandy's job, I rarely had a chance to take the weight off my feet. Celebrations for reaching the 500th slate soon seemed paltry. I went on to work on drama serials with so many episodes that they would have amounted to films four or five hours long.

I then became an assistant floor manager with camera-tape in hand. The BBC's equivalent to a second assistant director, I was also responsible for the action props working alongside one or two prop men. The few times that continuity props were forgotten or mislaid are painfully etched on my memory. That awful feeling, when a lost item like a wallet or car keys affects others, is magnified hugely when so many people are involved. Someone once stole the soap from the set of a drama I worked on. The prop buyer was furious. I quickly made up something that looked like the original, but I couldn't do the same when our prop man lost Gerald Durrell's pre-war binoculars on the island of Corfu during the filming of *My Family and Other Animals*. I remember him turning out his van in despair before finding them carefully stored in bubble-wrap behind the driver's seat.

I would not have had the physical strength to follow in Terry Needham's footsteps. It was his job – along with the action props and set dressing – that I was busy doing when I worked as an assistant floor manager on big costume dramas. I was exhausted after about four years. The walkie-talkie I had found so attractive aged twelve, became rather heavy on

Filming *My Family and Other Animals* on Corfu in 1987.

the hip. I have a Polaroid photograph that I kept of myself looking tired when I was working as a location manager in Bayswater, just to remind me not to accept the job again. Perhaps I should have taken the Bette Davis route after all. I might have had Terry looking after me.

I spent many months at Elstree Studios at Borehamwood when I worked in television production, this time at the BBC Studios across the road, where we recorded episodes of *EastEnders* and the wartime romance *Bluebell*, programmes that were never post-synced as *Swallows & Amazons* was. I'd drive past the old EMI-MGM Studios and never breathe a word that I'd worked there once as a child actress, re-dubbing my own lines.

The little pug we chose to play William, the hero of *Coot Club*, was appearing on *EastEnders* as Ethel's 'Little Willie'. It was so good to see him again. He was a playful little dog with a great sense of fun.

I was once walking along a path in our field at home when I saw what looked like a broken rubber fan-belt. I walked directly towards it, intending to pick it up, when I realised it was not a fan-belt but an adder. Young Billy's warning was ringing in my ears. The first documentary I directed for the BBC involved an adder. I was filming at a nature reserve in Dorset with a group of children who came across one immediately. It was huge, a black adder. The Billies would have declared this a great sign of luck.

With film editor Dave Good at Lime Grove Studios.

I'm not sure I thought much about *Swallows & Amazons* over the next few years, but I did produce an INSET documentary at a school in North Lancashire and loved being back in the Lakes. When I saw my first 'Producer' billing in the *Radio Times*, I was stunned to see my credit for *Swallows & Amazons* on the opposite page. There seemed to be no escape. Immediately afterwards, I bumped into my Head of Department in the lift. He enthusiastically asked to see my VHS tape. I thought he was referring to the series I had just produced, but all he wanted was a copy of *Swallows & Amazons* for his kids.

I've always thought that improvisation can be magical. When I started to direct dramas I made a short film on school bullies called *The Way People Talk* that turned out to be very powerful, purely because I let the children improvise. The only problem was that it came across as almost too frighteningly real. Although short scenes always worked well, it was up to me to write the story as we went along, which could be daunting.

When I went on a studio directors' course I tried improvising a scene where a couple go camping in true Mike Leigh style. I asked the actors to erect a tent, and left them to it while I spoke to the cameramen from the gallery, as normal, via intercom, with the vision mixer at my side, who also improvised. I used a dome tent of my own and had shown the couple just how easy it was to collapse it on top of them, to provide a comic moment at the end of the scene. This worked well. Once they grasped the

At Elstree Studios on the BBC Drama
Studio Directors' course.

idea, I ended up with the longest studio show-reel of all time.

I didn't need the help of visual FX for that story. I knew exactly how to bring down a tent. I never forgot the tricks that Terry Wells demonstrated with props, such as extended use of fishing line. People still ask me about the sequence in which the arrows were fired over our heads.

Ever mindful of my wooden performance in the train, I tried to schedule unimportant, 'running around' scenes first when directing serials that featured children. They learned about taking cues and could get used to working with the crew before tight close-ups and high drama were required. Even six-year-olds were unfazed by recording scenes out of story order; in fact they were probably less disorientated than the adults. I worked out that young people are naturally able to take direction and cope with action props with far more dexterity than older and more experienced actors. Their brains are still agile.

I started to direct on Beta-cam, attempting to shoot quite long scenes on a single shot by using a 'jib-arm' and camera track to move the camera. This was all the rage in the late 1980s. I remember using one long shot for the opening scene of a comedy drama called *Thinkabout Science* that starred Patsy Byrne – she who had become known to the nation as Nursie in the Rowan Atkinson sitcom *Blackadder II*.

In my little series, Patsy played a grandmother collecting two sisters and their friends from school. The children poured out of the front door, down some steps, met their granny and chatted to her as they skipped along the pavement. I had about 120 metres of camera track laid down the street, far more than any scene on *Swallows & Amazons*. We had a rehearsal and

On location in London
with Patsy Byrne.

shot the three-minute scene. It worked perfectly. It was fresh and funny and active. I was all set to move the whole crew to the next location when my producer descended from the scanner, the truck where she was watching on three monitors, to tell me that one of the extras had waved at the camera. I should have recorded the rehearsal. It took us twelve more takes to get the scene right after that. Luckily Beta tape costs were negligible in comparison with the Technicolor stock that Claude had been using.

Did the wishful lines given to Titty cast light on my future? After working at the BBC for eight years I fell ill and, much like Arthur Ransome, had to abandon my full-time job to work from home. My mother had an uncle junketing around in Africa, just like Captain Flint. I had a yearning for the great wilderness and soon set off to explore southern Africa with friends, camping and cooking on fires. I often saw Meyer's parrots in the palm trees above our camp in Botswana. They would clatter about looking for wild dates, while I sat painting just as Titty would have done.

Of all the subjects I'd studied at university, the ones I'd most enjoyed were cartography and water-colours. I started to earn my living by drawing birds, animals and decorative maps. The maps usually depicted game reserves and involved giving names to landmarks as places of interest. I must have drawn forty maps in the style of those on the original cover of *Swallows and Amazons*, using the same borders and design of lettering. I think that the chart on the cover of the first edition , originally drawn by Steven Spurrier, has been an inspiration to millions. I've gazed and gazed at it. Mine were all very much like Spurrier's. I added small pictures of settlements, trees, animals, and always a compass with a black and white border to give the scale. In the process, I was able to explore the most wonderful country. I have mapped areas of the Okavango Delta in Botswana, the Waterberg Plateau in South Africa, one of the Malilangwe Conservation Trust in Zimbabwe and a map showing how to cross the Namib Desert on a horse. I have also drawn maps of military zones, ski resorts and stately homes. Some have been for charities such as Save the Rhino Trust, others to illustrate books, others for marketing holidays. They have all given me the excuse to go on living a *Swallows and Amazons* lifestyle, camping in wild places and exploring wilderness areas – charting uncharted territory.

I then started writing about these maps and the adventures I had in making them. I'd sketch small scenes from the back of a horse or in a vehicle so I could add drawings of tents or remarkable trees to the finished book. I've since learned that Arthur Ransome worked in this

Sketching in Africa.

way. Soon I was migrating back and forth to the southern hemisphere literally with the swallows. It became a bit of a to-and-froing kind of life, but I was used to that. While I was travelling, I kept diaries or logs; *Mixed Moss by a Rolling Stone*, as Captain Flint would say.

I also freelanced for the BBC, mainly setting up wildlife programmes. A wry smile did pass my lips when I was asked to find South African items for *Blue Peter*. I was thinking back to my first interview at Theatre Projects with Claude Whatham, when he asked me what my favourite television programme was. After a while I fell into the pattern of flying back to England at Easter time and returning to Africa in the autumn like a migratory bird. This was partly through choice, partly to comply with visa regulations and work commitments.

What I have found really does shock people – shocks them so much that they admit to being shocked – is that I was once a missionary in Africa and Australia. I think they believe I tried to convert the natives, but of course it is not like that. You go, not knowing what will happen, and find yourself making life a bit more fun for people who belong to God but might be having a hard time, just as the Swallows managed to cheer up the Amazons who had been rejected by their uncle. I still go on short-term missions. We went to China with the Bible Society one March on a mission of encouragement that Titty would have loved. We met Christians who had not had European visitors for forty years. They

In rural China in 2011.

were excited to know that people in the wider world were interested in their welfare and had come to celebrate the word of God with them. The Chinese told us that the only Westerners they had seen before us were there to make money. Shocking, isn't it? Two of Arthur Ransome's aunts were missionaries in Peking at the turn of the last century. One was hit in her bonnet by an arrow during the Boxer Uprising.

What amazed me was that a few of the *Swallows & Amazons* fans followed the career I had in television behind the camera, noting when I appeared on the credits of *Doctor Who* or *One by One*, and would write very considerate letters telling me how Titty had been an inspiration for so much in their lives.

I came across a few perverts along the trail. It was the navy-blue elasticated gym knickers that did it. I could probably make a small fortune by selling them online. Someone in a sharp suit, who should have known better, started to tell me a tale about having appeared in a film as a cabin boy when he was young. I was obliged to hear how he'd been whipped before the mast before being keel-hauled. Deary me. I escaped unscathed but reported him to the police on the grounds that he seemed a bit of a liability.

I try to visit the Lake District whenever I can grab the chance. It is so good to be able to stay at Holly Howe. Mrs Batty explained to me that the bay window at Bank Ground Farm leaked terribly and she was glad to get rid of it. She built a dedicated *Swallows and Amazons* room instead where you can read books and drink tea. I was chatting to her back in 2003 when we were waiting for Ben Fogle and the BBC crew of *Countryfile* to return from looking for other locations used in the film, before interviewing Suzanna and myself at the farm. The only problem was that Zanna's train was terribly delayed. We waited and waited and waited for her. It got later and later. When her taxi finally arrived I was so excited, I made her run down the field to the lake and climb into *Amazon*, moored by the jetty. The poor director must have been at her wit's end. Ben Fogle had to come down to fetch us. My excuse was that Suzanna must have needed a stretch after such a long journey. I couldn't quite explain that running back into our childhood was something we had to do. The *Westmorland Gazette* captured the three of us plodding back up the field before we sat on the grass for our interview. I did the whole piece holding a bottle of grog given to me by Arthur Ransome enthusiasts staying at the farm. I don't think the director realised what it was.

It was into this profile of the movie presented by Ben Fogle that my father's 16mm behind-the-scenes footage of *Swallows & Amazons* was cut, with such success that the documentary was screened as both *Country Tracks*, a programme on the Lake District, and *Big Screen Britain*, a series about six all-time classic films shot on location in the United Kingdom. Both included interviews with Claude, Lucy Batty and Alan Smith, who had appeared as an Extra in one of the Rio scenes and is now an established presenter on Radio 4.

In 2005 I met Dr Bill Frankland, a former prisoner of war in Singapore, who was to become the historical consultant on a script I was developing. A Harley Street allergist, he mentioned that it was not advisable to keep a parrot in the house. Incredibly, I soon learned that Bill had been a good friend of Roger Altounyan, and had known his sister Titty. As young men they'd both worked for Alexander Fleming. I knew that Roger had taught fighter pilots for the RAF in World War II, but not that he had qualified as a doctor, and also became an allergist. He used his knowledge of propellers to develop the Intal spin-inhaler and effectively treat asthma. Having discovered that guinea pigs made him wheeze, he would experiment on himself – and was portrayed by David Suchet in a docudrama entitled *Hair Soup*, that was produced at the instigation of Barbara Altounyan. I was allergic to feathers as a child and prone to horrific asthma attacks, not from parrot feathers but old pillows and eiderdowns. I probably owe my life to Roger and his spin-inhaler. Nothing else brought peace to my lungs.

The asthma experimentation was responsible for Roger Altounyan's early death in 1987. Dr Frankland gave me a set of photos from his going-away party in the Lake District, when Roger insisted on smoking a pipe even while being reliant on oxygen.

What hugely influenced my life were the Amazons' bows and arrows. I, too, learned to shoot in front of the red double-decker buses, which proved useful when I auditioned to play Liz Peters, the archery champion in *The Copter Kids*. I had proper lessons for this, and reached a reasonable standard. As a result, many years later, I became Lady Champion of both the Worcestershire and West Berks archery societies and won the ladies' prize at the Woodmen of Arden.

Deb-archery.

About a week after I met my husband at an archery meeting, a lady arrived from Taiwan. She timidly knocked on the door, explaining that she was translating *Swallows and Amazons* into Chinese and would love to talk to me about the book. She came bearing gifts: a hand-quilted wedding bedspread and a pile of silk garments amounting to a bride's trousseau. At that stage my husband-to-be had not even thought of writing to thank me for making the scary speech for the prize-giving tea, and I had no idea we would marry.

For all this serendipity, the film did not loom large in my life until 2010 when my father alerted me to the fact that the dinghy used as the little ship *Swallow* in the feature film was up for auction. I found myself joining a group of film fans who clubbed together to purchase her. She has been renovated quite beautifully, and equipped so that anyone can take her out on the water. We took her to the London Boat Show in 2011, so that others could admire her varnish. My mother arrived with her old photographs and a DVD of the ciné footage taken behind the scenes. Quite a storm whipped up with everyone wanting to see more. I ended up looking for the Carnaby Street bag and sorting through my diaries, searching for the secrets of filming *Swallows & Amazons*.

Farewell and Adieu

I always feel a bit odd when people are expecting to see me as Titty, as they did when they came to pay homage to *Swallow* at the Boat Show. I'm not so very old, but I certainly look different from when I was only twelve. This always happens when I return to Westmorland. Everyone is a bit taken aback by my height:

'Eeh, lass, you've grown! But you sound juss the same!'

It is a bit like when Peter Pan flew back to see Wendy and found she looked just like her mother. Not that this phases the Japanese:

'Aa Titty! Titty! Titteee!' they exclaim, to the amazement of innocent bystanders. I still receive e-mails from Tokyo where I am assured there are more than two hundred fans.

'It is a great honour of me,' a girl called Tamami wrote. '. . . We LOVE your Titty very much.'

Americans tend to be more circumspect, asking politely if I have ever worked in the film industry before clasping me in a big friendly hug and declaring, 'Hey, but I knew Titty was around.' In France recently, a man I had never met before came over and greeted me as Titty, chatting away as if he knew me quite well. He paused for a moment, apologised and then went right on calling me Titty.

One very cold winter I went on a weekend with my friends from church. It was freezing. We found ourselves being invited in for tea and hot toast by a kind lady who had never met any of us and yet was more than generous with her hospitality. She started looking at me intently.

'You look just like the little girl in *Swallows & Amazons*,' she said.

'I *was* the little girl in *Swallows & Amazons*,' I admitted. She burst into tears. She'd always wanted to meet me and there I was, sitting by her fire.

I returned home to find *Swallows & Amazons* was being broadcast on television, twice on the same weekend. People often ask what it feels like to watch myself on screen. It can be poignant. There I am, my childhood distilled and preserved in bright sunlight. It is me, but it's not me. Me playing Titty, Suzanna being sensible and Susan-ish and poor Daddy watching us so very nearly hitting the steamer, the memory of which still takes my breath away.

'And we may never see you fair ladies again,' goes the sea shanty. As we get older it is the music that takes me back to those days on the lakes. I still have two little flags made by Bobby Props, two arrows winged with green feathers and even a bow I made myself from a hazel sapling and string. I treasure all the affection bestowed on us by everyone who signed my copy of the book. They have nearly all gone, those who worked so hard to bring the enduring sequences to the screen, but being so unusually young when the film was made, we Swallows and Amazons will hopefully be around to mark the 50th anniversary of its release in cinemas. I am just so glad that it was worth all the hard work; that we created something of a legacy that one generation after another has been able to enjoy.

I am not a famous person but my character has become dearly loved all over the world. She is a source of hope. The treasure chest she found for me did not hold gold ingots or pieces of eight, as one might expect, but mixed moss of eternal value – aspirations and voyages of discovery, sunlit memories and friendships forged by adventure, stories that have stood the test of time and the tradition of keeping a ship's log.

Little children often start calling me Titty. They put on her sand shoes, as it were, and run around in them, taking up her soaring spirit of enthusiasm. My only hope is that I have honoured their dreams, and honoured Arthur Ransome's dream. I hope that he would have been pleased with our efforts.

About the Author

An award-winning author, Sophie is an active member of the Nancy Blackett Trust and President of The Arthur Ransome Society. She joined forces with Sail Ransome to purchase *Swallow*, the original dinghy, which she sailed when she played Titty in 1973. Sophie still gives talks on making the film and how Arthur Ransome influenced her life. She lives with her husband on the south coast of England. They have three grown children, two boats, one dog, and like to travel as much as possible.

For more information:
Website *sophieneville.net*
Twitter *@Sophie_Neville*
Email *sophie@sophieneville.co.uk*

243

Acknowledgments

I nearly threw away my diaries and scrapbooks. Yet my parents had invested so much, taking expensive photographs, slides and ciné footage as well as storing albums of press cuttings and film memorabilia, that I hesitated, realising the collection had become historical and precious. My appreciation goes to them, for without their foresight there would not be much to show. I must thank Richard and Molly Pilbrow for sending encouragement, documents and photographs, Virginia McKenna for her support, Suzanna Hamilton for the loan of her hilarious diary, Sten Grendon for letting me see his scrapbooks and Simon West for sending his photographs and memories. David Wood kindly sent his words, which of course I have been quoting ever since.

I am deeply grateful to Random House Group Ltd and the Arthur Ransome Literary Estate for granting me permission to use quotes from Arthur Ransome's books. Thanks also to Christina Hardyment and Roger Wardale for their excellent reference books and correspondence. Many members of The Arthur Ransome Society have offered wise words and advice, including Lindy Castell, Peter Wright, Magnus Smith and Christopher Holmes who corrected first drafts, along with Billy Howard and Graham Edmiston who acted as proof readers.

Jill Goulder, Julia Jones, Duncan Hall, Barry Riddiford, Kevin Burn, Colin Salvage, Paul Endicott, Elizabeth Rondthaler Jolley, Peter Latham, Phil Dence, Patricia Buchanan, Ray Theron, Robert Slinn, Christopher Kenworthy, Donald Alexander, John White, Petr Korbel, Peter Walker, David Stott, Peter Willis and others have also helped me with information, or sent DVDs. Thank you all for encouraging me to keep writing. Such was Jamie Harris's love for the film that he had the faith to take an author photograph of me rowing on the lake ten years ago. Sylvain Guenot and Anthony Thompson honoured me by taking more recent portrait shots.

Transforming the diary of a twelve-year-old girl into a narrative, along with a morass of factual material, is not an easy task. Very many thanks go to Lisa Scullard for her patient work on my website, transforming a blog into a well-formatted draft whilst generously giving advice on film history. It is she I must thank for the success of the first ebook edition, which generated staggering publicity. I am sure that Claude Whatham would have been astonished at the response and only hope he would in interested in reading about what became of *Swallows & Amazons (1974)*

The most exciting thing was that StudioCanal graciously allowed us to use photographic stills from the movie in the year they released a restored version on DVD and Blu-ray with an unique extras package that will compliment this book.

Bibliography

Arthur Ransome books

Ransome, Arthur (1930), *Swallows and Amazons*, London: Jonathan Cape.

Ransome, Arthur (1931), *Swallowdale*, London: Jonathan Cape.

Ransome, Arthur (1932), *Peter Duck*, London: Jonathan Cape.

Ransome, Arthur (1933), *Winter Holiday*, London: Jonathan Cape.

Ransome, Arthur (1934), *Coot Club*, London: Jonathan Cape.

Ransome, Arthur (1936), *Pigeon Post*, London: Jonathan Cape.

Ransome, Arthur (1937), *We Didn't Mean to Go to Sea*, London: Jonathan Cape.

Ransome, Arthur (1939), *Secret Water*, London: Jonathan Cape.

Ransome, Arthur (1940), *The Big Six*, London: Jonathan Cape.

Ransome, Arthur (1941), *Missee Lee*, London: Jonathan Cape.

Ransome, Arthur (1943), *The Picts and the Martyrs*, London: Jonathan Cape.

Ransome, Arthur (1947), *Great Northern?*, London: Jonathan Cape.

Ransome, Arthur (1976), *The Autobiography of Arthur Ransome*, London: Jonathan Cape.

Wardale, Roger (2010), *Arthur Ransome: Master Storyteller*, Ilkley: Great Northern Books.

Wardale, Roger (2006), *In Search of Swallows & Amazons*, Ammanford: Sigma Press.

Wardale, Roger (1986), *Arthur Ransome's Lakeland*, Skipton: Dalesman.

Hardyment, Christina (2006), *Arthur Ransome and Captain Flint's Trunk*, London: Frances Lincoln.

Hardyment, Christina (2012), *The World of Arthur Ransome*, London: Frances Lincoln.

Kendall-Price, Claire (1993), *In the Footsteps of the 'Swallows and Amazons'*, York: Wild Cat Publishing.

Berry, John (2005), *Discovering Swallows & Ransomes*, Ammanford: Sigma Press.

Lovelock, Julian (2016), *Swallows, Amazons and Coots*, Cambridge: The Lutterworth Press.

Additional sources

Pilbrow, Richard (2011), *A Theatre Project*, New York: PLASA Media Inc.

McKenna, Virginia (2009), *The Life in My Years*, London: Oberon Books.

Doyle, Brian (1968), *The Who's Who of Children's Literature*, London: Hugh Evelyn.

Lee, Laurie (1959), *Cider with Rosie*, London: Penguin.

Palmer, Roy (ed.) (1986), 'The Log of the *Nellie*, 1796' from *The Oxford Book of Sea Songs*, Oxford: Oxford University Press.

Defoe, Daniel (1719), *The Adventures of Robinson Crusoe*, W. Taylor.

Stevenson, Robert Louis (1883), *Treasure Island*, London: Cassell & Co.

Mortimer, John (1994), *Murderers and Other Friends*, New York: Viking.

Altounyan, Taqui (1969), *In Aleppo Once,* London: John Murray Publishers.

Collingwood, Jeremy (2012), *A Lakeland Saga*, Ammanford: Sigma Press.

Collingwood, W.G. (1895), *Thorstein of the Mere*, London: Edward Arnold.

Dingle, Rodney (2005), *Roger: The Life and Distinguished Achievements of Dr Roger Altounyan*, Wild Reagents Publishing.

Jacobs, Joseph (1890), 'Titty Mouse and Tatty Mouse' from *English Fairy Tales*, London: David Nutt.

Barrie, J.M, (1911), *Peter Pan,* London: Hodder & Stoughton.

Further reading

The Arthur Ransome Society: www.arthur-ransome.org.uk

The Arthur Ransome Trust: www.arthur-ransome-trust.org.uk

All Things Ransome: www.allthingsransome.net

The Nancy Blackett Trust: nancyblackett.org

Sail Ransome: www.sailransome.org

Producer Richard Pilbrow's website: www.richardpilbrow.com

Picture Credits

Most of the photographs are from the author's private collection.

If you liked *The Making of Swallows & Amazons (1974)*, why not try. . .

Swallows, Amazons and Coots
A Reading of Arthur Ransome

Julian Lovelock

ISBN: 978 0 7188 9436 8
PDF ISBN: 9780718844646
ePub ISBN: 9780718844653
Kindle ISBN: 9780718844660

In 1929, Arthur Ransome (1884–1967), a journalist and war correspondent who was on the books of MI6, turned his hand to writing adventure stories for children. The result was *Swallows and Amazons* and eleven more wonderful books followed, spanning in publication the turbulent years from 1930 to 1947. They changed the course of children's literature and have never been out of print since. In them, Ransome creates a world of escape so close to reality that it is utterly believable, a world in which things always turn out right in the end.

Yet *Swallows, Amazons and Coots* shows that, to be properly appreciated today, the novels must be read as products of their era, inextricably bound up with Ransome's life and times as he bore witness to the end of Empire and the dark days of the Second World War. In the first critical book devoted wholly to the series, Julian Lovelock explores each novel in turn, offering an erudite assessment of Ransome's creative process and narrative technique, and highlighting his contradictory politics, his defence of rural England, and his reflections on colonialism and the place of women in society. Thus Lovelock demonstrates convincingly that, despite first appearances, the novels challenge as much as reinforce the pervading attitudes of their time.

Written with a lightness of touch and enlivened by Ransome's own illustrations, *Swallows, Amazons and Coots* is both fresh and nostalgic. It will appeal to anyone who has enjoyed the world of *Swallows and Amazons*, and there is plenty here to challenge both the student and the Ransome enthusiast.